MW00829979

The Evil Creator

The Evil Creator

Origins of an Early Christian Idea

M. DAVID LITWA

Institute for Religion and Critical Inquiry
Australian Catholic University, Melbourne

OXFORD
UNIVERSITY PRESS

OXFORD
UNIVERSITY PRESS

Oxford University Press is a department of the University of Oxford. It furthers
the University's objective of excellence in research, scholarship, and education
by publishing worldwide. Oxford is a registered trade mark of Oxford University
Press in the UK and certain other countries.

Published in the United States of America by Oxford University Press
198 Madison Avenue, New York, NY 10016, United States of America.

© Oxford University Press 2021

All rights reserved. No part of this publication may be reproduced, stored in
a retrieval system, or transmitted, in any form or by any means, without the
prior permission in writing of Oxford University Press, or as expressly permitted
by law, by license, or under terms agreed with the appropriate reproduction
rights organization. Inquiries concerning reproduction outside the scope of the
above should be sent to the Rights Department, Oxford University Press, at the
address above.

You must not circulate this work in any other form
and you must impose this same condition on any acquirer.

Library of Congress Cataloging-in-Publication Data
Names: Litwa, M. David, author.
Title: The evil creator : origins of an early Christian idea / M. David Litwa.
Description: New York, NY, United States of America :
Oxford University Press, [2021] |
Includes bibliographical references and index.
Identifiers: LCCN 2021013674 (print) | LCCN 2021013675 (ebook) |
ISBN 9780197566428 (hb) | ISBN 9780197566442 (epub)
Subjects: LCSH: God (Christianity)—History of doctrines—Early church, ca. 30-600. |
Good and evil—Religious aspects—Christianity. | Gnosticism. |
Marcion, of Sinope, active 2nd century. |
Bible. New Testament—Criticism, interpretation, etc.
Classification: LCC BT98 .L58 2021 (print) | LCC BT98 (ebook) |
DDC 231/.8—dc23
LC record available at https://lccn.loc.gov/2021013674
LC ebook record available at https://lccn.loc.gov/2021013675

DOI: 10.1093/oso/9780197566428.001.0001

I dedicate this book to my son, Darian

Contents

Preface

All translations in this volume, unless otherwise noted, are my own. All biblical translations, unless otherwise specified, come from the Septuagint (LXX). Throughout this work, I do not capitalize the "g" in "god" so as not to offer a value judgment, even implicit, as to which ancient deity is considered to be true or false, real or unreal. "Law" is capitalized when it refers to Jewish Law or Torah.

Here I gratefully acknowledge the readers who have provided comments on draft chapters of this work: my colleagues Ben Edsall, Stephen Carlson, Kylie Crabbe, Sarah Gador-Whyte, and Devin White offered feedback on Chapters 1, 4, 5, and 6. In addition, Dylan Burns, Tuomas Rasimus, Francis Watson, and John Barclay provided comments on Chapters 1, 2, and 4. An earlier version of Chapter 7 was presented as a paper at the 2018 ACU (Australian Catholic University) annual Rome seminar and published in a different form as "The Curse of the Creator: *Galatians* 3.13 and Negative Demiurgy," in *Telling the Christian Story Differently*, ed. Francis Watson and Sarah Parkhouse (London: Bloomsbury Academic Press, 2020), 13–30. Chapter 2 was offered as a seminar paper at the Biblical and Early Christian Studies Seminar at ACU in late 2019. It is published in a different form as "The Father of the Devil (John 8:44): A Christian Exegetical Inspiration for the Evil Creator, *VC* 74:5 (2020): 540–65. My plan to offer a shortened version of Chapter 4 at the North American Patristics Society Meeting in 2020 has now been shifted to 2021 (an Open Call session dedicated to the topic of negative demiurgy). I thank all the participants at these events for their generous feedback.

Abbreviations

AAH	Pseudo-Tertullian, *Against All Heresies*
AH	Irenaeus, *Against Heresies*
AM	Tertullian, *Against Marcion*
ANRW	*Aufstieg und Niedergang der römischen Welt*
CCSL	Corpus Christianorum Series Latina
Cels.	*Against Celsus*
DGWE	*Dictionary of Gnosis and Western Esotericism*, ed. Hanegraaff
EH	Eusebius, *Ecclesiastical History*
JBL	*Journal of Biblical Literature*
JSNT	*Journal for the Study of the New Testament*
LCL	Loeb Classical Library
LSJ	Liddell, Scott, Jones, eds. *Greek-English Lexicon*
LXX	Septuagint
NHC	Nag Hammadi Codices
NovT	*Novum Testamentum*
NTS	*New Testament Studies*
OLD	*Oxford Latin Dictionary*
OTP	*Old Testament Pseudepigrapha*, ed. James Charlesworth
PG	*Patrologia Graeca*
PGM	*Greek Magical Papyri*
Ref.	*Refutation of All Heresies*
SC	Sources Chrétiennes
VC	*Vigiliae Christianae*
ZAC	*Zeitschrift für Antikes Christentum*

PART I
EGYPTIAN AND JOHANNINE APPROACHES TO THE EVIL CREATOR

Introduction: Why the Evil Creator?

> Free will was the excuse for everything. It was God's alibi. They had
> never read Freud. Evil was made by man or Satan. It was simple that
> way. But I could never believe in Satan. It was much easier to believe
> that God was evil.
>
> —Graham Greene[1]

Of the many beliefs held by early Christians, the notion of an evil creator is perhaps the most scandalous. It was fundamental to Platonism—
the ascendant philosophy during Christianity's infancy—that the creator,
though distinct from the high god, was good.[2] Of all possible worlds,
the creator made this world following the finest of all possible models. The
creator's unstinting care for the universe—called providence—was widely
accepted in antiquity as the only pious option available.[3] The bright sun,
clear air, and fresh water were silent but eloquent witnesses of divine goodness, not to mention the very gift that made gratitude possible: human intelligence. Far from shutting out people from the richest of benefits, the

---

[1] Greene, *The Honorary Consul* (New York: Simon and Schuster, 1973), 239.
[2] Plato, *Timaeus* 29e. See further J. Halfwassen, "Der Demiurg: Seine Stellung in der Philosophie Platons und seine Deutung im Antiken Platonismus," in *Le Timée de Platon: contributions à l'histoire de sa réception*, ed. Ada Neschke-Hentschke (Leuven: Peeters, 2000), 39–62; Jan Opsomer, "Demiurges in Early Imperial Platonism," in *Gott und die Götter bei Plutarch: Götterbilder-Gottesbilder-Weltbilder*, ed. Rainer Hirsch-Luipold (Berlin: de Gruyter, 2005), 51–99; Adam Drozdek, "Plato and the Demiurge," in *Greek Philosophers as Theologians: The Divine* Arche (Hampshire: Ashgate, 2007), 151–68; Carl Séan O'Brien, *The Demiurge in Ancient Thought: Secondary Gods and Divine Mediators* (Cambridge: Cambridge University Press, 2015), 18–34. On the gradual dominance of Platonism, see Troels Engberg-Pedersen, ed., *From Stoicism to Platonism: The Development of Philosophy 100 BCE–100 CE* (Cambridge: Cambridge University Press, 2017); George Boys-Stones, *Platonist Philosophy 80 BC to AD 250: An Introduction and Collection of Sources in Translation* (Cambridge: Cambridge University Press, 2018), 1–80, and 148–49 (on divine goodness).
[3] Alcinous, *Handbook of Platonism* 12.1. On Providence, see further Gretchen J. Reydams-Schils, *Demiurge and Providence: Stoic and Platonist Readings of Plato's Timaeus* (Turnhout: Brepols, 1999); George Boys-Stones, "Providence and Religion in Middle Platonism," in *Theologies of Ancient Greek Religions*, ed. Esther Eidinow et al. (Cambridge: Cambridge University Press, 2019), 317–38; Dylan Burns, *Did God Care? Providence, Dualism and Will in Later Greek and Early Christian Philosophy* (Leiden: Brill, 2020), esp. 103–88.

The Evil Creator. M. David Litwa, Oxford University Press. © Oxford University Press 2021.
DOI: 10.1093/oso/9780197566428.003.0001

creator equipped them, according to Plato, to become as much like the divine as possible.[4]

By contrast, some early Christian groups thought that the creator of this world (known in Hebrew as "Yahweh," or "the lord") was an evil or hostile being opposed to the true and transcendent deity. To quote just a sample of some early Christian texts:

The chief creator was a fool. He despised condemnation and acted with audacity.[5]

The ruler was a joke, for he said, "I am god and no one is greater than I ... I am a jealous god ..." He is conceited and does not agree with our Father.[6]

What kind of god is this? First, he begrudged Adam's eating from the tree of knowledge. Second, he said, "Adam, where are you?" [This] god does not have foreknowledge. He has certainly shown himself to be a malicious envier.[7]

The concept of a wicked creator was the hallmark of Christians who today are still grouped under the global category of "gnostic."[8] We shall shortly

---

[4] Plato, *Theaetetus* 176b. On assimilation to god, see Julia Annas, *Platonic Ethics, Old and New* (Ithaca: Cornell University Press, 1999), 52–71. J. M. Armstrong, "After the Ascent: Plato on Becoming Like God," *Oxford Studies in Ancient Philosophy* 26 (2004): 171–83; George H. Van Kooten, *Paul's Anthropology in Context* (Tübingen: Mohr Siebeck, 2008), 129–99; Gretchen Reydams-Schils, "'Becoming Like God' in Platonism and Stoicism," in *From Stoicism*, ed. Engberg-Pedersen, 142–58.

[5] *Origin of the World* (Nag Hammadi Codices [NHC] II,5) 107.34–35.

[6] *Second Treatise of Great Seth* (NHC VII,2) 64.17–65.2.

[7] *Testimony of Truth* (NHC IX,3) 47.14–48.4. Hugo Lundhaug and Lance Jenott count twenty-one Nag Hammadi texts with a negative evaluation of the creator and ten with a positive evaluation (*The Monastic Origins of the Nag Hammadi Codices* [Tübingen: Mohr Siebeck, 2015], 86–87). The fact that negative evaluations are more than double the positive indicates to Jonathan Cahana-Blum that the negative readings predominated also in the case of the twenty-two texts wherein the evaluation of the creator is unclear (*Wrestling with Archons: Gnosticism as a Critical Theory of Culture* [London: Lexington, 2018], 40).

[8] The third century CE philosopher Porphyry presented a double title for Plotinus's treatise 2.9: "Against the Gnostics" (Πρὸς τοὺς Γνωστικούς), and "Against Those Who Declare the Creator of the World to Be Evil" (Πρὸς τοὺς κακὸν τὸν δημιουργὸν τοῦ κόσμου ... λέγοντας) (*Life of Plotinus* 5.33; 24.55). Within this treatise, Plotinus reproved these "Gnostics" for blaming the "governor of this universe" (2.9.6.60). According to Michael Williams, the demonizing of the demiurge was "the innovation of Gnostic myth" ("The Demonizing of the Demiurge: The Innovation of Gnostic Myth," in *Innovations in Religious Traditions*, ed. Michael A. Williams, C. Cox, and Martin S. Jaffe [Berlin: de Gruyter, 1992], 73–107 at 73). See further Gerard P. Luttikhuizen, "The Demonic Demiurge in Gnostic Mythology," in *The Fall of Angels*, ed. Christoph Auffarth and Loren T. Stuckenbruck (Leiden: Brill, 2003), 148–60 at 148; Christoph Markschies, *Gnosis: An Introduction* (London: T&T Clark, 2003), 16–17; Tuomas Rasimus, *Paradise Reconsidered in Gnostic Mythmaking: Rethinking Sethianism in Light of the Ophite Evidence* (Leiden: Brill, 2009), 158, 171–72; Winrich Löhr, "Gnostic and Manichean Interpretation," in *The New Cambridge History of the Bible* (Cambridge: Cambridge

take the opportunity to improve on this fuzzy and contested term. For now, it is sufficient to note that these early Christians were spread out in major urban centers across the Mediterranean world (Antioch, Alexandria, Rome, Carthage). Their founders and theologians were educated and gifted writers. They knew how shocking it was to proclaim an evil creator in their time, but they composed lengthy origin stories to depict him in living and lurid images—such as a lion-headed serpent.[9] The question is why—why did they affirm a malevolent creator, and how did they know that he was malign?

Scholars have searched for broader philosophical motives to explain the origin of the evil creator idea.[10] Some Platonists of the second century CE were prepared to contemplate evil emerging from nature, matter, or the erring fluctuations of a World Soul.[11] A distinctly evil creator, however, was generally not even considered as a philosophical option among the major schools, since it would conflict with divine providence.[12] Now educated early Christians often wished to appear philosophical. Yet philosophy was little

University Press, 2013), 584–604 at 584; George E. Karamanolis, *The Philosophy of Early Christianity* (London: Routledge, 2013), 21; Hebert Schmid, *Christen und Sethianer: Ein Beitrag zur Diskussion um den religionsgeschichtlichen und den kirchengeschichtlichen Begriff der Gnosis* (Leiden: Brill, 2018), 417; Jutta Leonhardt-Balzer, "Yaldabaoth und seine Bande. Die Gegner im Johannesapokryphon," in *Dualismus, Dämonologie und diabolische Figuren: Religionshistorische Beobachtungen und theologische Reflexionen*, ed. Jörg Frey and Enno Edzard Popkes (Tübingen: Mohr Siebeck, 2018), 351–66.

[9] See, e.g., *Ap. John, Nat. Rulers,* and *Orig. World,* all in Nag Hammadi codex II. For the "transgressive orientation" of early gnostics, see April D. DeConick, *The Gnostic New Age: How a Countercultural Spirituality Revolutionized Religion from Antiquity to Today* (New York: Columbia University Press, 2016), 256, 263.

[10] Jaap Mansfeld, "Bad World and Demiurge: A 'Gnostic' Motif from Parmenides and Empedocles to Lucretius and Philo," in *Studies in Gnosticism and Hellenistic Religions, Festschrift Gilles Quispel,* ed. R. van den Broek and M. J. Vermaseren (Leiden: Brill, 1981), 261–314; Einar Thomassen, "The Platonic and Gnostic 'Demiurge,'" in *Apocryphon Severini Presented to Søren Giversen,* ed. Per Bilde, Helge Kjaer Nielsen, and Jorgen Podemann Sorensen (Aarhus: Aarhus University Press, 1993), 227–44; Carl B. Smith, *No Longer Jews: The Search for Gnostic Origins* (Peabody: Hendrickson, 2004), 28–33; Zlatko Pleše, "Evil and Its Sources in Gnostic Traditions," in *Die Wurzel allen Übels: Vorstellungen über die Herkunft des Bösen und Schlechten in der Philosophie und Religion des. 1.– 4. Jahrhunderts,* ed. Fabienne Jourdan and Rainer Hirsch-Luipold (Tübingen: Mohr Siebeck, 2015), 101–32.

[11] Plato, *Laws* 896d–e and 898c; Plutarch, *Isis-Osiris* 369d, 370f; *On the Generation of the Soul in the Timaeus,* 1014e–1015e. See further Arthur H. Armstrong, "Dualism: Platonic, Gnostic, and Christian," in *Neoplatonism and Gnosticism,* ed. Richard T. Wallis and Jay Bregman (Albany: SUNY Press, 1992), 33–54 at 38–39; Karin Alt, *Weltflucht und Weltbejahung: Zur Frage des Dualismus bei Plutarch, Numenius, Plotin* (Stuttgart: Franz Steiner, 1993), 23–24; Jan Opsomer and Carlos Steel, "Evil Without a Cause: Proclus's Doctrine on the Origin of Evil and Its Antecedents in Hellenistic Philosophy," in *Zur Rezeption des hellenistischen Philosophie in der Spätantike: Akten der 1. Tagung der Karl-und-Gertrud-Abel-Stiftung vom 22.–25. September 1997 in Trier,* ed. Therese Fuhrer, Michael Erler, and Karin Schlapbach (Stuttgart: F. Steiner, 1999), 229–60 at 235–44; Karamanolis, *Philosophy,* 67; Burns, *Did God Care,* 111–12.

[12] One might cite Plutarch (*Isis-Osiris* 369d), Numenius (frag. 52.37–39, 44–64, Des Places), and Empedocles (Mansfeld, "Bad World") as exceptions here. Even so, they manage to prove the rule.

help for those Christians who imagined an evil creator. There must therefore have been other motives for some Christians to envision such a being.

The apostle Paul, following a trend in ancient Jewish theology, demonized the pantheons of all other peoples (1 Cor 10:20, following Ps 96:5). Paul lived in a world teeming with demons whom he called "rulers"—provincial potentates reigning from the lower heavens (Rom 8:38–39; 1 Cor 2:6–8).[13] Paul also believed in their chief ruler: a quasi-divine figure of evil who had various aliases: the devil, Beliar, Satan, and so on.[14] Here was a "homemade" anti-divine agent in Jewish lore whose oppositional role could readily be transferred to the creator.

Yet it is difficult to see why or how such a transfer would take place, since the creator in Jewish tradition was overwhelmingly conceived of as blessed and worthy of devotion. Jewish scriptures regularly called the creator compassionate, caring, and just. The Psalms sung at length of the abundance of divine mercy, forgiveness, and lovingkindness.[15] Thus to imagine the creator as a malicious being arrayed against a higher, benevolent deity required another, much bolder step.[16]

Yet what was it? Could it have been the experience of horrible social and political turmoil suffered by the Jews between 66 and 135 CE? During this period, Jewish groups drew up their battle lines against the Romans and thrice raised the ululations of war. In 66 CE, they proclaimed freedom in Jerusalem, slaughtered the Roman garrison, and defended their besieged city until mothers reportedly ate their own children.[17] A party of radicals held out three additional years in the fortress of Masada, committing mass suicide the

---

[13] See further Wesley Carr, *Angels and Principalities: The Background, Meaning and Development of the Pauline Phrase* hai archai kai hai exousiai (Cambridge: Cambridge University Press, 1981); Armin Lange, Hermann Lichtenberger, and Diethard Römheld, eds., *Die Dämonen: Die Dämonologie der israelitisch-jüdischen und frühchristlichen Literatur im Kontext ihrer Umwelt* (Tübingen: Mohr Siebeck, 2003); David Brakke, *Demons and the Making of the Monk: Spiritual Combat in Early Christianity* (Cambridge, MA: Harvard University Press, 2009); Chris Keith and Loren T. Stuckenbruck, eds., *Evil in Second Temple Judaism and Early Christianity* (Tübingen: Mohr Siebeck, 2016); Frey and Popkes, *Dualismus, Dämonologie und diabolische Figuren: Religionshistorische Beobachtungen und theologische Reflexionen* (Tübingen: Mohr Siebeck, 2018); Emma Wasserman, *Apocalypse as Holy War: Divine Politics and Polemics in the Letters of Paul* (New Haven: Yale University Press, 2018).

[14] See further Elaine Pagels, *Origins of Satan: How Christians Demonized Jews, Pagans, and Heretics* (New York: Vintage, 2011); Miguel A. de la Torre and Albert Hernández, *The Quest for the Historical Satan* (Philadelphia: Fortress, 2011).

[15] Michael Bergmann, Michal J. Murray, and Michael C. Rea, *Divine Evil? The Moral Character of the God of Abraham* (Oxford: Oxford University Press, 2011), 1.

[16] In this investigation, I exclude conceptions of the creator as a just (or righteous) being (as in Valentinian Christian thought). I only consider conceptions of the creator as an evil being. For the Valentinian creator, see, e.g., Ismo Dunderberg, *Beyond Gnosticism: Myth, Lifestyle and Society in the School of Valentinus* (New York: Columbia University Press, 2008), 119–58.

[17] Josephus, *Jewish War* 2.430 (capture of the garrison), 6.200–21 (eating of children).

night before an enraged Roman army rammed through their charred gates.[18] From 115 to 117 CE, Jewish militia in Libya, Egypt, and Cyprus took over entire cities, slaughtering at will and desecrating temples.[19] Finally, in 132 CE, Jews in Palestine carved out a rebel kingdom in the Judean foothills, using the tactics of guerilla warfare until they were hunted, starved, or flushed out from every underground hideout and rocky fort.[20]

Ancient Romans and Greeks could not understand why this tiny nation continually rebelled while larger and more powerful kingdoms lowed quietly under the Roman yoke. There were a bevy of socioeconomic and political reasons, but from the perspective of these Jews themselves, theological considerations played the most prominent role. These Jews acted as they thought their god had commanded—to rid the Holy Land of "heathen," to set up a kingdom governed by divine law, and to await the Messiah's iron rod reign.

But none of this ever happened. The Jewish deity did not intervene, and whole Jewish communities were drowned in their own blood. In Alexandria of 117 CE there was a virtual genocide, with Jews of all ranks murdered in the streets.[21] Further down the Nile, festivals were arranged celebrating the defeat and slaughter of the Jews for over a century.[22] Throughout the Mediterranean world, Jews were forced to pay a burdensome tax (the *fiscus Iudaicus*) simply because they were Jews or converts to Judaism.[23] By 135 CE, they were banned from living in Jerusalem—renamed Aelia Capitolina— then the location of a gleaming new temple to Zeus. Jews were prevented even from setting foot on the island of Cyprus. According to one report, Jews

---

[18] Josephus, *Jewish War* 7.389–406.

[19] For the Jewish revolt under Trajan (115–117 CE), see Victor A. Tcherikover and Alexander Fuks, *Corpus Papyrorum Judaicarum*, 3 vols. (Cambridge, MA: Harvard University Press, 1957– 1964), 2.225–60; Joseph Mélèze Modrzejewski, *The Jews of Egypt from Ramses II to Emperor Trajan*, trans. Robert Cornman (Edinburgh: T&T Clark, 1995), 198–225; Smith, *No Longer Jews*, 72–112; Miriam Pucci Ben Zeev, *Diaspora Judaism in Turmoil 116–117 CE: Ancient Sources and Modern Insights* (Leuven: Peeters, 2005); William Horbury, *Jewish War Under Trajan and Hadrian* (Cambridge: Cambridge University Press, 2014), 164–277.

[20] See further Werner Eck, "The Bar Kokhba Revolt: The Roman Point of View," *Journal of Roman Studies* 89 (1999): 76–89; Peter Schäfer, *The History of the Jews in the Graeco-Roman World* (London: Routledge, 2003), 145–62; Schäfer, ed. *The Bar Kokhba War Reconsidered: New Perspectives on the Second Jewish Revolt Against Rome* (Tübingen: Mohr Siebeck, 2003); Hanan Eshel, "The Bar Kochba Revolt, 132–135," *Cambridge History of Judaism Vol. 4: Late Roman- Rabbinic Period*, ed. Steven T. Katz (Cambridge: Cambridge University Press, 2008), 105–27.

[21] See further Modrzejewski, *The Jews of Egypt*, 198–230; Roger S. Bagnall, *Egypt in Late Antiquity* (Princeton: Princeton University Press, 1993), 276–78; Ben Zeev, *Diaspora Judaism in Turmoil*; Horbury, *Jewish War*, 164–277.

[22] Annemarie Luijendijk, *Greetings in the Lord: Early Christians and the Oxyrhynchus Papyri* (Cambridge, MA: Harvard Theological Studies, 2008), 16–17.

[23] Marius Heemstra, *Fiscus Iudaicus and the Parting of the Ways* (Tübingen: Mohr Siebeck, 2010).

that were shipwrecked there could be hacked to pieces on the shores with impunity.[24]

Thus in the first forty years of the second century, political events turned sour, to say the least, for many Jews in Palestine, Syria, and Egypt. Yet despite apocalyptic prophecies new and old, the world never ground to a halt, and the thick veil of heaven remained untorn. Targeted by the tax system, and stigmatized by failed rebellions, Jews, according to one theory, looked around and began to see themselves "as strangers and afraid in a world their God had never made."[25]

Despite the enticements of this lachrymose tale, however, it does not actually explain how the notion of an evil creator arose. After all, Jews with apocalyptic and Messianic hopes—as is typical in Abrahamic religions—overwhelmingly blamed their sins for disasters, not the creator.[26] If Jews became alienated from the world, this hardly meant alienation from god or the belief that their deity did not create the world. Failure on earth might, indeed, have tied their hearts more tightly to heaven. Even if it did not, why would Jews—whose sole hope and commitment was to exalt their putatively unique lord—rewrite scripture to portray Yahweh as foolish and evil? It would have been simpler for them to renounce the faith, assimilate to the larger society, and move on. (And indeed, some did.)

Perhaps, however, we have been looking for an answer in the wrong place. Perhaps it was not the Jews at all who turned in desperation against their deity. Christians, after all, had just entered history in significant numbers.[27] Newly converted Gentile Christians had no original love or loyalty for the Jewish god, and they already had a vested interest in criticizing the rules and regulations of Yahweh's Law, the so-called yoke of compulsion.[28] Early Christians also paraded their Messiah as the true object of worship, declaring

[24] Dio Cassius, *Roman History* 68.32.3.

[25] R. M. Grant, *Gnosticism and Early Christianity*, 2nd ed. (New York: Columbia University Press, 1966), 37. For similar theories, cf. Birger Pearson, *Gnosticism, Judaism, and Egyptian Christianity* (Minneapolis, Fortress, 1990), 51; Bart Ehrman, *Lost Christianities: The Battles for Scripture and the Faiths We Never Knew* (Oxford: Oxford University Press, 2003), 119; Smith, *No Longer Jews*, 53–58.

[26] E.g., Dan 9:9–10; 4 Ezra 3:21–27; 2 Bar 1:2. See further A. Laato and Johannes C. de Moor, eds., *Theodicy in the World of the Bible* (Leiden: Brill, 2003); Christopher Rowland, "The Parting of the Ways: The Evidence of Jewish and Christian Apocalyptic and Mystical Material," in *Jews and Christians: The Parting of the Ways A.D. 70 to 135*, ed. James D. G. Dunn (Grand Rapids: Eerdmans, 1993), 213–38 at 236–37.

[27] For (very) rough estimates, see Rodney Stark, *The Rise of Christianity: A Sociologist Reconsiders History* (Princeton: Princeton University Press, 1996), 3–29.

[28] E.g., *Epistle of Barnabas* 2.6 (ζυγοῦ ἀνάγκης). See further William Horbury, "Jewish- Christian Relations in Barnabas and Justin Martyr," in Dunn, ed., *Jews and Christians*, 315–46.

the Jews to be blind for misinterpreting their own prophecies.[29] If any group could suddenly turn on the Jewish god, it was the Christians, who had already turned against Yahweh's people to carve out a space for their own identity as priests and kings in a new "kingdom of god."[30]

Who were, we might ask, the Christians most hostile to the Jews? It was, we were once told, those Christians who were expelled from the synagogues.[31] They were expelled because the Jews pointed out that they worshiped *one* god, not a divine Messiah and his reputed Father. One could not confess "the Lord is one" if one worshiped *two* distinct beings—or so the earliest rabbis thought. Against such reasoning, a group of Christians supposedly identified the Jews with "the world" and concluded that the world itself was evil because it had rejected and isolated early Christians.[32]

Yet here again we run into the same problem we did before: the conception of a bad world does not necessarily or immediately lead to a bad *god-who-made-the-world*. Besides, a large contingent of Christians simply claimed the Jewish god for themselves, identifying him with their all-good and merciful father. They even appropriated Jewish scriptures, claiming that the Messianic prophecies were about Jesus and that the lord had in fact chosen them—not unbelieving Jews—before the foundation of the world (Eph 1:4).

To be sure, the Jewish scriptures themselves could sometimes speak of other divine beings in the heavens. The book of Exodus speaks of an "Angel of Yahweh" who bears Yahweh's name and—according to later tradition— participates in the work of creation. This angel sometimes punishes sin, but he is never described as evil, nor is it clear why or how such an angel would ever become evil and be equated with the Jewish deity.[33] This logic,

---

[29] 2 Cor 3:14; Justin Martyr, *Dialogue with Trypho*; Tertullian, *Against the Jews*.

[30] See further Judith M. Lieu, *Image and Reality: The Jews in the World of the Christians in the Second Century* (Edinburgh: T&T Clark, 1996), 261–76; Stephen G. Wilson, *Related Strangers: Jews and Christians 70–170 CE* (Minneapolis: Fortress, 1995); Pierluigi Lanfranchi and Joseph Verheyden, ed., *Jews and Christians in Antiquity: A Regional Perspective* (Leuven: Peeters, 2018).

[31] This trajectory of interpretation was initiated by J. Louis Martyn, *History and Theology of the Fourth Gospel*, 3rd ed. (Louisville: Westminster/John Knox, 2003), 46–100. See more recently Martinus C. De Boer, "Expulsion from the Synagogue: J. L. Martyn's *History and Theology in the Fourth Gospel* Revisited," *New Testament Studies (NTS)* 66 (2020): 367–91.

[32] Alan Segal, "Ruler of This World: Attitudes Toward Mediator Figures and the Importance of Sociology for Self-definition," in *Jewish and Christian Self-definition Vol. 2*, ed. E. P. Sanders (Philadelphia: Fortress, 1980), 245–68, esp. 259.

[33] Jarl E. Fossum, *The Name of God and the Angel of the Lord: Samaritan and Jewish Concepts of Intermediation and the Origin of Gnosticism* (Tübingen: Mohr Siebeck, 1985), 336. Fossum's studies (including his "Origin of the Gnostic Concept of the Demiurge," *Ephemerides Theologicae Lovanienses* 61 [1985]: 142–52) employ late Samaritan sources (from the fourth to the fourteenth century CE) along with speculative interpretations of texts widely scattered in space and time. For

though argued vigorously, is missing several steps and is often based on late evidence.[34]

Nevertheless, paying close attention to scriptural interpretation does, I believe, set us on the right track. There were, after all, numerous "hard sayings" and stories in scripture—texts that seemed like thorns in the eyes of educated and philosophically informed readers.[35] Typical examples come from the first six chapters of Genesis. Why, for instance, did the Jewish god prohibit the first humans from eating the fruit of the tree of knowledge (Gen 2)? Why did he not seem to know Adam's location in the garden of Eden? Why did he eventually cast Adam and Eve out of Eden (Gen 3)? Why did he later send a flood to wipe out most of humanity (Gen 6-8)? And—beyond the book of Genesis—why did Yahweh repeatedly say that he was jealous? Assuming he was the most powerful being in the universe, whom could he possibly envy?[36]

These were questions that early Jews and Christians were asking already in the late first and early second centuries CE. Most Jews and Christians, it seems, found a way to answer them while preserving the glory and goodness of the Jewish lord. For other Christians, however, these problematic sayings and stories produced a cumulative case against the benevolent character of the creator. As more and more negative stories were told about the creator based on his own scriptures, the reading of these scriptures helped to cultivate a deep-rooted suspicion that the creator was not benign after all.

Although this hypothesis is hardly new, it has not, to my knowledge, been the subject of a book length investigation. Naturally, able scholars have written dozens of essays on individual scriptures that could be taken to support an evil creator, but these have mostly focused on passages from *Jewish* texts.[37] In this book, I ultimately grant more weight to distinctly *Christian*

---

critique, see Michael Williams, *Rethinking "Gnosticism": An Argument for Dismantling a Dubious Category* (Princeton: Princeton Univeristy Press, 1996), 222–24; Smith, *No Longer Jews*, 40–41.

[34] See the more detailed history of research in M. David Litwa, "The Curse of the Creator: Gal 3.13 and Negative Demiurgy," in *Telling the Christian Story Differently: Counternarratives from Nag Hammadi and Beyond*, ed. Francis Watson and Sarah Parkhouse (London: Bloomsbury Academic Press, 2020), 13–30 at 13–15.

[35] Noted Williams, "Demonizing," 87–91.

[36] Williams, *Rethinking*, 265–66. Note also Williams' comments on Guy Stroumsa, *Another Seed: Studies in Gnostic Mythology* (Leiden: Brill, 1984), in *Rethinking*, 221–23.

[37] See, e.g., Elaine Pagels, *Adam, Eve and the Serpent* (New York: Random House, 1988), 55–77; G. P. Luttikhuizen, *Gnostic Revisions of Genesis Stories and Early Jesus Traditions* (Leiden: Brill, 2006); Jaan Lahe, *Gnosis und Judentum: Alttestamentliche und jüdische Motive in der gnostischen Literatur und das Ursprungsproblem der Gnosis* (Leiden: Brill, 2006); Ismo Dunderberg, "Gnostic Interpretations of Genesis," in *The Oxford Handbook of the Reception History of the Bible*, ed. Michael Lieb, Emma Mason, and Jonathan Roberts (Oxford: Oxford University Press, 2011), 383–96; Karen King, "A Distinctive Intertextuality: Genesis and Platonizing Philosophy in the Secret Revelation of John,"

scriptures (the "New Testament"), in part because the Christian interpretation of these texts gives a sense for the *hermeneutical frameworks* that were then applied to Jewish scriptures.[38]

Figures and Sources

Before we dive into the maelstrom of early biblical interpretation, however, we must inquire about the Christians who used scripture to derive the evil creator. In many cases, their names have been utterly forgotten. We can reasonably refer to *certain* Christian conventicles as "Sethians" (aka the Seed of Seth, the Immovable Generation, the Generation Without a King) in the sense of a distinct sociological group.[39] It is inaccurate, however, to speak globally of "G/gnostics" as if this label included every supporter of the evil creator idea. It did not, for instance, typically include Marcion, a key second-century Christian theologian and our focus in Part II.

Here in Part I, I examine the origin of the evil creator idea among other early Christian groups. In Chapter 1, I refer to people whom Epiphanius of Salamis (about 315–403 CE) called "Phibionites" in Egypt.[40] I will compare the views of these Phibionite Christians with the description of the evil world rulers in the *Secret Book of John* and the so-called Ophite diagram. The *Secret*

---

in *Gnosticism, Platonism, and the Late Ancient World: Essays in Honor of John Turner* (Leiden: Brill, 2013), 3–22.

[38] See further Gerhard Luttikhuizen, "Sethianer?" *Zeitschrift für Antikes Christentum (ZAC)* 13:1 (2009): 76–86 at 82–85; Luttikhuizen, *Gnostic Revisions*, 17–28; Michael Waldstein, "The Primal Triad in the *Apocryphon of John*," in *The Nag Hammadi Library After Fifty Years*, ed. John D. Turner and Anne McGuire (Leiden: Brill, 1997), 154–87 at 174–75; Alistair H. B. Logan, *Gnostic Truth and Christian Heresy: A Study in the History of Gnosticism* (Edinburgh: T&T Clark, 1996), 182–83, 283, and in general Christoph Markschies's attempt to reintegrate Gnosis into second-century ecclesiastical history (*Gnosis und Christentum* [Berlin: Berlin University Press, 2009], 34–82).

[39] I agree with David Brakke that we can speak etically of a "Gnostic" school of thought roughly equivalent to what other scholars designate by the term "Sethian" (*The Gnostics: Myth, Ritual, and Diversity in Early Christianity* [Cambridge, MA: Harvard University Press, 2010]). But the conception of the evil creator was not limited to this particular school, and the writings of this group do not clearly reveal how its theologians arrived at this conception.

[40] Epiphanius, *Panarion* 25.2.1; 26.3.7; cf. 26.4.6. Epiphanius himself testified that he had met these people between about 330 and 335 CE (*Panarion* 26.17.4, 8). Van den Broek considers Epiphanius's Phibionites to be an "offshoot" of the "Gnostics" who adhered to the system described by Irenaeus (*AH* 1.29) and the *Secret Book of John* ("Borborites," in *DGWE (Dictionary of Gnosis and Western Esotericism)*, ed. Wouter Hanegraaff [Leiden: Brill, 2006], 196). Hans Martin Schenke grouped Epiphanius's "Phibionites" and "Archontics" into his Sethian category ("The Phenomenon and Significance of Gnostic Sethianism," in *Rediscovery of Gnosticism*, ed. Benton Layton [Leiden: Brill, 1981], Vol. 2, 588–616 at 589. See also Williams, *Rethinking*, 179–84.

Book is widely held to be the classic work of the Sethian school of Christian thought.[41] The "Ophite diagram" was named after a group that heresiologists called "Ophite" ("Serpentine"). We do not know how the latter group labeled itself, although "Christian" seems a fair guess since Celsus, a Platonist writing about 178 CE, assumed their Christian identity.[42]

In Chapter 2, we encounter other types of Christians labeled "Peratic," "Archontic," "Severian," and "Manichean." Once again, it would be a mistake to clump together these systems under one global category, "gnostic," since none of them belonged to a single school of thought or shared a coherent spirituality.[43] What united them in this case were certain hermeneutical strategies for interpreting John 8:44. They all agreed, as it turned out, that John 8:44 spoke of "the father of the devil," a being whom they identified with the putatively wicked god of the Jews. [44]

Method

In large part, this is a work of reception history—more specifically the history of interpretation. I define the latter as the study of the activated meanings of a text in a given historical context.[45] The historical focus of this book is the period between the mid–second and the late fourth century CE. Accordingly, I do not aim to uncover the earliest ("original") meanings of biblical texts. Rather, I attempt to recover what they meant at a particular time frame to the particular Christian interpreters studied here.

---

[41] Brakke, *Gnostics*, 36–37, 54–70. The label "Classic Gnostic" is proposed by Rasimus, (*Paradise*, 5) to signify the fusion of Sethite, Ophite, and Barbeloite mythology so tightly interwoven in the *Secret Book*.

[42] Origen, *Against Celsus* (*Cels*). 6.24. For Ophite mythology, see Rasimus, *Paradise*, 41–64, 283–94.

[43] Roelof van den Broek, "Archontics," in *DGWE* 89–91 at 90; Brakke, *Gnostics*, 45, 51. See further Michael A. Williams, "Sethianism," in *A Companion to Second-Century Christian "Heretics,"* ed. Antti Marjanen and Petri Luomanen (Leiden: Brill, 2005), 32–63.

[44] Chapters 3–7 of this work will be summarized in the Introduction to Part II.

[45] For reception history, see further Emma England and William John Lyons, eds., *Reception History and Biblical Studies: Theory and Practice* (London: Bloomsbury, 2015), 45–46; Robert Evans, *Reception History, Tradition and Biblical Interpretation: Gadamer and Jauss in Current Practice* (London: Bloomsbury, 2014); David Paul Parris, *Reception Theory and Biblical Hermeneutics* (Eugene: Pickwick, 2008). On the reception history of Paul, see Margaret M. Mitchell, *Paul, the Corinthians and the Birth of Christian Hermeneutics* (Cambridge: Cambridge University Press, 2010); Benjamin L. White, *Remembering Paul: Ancient and Modern Contests over the Image of the Apostle* (Oxford: Oxford University Press, 2014); Jennifer R. Strawbridge, *The Pauline Effect: The Use of the Pauline Epistles by Early Christian Writers* (Berlin: de Gruyter, 2015).

As a scholar, I acknowledge that I have my own interpretive horizon, best disclosed, perhaps, through a discussion of hermeneutical presuppositions. I assume, first of all, that there is no "plain" reading of biblical texts, but simply readings that make sense in certain cultural environments to certain persons or groups for certain reasons.[46] No text is hermeneutically determined. There is a hermeneutical fullness—caused in part by semantic gaps—in biblical texts that allow searching minds to fill in the blanks and make inferences. In new contexts, interpreters ask different questions and bring out distinctive facets of a text not readily visible to those in different times and intellectual traditions.[47]

I presuppose, furthermore, that interpretation is always selective and limited by the horizon of the interpreter (whether ancient or modern). As a result, reception history is always *our* reception of an *earlier* reception. We are the ones who imagine and reconstruct the earlier interpretive horizon that is to some degree fused with our own.[48]

It used to be thought that so-called gnostic exegesis was an intentionally perverse kind of "protest exegesis." This view has been thoroughly criticized and is no longer tenable, at least as a generalization.[49] When the earliest Christian interpreters read John 8:44, for instance, it was not to counter a standard or "normative" reading of the verse, since such a reading had not yet emerged.

The greatest benefit of reception history for this study is that it allows a clearing of the table—a suspension (though obviously not a complete liquidation) of our value judgments in the interest of reading and hearing biblical texts as they were interpreted in antiquity. This suspension is especially needed when dealing with a theologically charged topic like the evil creator. Traditional ("orthodox") readings of Christian scripture have in effect made the evil creator an impossible idea—or if possible, then blasphemous and dangerous. To the best of our ability, we must bracket these traditional readings to endeavor to understand interpretations from a fundamentally different—though still Christian—preunderstanding. It is pointless to *defend*

---

[46] See, e.g., Stanley Fish, "With the Compliments of the Author: Reflections on Austin and Derrida," in *Doing What Comes Naturally* (Durham: Duke University Press, 1989), 37–67.

[47] See further David W. Jorgensen, *Treasure in a Field: Early Christian Reception of the Gospel of Matthew* (Berlin: de Gruyter, 2016), 20–30; Benjamin A. Edsall, *The Reception of Paul and Early Christian Initiation: History and Hermeneutics* (Cambridge: Cambridge University Press, 2019), 253.

[48] Hans-Georg Gadamer, *Truth and Method* (New York: Continuum, 2003), 278–388.

[49] See esp. Williams, *Rethinking*, 54–79; Jorgensen, *Treasure*, 266–77; Austin Busch, "Characterizing Gnostic Scriptural Interpretation," *ZAC* 21:2 (2017): 243–71; Busch, "Gnostic Biblical and Second Sophistic Homeric Interpretation," *ZAC* 22:2 (2018): 195–217.

readings that construct an evil creator. At the same time, it is historically important charitably to *understand* them, in part because—as I point out in the Conclusion—analogous readings have resurfaced in the modern world.

In our quest for understanding, however, I must offer the following caveat. The early Christian interpreters discussed in this book were no friends of the Jewish deity and were likely no friends of the Jewish people either. Some of them were staunch critics of Jewish scriptures, at least insofar as these scriptures portrayed the creator as the true deity. A great deal of what these Christians wrote might seem (sometimes crassly) anti-Jewish in modern ears. As historians, we owe it to the ancients to understand them on their own terms and faithfully to report their words, their logic, and their inferences. It should go without saying, however, that I myself do not support or condone any interpretation that might lead to anti-Judaism in any form at any time for any reason. This point should be obvious, yet the terrible forces of racism that still lurk in our world compel the clearest of speech. In investigating the nature and sources of evil, we must never succumb to it.

1

The Donkey Deity

Snout: O Bottom, thou art changed! What do I see on thee?
Bottom: What do you see? You see an asshead of your own, do you?
—Shakespeare, *A Midsummer Night's Dream*, 3.115–18

Introduction

There was an ancient story recorded in two gospels that Jewish leaders murdered a righteous man called Zechariah between the inner shrine of the temple in Jerusalem and the bronze altar of its outer court (Matt 23:35; Luke 11:51). Although the tradition is mentioned as if well known, the circumstances of the murder and its motives went unstated. Indeed, even the identity of this "Zechariah son of Berachiah," as recorded in Matthew, remains unclear.[1]

By the early second century CE, Christians identified Zechariah with the father of John the Baptist, who—according to the gospel called Luke— briefly served as the Jewish high priest. When this Zechariah was wafting incense in the Holy of Holies, his priestly service was delayed by the sudden apparition of the angel Gabriel. Gabriel prophesied the birth of Zechariah's son. Yet when Zechariah asked a seemingly innocent question ("How will I know this?"), the angel's wrath flared; he numbed Zechariah's tongue for the next nine months. Accordingly, when the priest emerged from the temple doors, he could not explain the wonders he saw except by signals of his hands (Luke 1:5–25).

In this episode, however, Zechariah was not murdered—nor was there cause. Such a cause was later invented, however, and appeared in the account called the *Birth of Mary* (aka the *Protoevangelium of James*, mid–second

---

[1] See further Jean-Daniel Dubois, "La mort de Zacharie: mémoire juive et mémoire chrétienne," *Revue des Études Augustiniennes* 40 (1994): 23–38, with earlier sources on 31–32.

The Evil Creator. M. David Litwa, Oxford University Press. © Oxford University Press 2021.
DOI: 10.1093/oso/9780197566428.003.0002

century CE).[2] The launch point of this tale was Matthew's story of the infants in Bethlehem slaughtered by king Herod (2:1–18). In the *Protoevangelium*, Herod further sent representatives to the priest Zechariah demanding the whereabouts of his son John—a presumed royal pretender. Zechariah pled ignorance, a tactic that inspired an enraged Herod to dispatch soldiers to slaughter Zechariah. This unholy rite the soldiers performed in the very forecourt of the temple. Eerily, however, Zechariah's body vanished and his blood congealed into stone—a permanent witness to murder licking the base of the temple altar.[3]

Yet this spicier tale still proved unsatisfactory since it did not explain why Jesus said that "*you*"—Judean people, not Herod's soldiers—"murdered Zechariah" (Matt 23:35). Accordingly, in another text called *The Birth* (or *Offspring*) *of Mary*, we find a competing narrative that in some ways is closer to what we find in Luke, though in other ways distant.[4]

As in Luke, Zechariah entered the temple, beheld a vision, and was made dumb. As he was releasing a cloud of incense from his censor, he beheld, to his surprise, a person standing in the Holy of Holies. This mysterious being lurking in the smoke was no Gabriel, however, but a being with the face or form of a donkey (*onou morphēn*). This was the creature who silently—and secretly—received the devoted worship of the Jewish people.

The stunned Zechariah stormed out of the temple intending to shout to the bystanders: "Woe to you! Whom are you worshiping?!" He would have done so, had not the ass deity—much like Gabriel—stopped up his mouth. But the powers of the donkey god were evidently frail, because Zechariah managed to soften his stony tongue and relate to the Jews the horror he beheld inside.[5]

---

[2] Émile de Strycker, *La forme la plus ancienne du Protévangile de Jacques* (Brussels: Bollandist Society, 1961), 211–12.

[3] *Protoevangelium* 23. Origen reported that Zechariah, father of John the Baptist, defended Mary the mother of Jesus's right to pray in the place of virgins and was killed by "the men of that generation" (*Series Commentary on Matthew* 25, translated by Ronald E. Heine, *The Commentary of Origen on the Gospel of Matthew* 2 vols [Oxford: Oxford University Press, 2018], 2.575–76).

[4] The title of the work is Γέννα Μαρίας. Liddell-Scott-Jones, *Greek-English Lexicon (LSJ)*, lists under the headword γέννα: "descent, birth, origin" (I), but also "offspring, son, creation, family" (II).

[5] Zechariah's intended proclamation puts him into the mold of a prophet and in particular the mold of the prophet Zechariah killed in 2 Chronicles 24:20–22. Before his death, this Zechariah claimed that the Jewish people had abandoned Yahweh, so Yahweh abandoned them.

The people were aghast—not (or not only) to learn of the perverse shape of their deity—but that Zechariah the high priest would say things so disturbing as to strike at the root of their religious worship. And so—as if Zechariah himself were some sacrificial bull or goat—they cut him down then and there at the foot of the temple altar.[6]

This story from the *Birth of Mary* was used by a Christian sect that Epiphanius, bishop of Cyprus, called "Phibionite."[7] These Epiphanian Phibionites lived somewhere in Egypt around the year 335 CE. The prehistory of this group, however—along with the composition of the *Birth of Mary*—is masked in shadows.[8] Previous scholars have proposed a mid-second century date for what became the Phibionite *Birth of Mary*, slightly before the *Protoevangelium of James*.[9]

Yet the Phibionite *Birth of Mary* depends upon a much older Egyptian tradition, one that depicted the Jewish deity as a donkey god (or rather, donkey demon). In this chapter, I trace the roots of this tradition before judging its significance for the early Christian notion of the evil creator. My proposal is that whoever wrote and used the Phibionite *Birth of Mary* came to accept Egyptian revisionary lore polemically aimed at the Jews. The writers maintained, in short, that the Jewish deity was a form of the Egyptian god Seth. Long before Christianity was born, Seth's wicked character and donkey-shaped appearance had been transferred to the god of the Jews such that it

---

[6] Epiphanius, *Panarion* 26.11.12–26.12.4.

[7] Epiphanius, *Panarion* 25.2.1; 26.3.7. For their background, see Stephen Benko, "The Libertine Sect of the Phibionites according to Epiphanius, *Vigiliae Christianae (VC)* 21:2 (1967): 103–19; Michel Tardieu, "Épiphane contre les Gnostiques," *Tel Quel* 88 (1981): 64–91, esp. 88; Williams, *Rethinking*, 179–84; Birger Pearson, *Ancient Gnosticism* (Minneapolis: Fortress, 2007), 54–59; Christoph Markschies, "Die Geburt Mariens," in *Antike christlichen Apokryphen in deutscher Übersetzung*, ed. Jens Schröter and Christoph Markschies (Tübingen: Mohr Siebeck, 2012) I/1, 416–19.

[8] Epiphanius implied that his "Phibionites" forged the *Birth of Mary* (*Panarion* 26.11.12), but he cannot be taken as reliable. Stephen Gero, believing Epiphanius too much, traces these "Phibionites" back to second-century Nicolaitans ("With Walter Bauer on the Tigris: Encratite Orthodoxy and Libertine Heresy in Syro-Mesopotamian Christianity," in *Nag Hammadi Gnosticism and Early Christianity*, eds. C. W. Hedrick and R. Hodgson [Peabody: Hendrickson, 1986], 287–307, at 304). See further van den Broek, "Borborites," in *DGWE*, 194–96.

[9] A. Berendts, *Studien über Zacharias-Apokryphen und Zacharias-Legenden* (Leipzig: Deichert'sche, 1895), 36–37; Jean-Daniel Dubois, "Hypothèse sur l'origine de l'apocryphe *Genna Marias*," *Augustinianum* 23 (1983): 263–70; Enrico Norelli, *Marie des apocryphes: Enquête de la mère de Jésus dans le christianisme antique* (Geneva: Labor et Fides, 2009), 91–92.

was possible for early Gentile Christians in Egypt immediately to associate him with chaos and evil.[10]

The Egyptian Seth

Since the time of the Assyrian occupation of Egypt (670 BCE), Egyptians recognized their native god Seth as a source of evils and misfortunes. He was god of violent storms and unforgiving desert sands. He protected nomads, watched over foreign countries, and provided for resident aliens in Egypt.[11] Even before the Persians assaulted the land of the Nile, Seth was identified with the Phoenician storm god Baal—the theological cousin, so to speak, of Yahweh in Judea.[12]

Important for our purposes, Seth was frequently described as having the form or skin of a donkey.[13] From ancient times, he appeared in Egyptian art as a human figure with the head (or mask) of a creature showing long, cropped ears and a drooping snout.[14] The Greeks, at least, identified this creature with a donkey, and the donkey was portrayed—along with the pig—as Seth's sacred animal (see Figure 1.1).[15]

---

[10] See further Wolfgang Fauth, "Seth-Typhon, Onoel und der eselköpfige Sabaoth: Zur Theriomorphie der ophitsichen-barbelognostischen Archonten," *Oriens Christianus* 57 (1973): 79–120.

[11] H. Te Velde, *Seth, God of Confusion* (Leiden: Brill, 1967), 91–94, 118, 128, 139–40, 145–46, 148–49; Birger Pearson, "Egyptian Seth and Gnostic Seth," in *Society of Biblical Literature 1977 Seminar Papers*, ed. Paul J. Achtemeier (Missoula: SBL, 1977), 25–43 at 25–30; K. van der Toorn, "Seth" in *Dictionary of Deities and Demons in the Bible (DDD)*, ed. Karel van der Toorn, Bob Becking, and Pieter W. Van der Horst (Leiden: Brill, 1999), 748–49; J. W. van Henten, "Typhon" in ibid., 879–81; Yuri Stoyanov, *The Other God: Dualist Religions from Antiquity to the Cathar Heresy* (New Haven: Nota Bene, 2000), 17–21; Jan Assmann, *Of God and Gods: Egypt, Israel, and the Rise of Monotheism* (Madison: University of Wisconsin Press, 2008), 28–52.

[12] Te Velde, *Seth*, 109, 119–20, 124–29.

[13] Plutarch, *Isis-Osiris* 362f–363b.

[14] The exact nature of the creature is still disputed. See Te Velde, *Seth*, 7–26; Bezalel Bar-Kochva, *The Image of the Jews in Greek Literature* (Berkeley: University of California Press, 2010), 236, n.99. For images, see Richard Wünsch, *Sethianische Verfluchungtafeln aus Rom* (Leipzig: Teubner, 1898), 16, 40; A. Procopé-Walter, "Iao und Set (Zu den figurae magicae in den Zauberpapyri)," *Archiv für Religionswissenschaft* 30 (1933): 34–69 at 49, 60; Hans Dieter Betz, ed., *The Greek Magical Papyri in Translation*, 2nd ed. (Chicago: University of Chicago Press, 1992), 169; G. Michailides, "Papyrus contenant un dessin du dieu Seth à tête d'âne," *Aegyptus* 32:1 (1952): 45–53.

[15] Plutarch, *Isis-Osiris* 362f; 363c; 371c. See further J. Gwynn Griffiths, *Plutarch's De Iside et Osiride* (Cardiff: University of Wales, 1970), 409–10, 418; Te Velde, *Seth*, 3–26; Bar-Kochva, *Image*, 245. Seth-Typhon is symbol of superstitious fear and hatred (Ps.-Plutarch, *Banquet of Seven Sages* 150f; Apuleius, *Metamorphoses*, 11.6). Practitioners of spells, when they referred to the "blood of Typhon," referred to donkey blood (*Greek Magical Papyri [PGM]* 4.3260).

SĒTH

BOLCHOSĒTH

[I]ŌERBĒTH

OSESRO

Figure 1.1. The Seth animal. Reproduced by permission from Hans Dieter Betz, ed., *The Greek Magical Papyri in Translation Including the Demotic Spells*, 2nd ed. (Chicago: University of Chicago Press, 1992), 169.

Interpretatio Graeca

Since the fifth century BCE (and probably earlier), there was a Greek cultural practice of identifying foreign gods now dubbed *interpretatio Graeca*.[16] In short, Greeks would identify two different gods from two different cultures based on shared traits. For instance, the Egyptian god Thoth was identified with the Greek Hermes because both were considered clever;[17] Hathor was fused with Aphrodite because both were goddesses of love; Horus morphed with Apollo since both shared solar characteristics, and so on.

[16] See Mark S. Smith, *God in Translation: Deities in Cross-Cultural Discourse in the Biblical World* (Grand Rapids: Eerdmans, 2008), 5–9, 243–83; Clifford Ando, *The Matter of the Gods: Religion and the Roman Empire* (Berkeley: University of California Press, 2008), 43–58; Alexandra von Lieven, "Translating Gods, Interpreting Gods," in *Greco-Egyptian Interactions: Literature, Translation, and Culture 500 BC–AD 300*, ed. Ian Rutherford (Oxford: Oxford University Press, 2016), 61–83; Océane Henri, "A General Approach to *interpretatio Graeca* in the Light of Papyrological Evidence," in *Platonismus und spätägyptische Religion: Plutarch und die Ägyptenrezeption in der römischen Kaiserzeit*, ed. Michael Erler and Martin Andreas Stadler (Berlin: de Gruyter, 2017), 43–54. See also Peter Schäfer, *Judeophobia: Attitudes Toward the Jews in the Ancient World* (Cambridge: Harvard University Press, 1997), 50–54.

[17] See further M. David Litwa, *Hermetica II: The Excerpts of Stobaeus, Papyrus Fragments, and Ancient Testimonies* (Cambridge: Cambridge University Press, 2018), 2–9.

When it came to Seth, the Greeks had long identified him with Typhon, lord of chaos.[18] Typhon was more of a monster than a god. The archaic poet Hesiod had described him as a hundred-headed dragon with sparks shooting from his eyes, roaring surreally.[19] Another Greek poet described him as "enemy of gods."[20] Yet another said that he withstood all the gods, furiously hissing terror with his horrid jaws.[21] Typhon, an unstoppable blitzkrieg, was known for boasting loudly against the great gods, and for a time he even overcame their king, Zeus, by stealing his sinews.[22]

Analogously, Seth buried alive the king god Osiris and later hacked up his body in order to taste the sweetness of a fleeting rule.[23] Even though both Seth and Typhon were reconquered, they continued to wreak havoc by sending powerful storms. Thus it was logical for Greeks to identify Seth with Typhon, and in scholarly literature his name regularly appears in hybrid form as "Seth-Typhon."

Hellenized Egyptians capitalized on this cultural practice of translation by viewing the Jewish god Yahweh as a form of Seth. In this case, however, malice seems to have been the chief motive, and the translational practice was part of a larger program of mythmaking. Put briefly, Yahweh became Seth for Egyptians when they revised their historical memory to oppose the perceived political and cultural threat posed by Jewish lore in Egypt.

Exodus Lore

The Jewish story of the Exodus was translated into Greek (third century BCE) and retold in iambic trimeter by Ezekiel the Tragedian (probably second century BCE).[24] The case of Ezekiel is important because he adapted the story for the stage. Theater was enjoyed, not just by Jews, but by Egyptians, Greeks, and

---

[18] The identification is already made by Herodotus, *Histories* 2.144, 156, and apparently by Pherecydes according to Celsus in Origen, *Cels.* 6.42.

[19] Hesiod, *Theogony*, 820–80.

[20] Pindar, *Pythian Odes* 1.15.

[21] [Aeschylus], *Prometheus Bound*, 353–63; cf. Aeschylus, *Seven Against Thebes*, 493–4.

[22] Pseudo-Apollodorus, *Library* 1.6.3 with Timothy Gantz, *Early Greek Myth: A Guide to Literary and Artistic Sources*, 2 vols. (Baltimore: Johns Hopkins University Press, 1993), 1.48–51.

[23] Plutarch, *Isis-Osiris* 356b–359d; Diodorus, *Library of History* 1.21.

[24] R. G. Robertson, "Ezekiel the Tragedian," in *The Old Testament Pseudepigrapha (OTP)*, ed. James H. Charlesworth (New York: Doubleday, 1985), 2.803–20. Greek text in Carl Holladay, *Fragments from Hellenistic Jewish Authors II: Poets* (Atlanta: Scholars Press, 1989), 376–78. See further John M. G. Barclay, *Jews in the Mediterranean Diaspora: From Alexander to Trajan (323 BCE–117 CE)* (Edinburgh: T&T Clark, 1996), 35–47, 132–38; Tim Whitmarsh, "Politics and Identity in Ezekiel's *Exagoge*," in *Beyond the Second Sophistic: Adventures in Greek Postclassicism* (Berkeley: University of California Press, 2013), 211–27.

by the many peoples of mixed cultural heritage in Egypt. If Ezekiel's play was staged (as its form indicates[25]), it was probably presented to a wide audience.[26]

The biblical Exodus spoke of the Hebrews as an innocent people, about seventy strong, invited to stay in Egypt to escape starvation but later betrayed and oppressed by a hostile Pharaoh. As a ploy to stave off the Israelite population explosion, Pharaoh ordered the slaughter of Israel's male infants by having them tossed, helpless, into the Nile (Exod 1–4).

After 400 years, the Jewish deity responded by unleashing ten horrific plagues against Egypt—epidemics that decimated the countryside, Egypt's sacred river, and its youth. In the words of the Wisdom of Solomon (first century BCE or CE), the Egyptians were "whipped by foreign showers of rain and hail, pursued by relentless storms, and utterly torched by fire" (16:16).

Finally broken by the tenth plague—which destroyed his own son—Pharaoh agreed to release the Hebrews, who burst forth from Egypt wearing the gold and silver bangles of the Egyptians (Exod 11:2; 12:35–36). Their final triumph was enacted at the Red Sea where Yahweh opened a dry channel for his people's safe crossing but let the waters come crashing down on Pharaoh's army.

When, toward the beginning of the third century BCE, the Jews became established in Egypt, native Egyptians and Greeks became increasingly aware of the god of Exodus and his plagues. In the fragments of Ezekiel's play, this deity speaks to Moses:

> By this wand all these evils you shall create:
> The river [Nile] shall run with blood in spate
> Along with all the springs, pools, and bogs.
> I'll cast on the ground teeming lice and frogs;

---

[25] Robertson notes that the "possibility that the play was intended for the stage is enhanced by the evidence which indicates that Ezekiel transformed certain material from the Exodus account which would have been virtually impossible to present upon the stage. The plagues, for example, have been completely relegated to a speech delivered by God to Moses" (*OTP* 2.806).

[26] Howard Jacobson, "The *Exagoge* was written for non-Jews as well as Jews" (*The Exagoge of Ezekiel* [Cambridge: Cambridge University Press, 1983], 8). Jacobson thought that there was already "present an element of polemic against anti-Semitic Exodus-traditions. Further, Ezekiel leaves out material from the Biblical narrative that would be offensive to non-Jews or that would put the Jews in a bad light" (*ibid.*, 18). A similar point is made by Holladay, *Fragments II* 303: "Ezekiel's concern [was] to commend the Jewish faith to a *Greek* audience" (311, emphasis his). Likewise K. B. Free, "Thespis and Moses: The Jews and the Ancient Greek Theater," in *Theatre and Holy Script*, ed. Shimon Levy (Brighton: Sussex Academic Press, 1999), 149–58 at 153; Allen, "Ezekiel the Tragedian and the Despoliation of Egypt," *Journal for the Study of the Pseudepigrapha* 17:1 (2007): 3–19, at 9. For opposing views, see Erich Gruen, *Heritage and Hellenism: The Reinvention of Jewish Tradition* (Berkeley: University of California Press, 1998), 136; Pierluigi Lanfranchi, *L'Exagoge d'Ezéchiel le Tragique: Introduction, texte, traduction et commentaire* (Leiden: Brill, 2006), 157–64.

> Then sprinkle ashes from the oven
> So ulcerous sores burst upon men.
> Next, dog-flies shall come and prick
> The hides of Egyptians fast and thick.
> They of hardened heart shall expire
> When I from heaven send hail and fire
> When mortal corpses rot and burn;
> Against their crops and cattle I'll turn
> Darkness I'll create for three days successive,
> Then locusts, fearsome and aggressive
> Will chew up every green shoot grown wild.
> To top it all, I'll kill everybody's firstborn child.[27]

Egyptian priests, including famous historians like Manetho and Chaeremon, would have been horrified by the Exodus myth's rhetorical violence wielded against Egypt, its people, and its gods.[28] The Egyptian gods were depicted as powerless to defend themselves against the relentless attacks of a foreign deity, a being who showed open favoritism to his own people while unleashing the equivalent of biological warfare against the Egyptian populace.[29]

Beginning in the first century BCE, Hellenized Egyptian literati punched back to refute and reverse elements of the Exodus story using the resources of their own millennia-long cultural memory. In their retellings, the Egyptians were not plagued; it was the Hebrews who were afflicted with leprosy and boils.[30] Instead of the Egyptians drowned in the Red Sea, it was the Hebrews drowned in lakes on leaden rafts. Instead of the Hebrews bursting out of Egypt weighted with gold, they were disgorged into the desert—the realm of

---

[27] Ezekiel, *Exagoge*, 1.132–47.

[28] For Manetho, see John Dillery, *Clio's Other Sons: Berossus and Manetho* (Ann Arbor: University of Michigan Press, 2018). Manetho in the third century BCE did not depend on Septuagintal traditions (Gruen, *Heritage* 62–68; Russell E. Gmirkin, *Berossus and Genesis, Manetho and Exodus: Hellenistic Histories and the Date of the Pentateuch* [London: Bloomsbury, 2006], 187; Jan Assmann, *Moses the Egyptian: The Memory of Egypt in Western Monotheism* [Cambridge, MA: Harvard University Press, 1997], 23–44). Nevertheless, the reworking of Manetho's history and its reception by Josephus and Theophilus (*Autolycus* 3.21) show that later readers used Manetho's account to support anti-Jewish attitudes and policies. On Chaeremon, see Pieter W. van der Horst, *Chaeremon: Egyptian Priest and Stoic Philosopher* (Leiden: Brill, 1983), esp. 9, 50–51. Chaeremon evidently derived the names "Moses" and "Joseph" from Genesis and Exodus. He possibly obtained the name "Ramesses" from Exodus 12:37, and his total number for the forces against Egypt (630,000) is close to the 600,000 men in Exodus 12:37.

[29] Josephus's comment may be significant here: "At Alexandria there had been constant strife (ἀεὶ . . . στάσις) between the natives and the Jewish element ever since Alexander [the Great, died 323 BCE]" (*Jewish War* 2.487).

[30] Josephus, *Against Apion* 2.21–24.

Seth—and left there to wander with nothing.[31] The flight of a liberated people was retooled as an expulsion of a diseased and doomed tribe.[32]

Seth-Yahweh

Our focus, however, is on the Egyptian depiction of the Jewish deity. From the Greco- Egyptian perspective, Yahweh and Seth shared several traits: they were both gods of foreigners, of the desert, and of frightening storms. They both sent calamities. Indeed, Egyptians could not help but notice that some of the plagues unleashed by Yahweh resembled disasters customarily inflicted by Seth: darkness, eclipse, and pestilence.[33] Red was the distinctive hue of Seth,[34] and Yahweh turned the Nile crimson before ordering the Hebrews to paint their lintels with blood.[35] Mount Sinai, the desert crag from which Yahweh revealed his Law, quaked as it was enveloped in thunder, lightning, and fire—all phenomena associated with Seth.[36] Finally, the Greek word for Yahweh (*Iaō*)—with a perverse twist of the tongue—sounded like the native Egyptian word for donkey (*eiō* or simply *iō*).[37] These factors, even if judged artificial today, were more than enough for Hellenized Egyptians to portray Yahweh as a form of Seth.[38]

---

[31] The last three sentences represent the account of the Alexandrian writer Lysimachus, whose work on the history of Egypt Bar-Kochva (*Image* 336) dates from 110 to 100 BCE. Its contents are partially transmitted by Josephus, *Against Apion* 1.305–11, with translation and discussion in Menahem Stern, *Greek and Latin Authors on Jews and Judaism*, 3 vols. (Jerusalem: Israel Academy of Science and Humanities, 1974), 1.382–88. See further John G. Gager, *Moses in Greco-Roman Paganism* (Nashville: Abingdon, 1972), 113–33; C. Aziza, "L'utilisation polémique du récit de l'Exode chez les écrivains alexandrins (IV siècle av. J.-C.-1 siècle ap. J.C.," *Aufstieg und Niedergang der römischen Welt* (*ANRW*), ed. Wolfgang Haase, II.20.1 (Berlin: de Gruyter, 1987), 41–65, esp. 46–61; Schäfer, *Judeophobia* 15–33.

[32] On the cultural logic of this anti-Jewish mythmaking, see John M. G. Barclay, "Hostility to Jews as a Cultural Construct: Egyptian, Hellenistic, and Early Christian Paradigms," in *Josephus und das Neue Testament: Wechselseitige Wahrnehmungen*, ed. Christfried Böttrich and Jens Herzer (Tübingen: Mohr Siebeck, 2007), 365–86, esp. 370–75.

[33] Plutarch, *Isis-Osiris* 368f; 369a; 373d; cf. Exod 9:15–35; 10:21–23; 11:4–6.

[34] Plutarch, *Isis-Osiris* 359e; 362e; 363b; 364b; Diodorus of Sicily, *Library of History* 1.88.4.

[35] Exod 12:7, 13, 22–23.

[36] Plutarch *Isis-Osiris* 373d; 364a; 366d; 376f; cf. Exod 19:16–18; *PGM* 4.180–96.

[37] W. E. Crum includes ιλω as a variant spelling for ειω (*A Coptic Dictionary* [Oxford: Clarendon, 1939], 75). Adolf Jacoby speculated that the Hebrew Yahu (a form of Yahweh) was morphed with the Coptic ειλ 20 or "donkey head" ("Der angebliche Eselskult der Juden und Christen," *Archiv für Religionswissenschaft* 25 [1927]: 265–82 at 273); Griffiths (*De Iside*, 409) notes that the spelling of the donkey noise was sometimes written *iao*. See also Stern, *Authors*, 1.98; Assmann, *Moses*, 37. For a different opinion, see Bar-Kochva, *Image*, 244. On Greek and Roman knowledge of the name "Iao," see Diodorus, *Library of History* 1.94.1–2; Varro in Augustine, *Agreement of the Gospels* 1.27.42.

[38] It may also be significant that Yahweh, perhaps identical to the "angel of Yahweh," chose a donkey to speak for him in the story of Balaam's ass (Num 22:22–35). Other talking donkeys akin to this one appear in early Christian literature, for instance, in the *Acts of Thomas* 39–41, 68–80. See further Janet E. Spittler, *Animals in the Apocryphal Acts of the Apostles: The Wild Kingdom of Early Christian*

There was an additional motivation. For centuries, Jews had scorned the religion of Egypt as the worship of dumb beasts.[39] One way for learned Egyptians to fight back was to depict the Jewish deity as himself the most vile and ridiculous beast.[40] If Yahweh was a form of Seth, then he could be portrayed in Seth's ass-like shape. Thus there arose the tradition that the Jews (secretly) worshiped Yahweh as a donkey or as a man standing upright with an ass's head.[41]

The Ass God

We see this tradition recounted by several writers. Around 200 BCE, a man called Mnaseas (an Alexandrian originally from what is now southern Turkey), told a story of an Idumean (southern Palestinian) who entered the Judean temple and tore off the golden head of a pack ass from the inner sanctuary.[42] This head was evidently attached to a body, whether human or

---

Literature (Tübingen: Mohr Siebeck, 2008), 199–223. Already in the third century BCE translation of the Pentateuch, Jewish translators avoided the word "donkey" when connected with Moses, as in Exod 4:20; Num 16:15 (LXX). The avoidance is noted in b. *Megillah* 9b.

[39] Rom 1:23–28; Wisd 11:15; 12.24, 27; 13:14; 15:18–19; *Letter of Aristeas* 135; Philo, *Decalogue* 76–80; *Contemplative Life* 8–10; *Embassy* 139, 163; Josephus, *Against Apion* 1.225, 254; 2.66, 81, 86, 128–29, 139. See further K. A. D. Smelik and E. A. Hemelrijk, "'Who Knows Not What Monsters Demented Egypt Worships?' Opinions on Egyptian Animal Worship in Antiquity as Part of the Ancient Conception of Egypt," *ANRW*, ed. Haase, II.17.4, 1920–1981 at 1910–19. According to Erik Hornung, ancient Egyptians viewed animals not as gods but as dwelling places, vehicles, and living images of the gods (*Conceptions of God in Ancient Egypt: The One and the Many*, trans. John Baines [Ithaca: Cornell University Press 1982], 137–38). Ingvild Saelid Gilhus speaks of Egyptian animals sharing the divine essence of the gods (*Animals, Gods and Humans: Changing Attitudes to Animals in Greek, Roman, and Early Christian Ideas* [London: Routledge, 2006], 100).

[40] Plutarch observes that the donkey is the stupidest of tame animals (*Isis-Osiris* 371c).

[41] For what follows, see John M. G. Barclay, *Against Apion: Translation and Commentary* (Leiden: Brill, 2007), 350–52; Louis Feldman, *Jew and Gentile in the Ancient World: Attitudes and Interactions from Alexander to Justinian* (Princeton: Princeton University Press, 1993), 499–501, n.12; Schäfer, *Judeophobia* 55–62; Jan Willem van Henten and Ra'anan Abusch, "The Depiction of the Jews as Typhonians and Josephus' Strategy of Refutation in *Contra Apionem*," in *Josephus' Contra Apionem: Studies in Its Character and Context with a Latin Concordance to the Portion Missing in Greek*, ed. Louis H. Feldman and John R. Levison (Leiden: Brill, 1996), 271–309 at 284–88; Gmirkin, *Berossus*, 277–96; Gilhus, *Animals*, 231–34; Philippe Borgeaud, "Quelques remarques sur Typhon, Seth, Moïse et son âne, dans la perspective d'un dialogue reactive transcultural," in *Interprétations de Moïse: Égypte, Judée, Grèce et Rome*, ed. Borgeaud et al. (Leiden: Brill, 2009), 173–85; Bar-Kochva, *Image*, 206–516.

[42] Josephus, *Against Apion* 2.112–14 = §28 in Stern, *Authors*, 99–100 (in the Greek text ἀκανθῶνος has been emended to κάνθωνος to agree with the Latin *asini*). For commentary, see Barclay, *Apion*, 228–29. Mnaseas had an Egyptian connection as a pupil of Eratosthenes, who thrived in the late third century BCE (*Suda s.v.* "Eratosthenes"). Probably Mnaseas told the story in his *Periplus*, a work that Bar-Kochva claims had wide circulation (*Image*, 206–31 at 207). See also P. M. Fraser, *Ptolemaic Alexandria*, 2 vols. (Oxford: Clarendon, 1972), 1.524–25, 781–82; Pietro Cappelletto, *I Frammenti di Mnasea: Introduzione testo e commento* (Milan: LED, 2003), 14–39, 89–90, 266–71.

donkey. The reader would have understood that the Jews (secretly) wor-shiped Yahweh as a donkey in the Jerusalem temple, since gold was char-acteristically used for cult statues of gods.[43] Egyptians knew only one other deity in ass-like form: Seth. We presume that Mnaseas adapted this story from someone, if not ethnically Egyptian, then at least embedded in Egyptian culture—which would include Mnaseas himself.[44]

Over a hundred years later, two respected scholars teaching on the island of Rhodes—the rhetor Apollonius Molon and the philosopher Posidonius (both flourishing from 100 to 70 BCE)—passed on a tradition that the Jews vener-ated their deity in the form of a golden donkey head.[45] According to their ver-sions (whose differences we cannot precisely discern), it was the Macedonian king—archenemy of the Jews—Antiochus IV Epiphanes who discovered the donkey head when he ransacked the Jewish temple around 167 BCE.[46] This tradition was recalled—or perhaps invented—when Antiochus's later suc-cessor (called Sidetes) was also poised to take over Jerusalem around 134 BCE.

Variants of this story fusing the form of Seth and Yahweh spread like a cancer. Probably in the first century BCE or CE, a man called Damocritus wrote a treatise *On the Jews*, in which he stated that the Jews worshiped the golden head of an ass.[47] In the 90s CE, Josephus the Jewish historian opened rhetorical fire against these traditions when they were recycled and adapted by his archenemy Apion (flourished 20–45 CE). Despite the efforts of Josephus, the tradition continued to be repeated by educated elites, including the eminent Roman historian Tacitus, who wrote (early in the second cen-tury CE) that the Jews dedicated in their holiest shrine a statue of a wild ass.[48]

---

[43] The story assumes that by stealing the god, the Idumean deprived the Jews of their power to fight a war (cf. 1 Sam 5:2). Here I oppose Bar-Kochva (*Image*, 237), who leans toward the view that for Mnaseas the donkey head/statue was a mere votive offering.

[44] Stern, *Authors*, 1.97–98; Bar-Kochva, *Image*, 224; cf. 217.

[45] The fragments of Apollonius Molon relating to the Jews are gathered by Stern, *Authors*, 1.148–56. See further Bar-Kochva, *Image*, 469–516, with earlier sources cited on 470, n.4. Bar-Kochva has a lengthy discussion of Posidonius (*Image*, 338–457, esp. 443–57). In part because he sees Posidonius as the source for Diodorus, Bar-Kochva concludes that Apion falsely named Posidonius as his refer-ence for the ass-head story (443). Contrast Stern, *Authors*, 1.141–47; Barclay, *Apion*, 350–52.

[46] Apion passed on the report of Molon and Posidonius according to Josephus, *Against Apion* 2.80. See Barclay, *Apion*, 350–52. Compare the tradition in Diodorus, *Library of History* 34/35.1.1–5. In this passage, Epiphanes finds a stone statue of Moses riding a donkey. But here the Jewish *deity* is not in focus.

[47] *Suda s.v.* "Damocritus" in Ada Adler, *Suidae Lexicon*, 5 vols. (Leipzig: Teubner, 1931), 2.5, n.49. See further Stern, *Authors*, 1.531.

[48] Tacitus, *Histories* 5.4.2, with Stern, *Authors*, 2.2–25. Tacitus referred to his story of a pack of wild asses guiding Moses to water in the desert, allowing him to assuage the thirst of the dying Israelites (*Histories* 5.3.2). This is also a tradition known from Plutarch, *Table Talk* 4.5.2 (670d). See further Heinz Heinen, "Ägyptische Grundlagen des antiken Antijudaismus: Zum Judenexkurs des Tacitus,

We gather that the tradition of the Jews (secretly) worshiping their god in donkey form was widely known by the early second century CE. Whoever originally invented the tales of the statue(s) was probably a person of Egyptian cultural heritage attempting to depict Yahweh as a form of Seth.[49] But the image had gone viral and could be learned in Syria, Rhodes, Greece, Egypt, Rome—and evidently the places in between.

Thinking of Yahweh as donkey shaped was perverse because educated Greeks and Romans knew that the Jews claimed to use no pictures or statues to represent their deity.[50] But claiming that the Jews were in fact hypocrites in this regard was part of the polemical twisting of the knife. The donkey-god tradition also "explained" why Jews were so selective about who entered their temple—they were ashamed of the shape of their deity.

Apart from broader knowledge of the Sethianization of Yahweh, it was unclear why Jews would have worshiped an ass god. But the same writers (like Apion and Tacitus) who told the donkey god stories also knew the revisionary Exodus stories (Jews as lepers expelled from Egypt). Even if some writers did not fully grasp the context of the Seth–Yahweh fusion, they had enough information to link the two deities, as is shown by the Greek polymath Plutarch.

In his treatise *On Isis and Osiris* (composed 100–120 CE), Plutarch recorded a tradition that Seth escaped a battle by fleeing Egypt on the back of a donkey.[51] Now a donkey is no glamorous getaway vehicle, but educated readers would recognize the braying beast of Seth.[52] This particular tradition was directed against the Jews, for it included an etiology of the Sabbath (Seth's

---

Historien V2 2–13," *Trierer Theologische Zeitschrift* 102 (1992): 124–49, esp. 137–40. There were also authors who knew the Egyptian revisionary mythology of the Hebrew Exodus but did not mention Jewish onolatry (e.g., Pompeius Trogus, *Philippic History*, in Stern, *Authors*, 1.332–43).

[49] Following Tcherikover, *Hellenistic Civilization and the Jews* (Philadelphia: Jewish Publication Society, 1961), 365–66, Feldman, *Jew and Gentile*, 500–501; Schäfer, *Judeophobia*, 55–72; Barclay, *Apion*, 352; Bar-Kochva, *Image*, 244, n.126.

[50] E.g., Hecataeus in Diodorus, *Library of History* 40.3.4, and in Josephus, *Against Apion* 1.199; Strabo, *Geography* 16.2.35 (Stern, *Authors*, 1.300).

[51] Plutarch, *Isis-Osiris* 363c–d, in Stern, *Authors*, 1.563.

[52] *Pace* Bar-Kochva (*Image*, 243–46), it is methodologically incorrect to blend this story of Plutarch with the tradition passed on by Diodorus (that there was a statue of *Moses* riding a donkey set up in the Jewish temple). The argument that Plutarch, or the inventor of the tradition he passed on, considered *Moses* to be Seth is unconvincing (Bar-Kochva, *Image*, 241–43). Bar-Kochva's statement that Tacitus viewed the *effigiem* not as a depiction of the Jewish god but as a votive offering is incorrect. The Latin term *votiva* mentioned by Bar-Kochva (*Image*, 242) is not found in the passage he cites (Tacitus, *Histories* 5.4.2). The fact that Artapanus described Moses as "fiery red" (in Eusebius, *Preparation for the Gospel* 9.37) indicates that Moses was Typhonic, not Seth-Typhon.

journey took seven days).[53] It also made Seth the father of Hierosolym
Judaeus (fictive ancestors of the Judeans who lived in Jerusalem).[54]

We do not know who first told this particular tale. We infer that the story's
author was familiar with Egyptian political myth and wanted to depict Seth
as the forefather of the Jews. The Jews, according to the story's logic, later dei-
fied their ancestor Seth.[55] That is to say, the Jews worshiped Seth as their god
Yahweh, just as the Greeks worshiped Zeus, king and culture-bringer of old.
Plutarch knew that Jewish elements were "dragged into" this story, though he
may have assumed that Jews themselves were the culprits.[56]

Onocoetes

The Seth–Yahweh fusion is also illustrated by early Christian writers. Many
early Christians adopted the Jewish creator as their supreme deity. Due in
part to this adoption, the accusation of donkey worship was easily transferred to them. Early readers of Tacitus assumed that the donkey-headed
deity in the Jewish temple was the Christian god as well.[57] Yet one did not
have to be a reader of Tacitus to be familiar with the ass god of the Christians.

According to a late second-century report, a former Jew hired himself
out in the wildly popular animal shows at Carthage (or possibly Rome).
Apparently he was a kind of bullfighter and entertainer all rolled into one.
This particular individual was known for holding up a placard exhibiting a
being with donkey ears and a cloven hoof poking out of his toga. This being
was labeled: "ONOCOETES, GOD OF THE CHRISTIANS."[58]

[53] This is the length of time it took the Israelites to reach Israel from Egypt (according to Apion in
Josephus, *Against Apion* 2.21; cf. Ezekiel, *Exagoge* 169 (*OTP* 2.815); Tacitus, *Histories* 5.4.3 (Stern,
Authors, 2.25).

[54] Plutarch, *Isis-Osiris* 363c–d. Tacitus wrote that the Jews came from Egypt during the reign of
Isis under the leadership of Hierosolymus and Juda (*Histories* 5.2.2). See further Theodor Hopfner,
Plutarch Über Isis und Osiris Zweiter Teil: Dei Deutungen der Sage (Darmstadt: Wissenschaftliche,
1967), 143–47; Griffiths, *Iside*, 418–19.

[55] For the deification of great ancestors, see Franco de Angelis and Benjamin Garstad, "Euhemerus
in Context," *Classical Antiquity* 25:2 (2006): 211–42; Marek Winiarczyk, *The "Sacred History" of
Euhemerus of Messene* (Berlin: de Gruyter, 2013); Nickolas P. Roubekas, *An Ancient Theory of
Religion: Euhemerism from Antiquity to the Present* (London: Routledge, 2017).

[56] Plutarch, *Isis-Osiris* 363d.

[57] Tertullian, *Apologeticum* 16.1.

[58] Tertullian, *Against the Nations* 1.14.1–2; *Apologeticum* 16.12. Manuscripts of *Against the Nations*
vary on the spelling of the donkey god. The names *onocholtes* and *oenocholtes* have been corrected
by the later use of *onochoetae*. See further Jean-G. Préaux, "Deus christianorum Onocoetes," in
Hommages à Léon Hermann (Brussels: Latomus, 1960), 639–54 at 639–41; Lukas Vischer, "Le prétendu 'culte de âne' dans la Église primitive," *Revue de l'histoire des religions* 139:1 (1951): 14–35;

nocoetes is obscure. *Onos* is the Greek word for
a common word for "(marriage) bed." The fusion
ld signify that the Christian god was born from the
a woman. (In the mid–second century, the novelist
:ivious upper-class lady who enjoyed intercourse with
ins associated the donkey with sexuality. According
eror Commodus (reigned 180–192 CE) nicknamed a
man known to have a large penis "Donkey."[60]

In the placard, the Christian deity was depicted as a donkey hybrid. Since, however, the donkey was the token of Seth-Typhon, he was no less a god. It was this ass deity who was regularly exhibited to thousands of spectators, a spectacle that reportedly inspired much guffawing in the audience.[61]

Minucius Felix (died around 250 CE) revealed how a Roman intellectual could think that Christians worshiped a donkey-headed figure. In his dialogue *Octavius*, he portrayed two Roman elites who locked horns in debate: Caecilius, the opponent of Christianity, and its champion Octavius. In the debate, Caecilius accuses Christians of worshiping a donkey head. Caecilius does not (or feigns not to) know why Christians do this. He simply assumes that they are stupid and worship a deity who fits their perverse morality.[62]

In his rebuttal, Octavius mentions Egypt—best known for animal worship (he mentions the Apis bull, for instance, and "dog-headed deities").[63] Octavius portrays Egyptian worship as foreign and perverse in order to distance its practices from Christian worship.[64] At the same time, he links

Claude Aziza, "Recherches sur l'Onokoites' des écrits apologétiques de Tertullien," in *Hommage a Pierre Fargues (Philologie, Littératures et histoire anciennes)*, ed. Wolfgang Haase (Paris: Belles Lettres, 1974), 283–90; Odile Ricoux, "Des Chrétiens accusés d'onolâtrie à Carthage," *Lalies* 16 (1996): 53–73; Xavier Levieils, *Contra Christianos: La critique sociale et religieuse du Christianisme des origines au Concile de Nicée* (Berlin: de Gruyter, 2007), 321–30.

[59] Apuleius, *Metamorphoses* 10.21–23; cf. Juvenal, *Satires* 6.332–34.

[60] *Historia Augusta, Commodus* 10.9.

[61] Tertullian, *Against the Nations* 1.14.2.

[62] Minucius Felix, *Octavius* 9.4.

[63] Minucius Felix, *Octavius* 28.7–9; cf. 25.6 (Egyptian gods as ominous monsters); 22.1–2 (Isis worship in Rome).

[64] Christians preserved the cultural memory that Egyptians worshiped the donkey, for instance, Athanasius, *Against the Nations* 9: "They [non-Christians] . . . venerate . . . the donkey-heads of the Egyptians" (οἱ παρ' Αἰγυπτίοις . . . ὀνοκέφαλοι). Cf. Jerome, *Commentary on Isaiah* 4.13: *gens Aegyptiorum . . . asinos divino nomine consecrarent* ("the Egyptian race . . . worship donkeys with the divine name"); Epiphanius mentions rites at Diospolis performed τῷ ὄνῳ εἰς ὄνομα τοῦ Σήθ, δῆθεν τοῦ Τυφῶνος ("for the donkey in the name of Seth, that is Typhon"; *On Faith* 12.3).

supposedly Christian ass worship with the memory of Egypt. Was he gesturing toward the tradition of Seth-Yahweh?

Excursus: Seth-Yahweh in Spells and Gems

In at least four surviving spells, Seth and Yahweh are invoked in such a way as to suggest their close association and perhaps identity. The spells come from papyrus books discovered in Egypt and now held in Paris. The books are dated to the fourth century CE, but many of their spells are thought to come from second- or third-century prototypes.

In a multipurpose spell for restraining charioteers, sending dreams, and inspiring love, a cat-headed sun god is invoked under various names. One of the names inscribed on a metal leaf and inserted into the earholes of a drowned cat is "IŌ SETH."[65] The spell is relevant only if IŌ is a form of IAŌ (the Greek form of Yahweh). Even if IŌ represents the Egyptian word for donkey (EIŌ) or the donkey's bray, however, a double meaning (IŌ = IAŌ) could be in play.[66]

A second spell, written in the form of a letter from Nephotes (an Egyptian sage) to a Pharaoh of the seventh or sixth century BCE, promises Pharaoh the power to get special information from a deity revealed through bowl divination. The deity is a sun god identified with "mighty Typhon, ruler of the realm above and master, god of gods."[67] A long list of names for the god follows. Among the names can thrice be distinguished IAŌ.[68] In this spell, Birger Pearson considered it "clear" that "Seth-Typhon is identified with the god of the Jews."[69] Pearson upheld a similar identification in the following two spells.

The first is an incantation of Typhon's soul represented by the Great Bear constellation. The practitioner anoints his or her lips with the fat of a black donkey and uses hairs from the same donkey to make a plaited cord wrapped

---

[65] *PGM* 3.77: ιωσηθ. For Seth as god of the blazing (vaporizing) sun, see Plutarch, *Isis-Osiris* 367d–e.

[66] See further Reinhold Merkelbach, *Abrasax: ausgewählte Papyri religiösen und magischen Inhalts. Band III: Zwei griechisch-ägyptsiche Weihezeremonien (Die Leidener Weltschöpfung-Die Pschai-Aion-Liturgie* (Opladen: Westdeutscher, 1992), 19–20, 44, 124–25, 214; Raquel Martín Hernández, "More than a Logos: The ΙΩΕΡΒΗΘ Logos in Context," in *Litterae Magicae: Studies in Honour of Roger S. O. Tomlin*, ed. Celia Sánchez Natalías (Zaragoza: Libros Pórtico, 2019), 187–210.

[67] *PGM* 4.179–80.

[68] *PGM* 4.204, 208.

[69] Pearson, "Egyptian Seth," 28.

as a crown.[70] The practitioner then kneels and prays to daemonic rulers, among them being SABAŌTH IAŌ. He or she then writes the hundred-lettered name of Typhon on papyrus and ties it to the cord used as a crown.[71]

Another spell was designed to afflict a woman with terrible pains. The practitioner is bid to draw on an unbaked brick the picture of a running donkey with the title IAŌ IŌ on its face.[72] The spell inscribed on the brick begins with the names of the deity addressed. The key deity invoked is "the great, great Typhon!"[73]

Despite Pearson's judgment, in none of these spells is it actually "clear" that Typhon is a form of Yahweh. The name of Yahweh may be invoked in its Greek form (Iao), but is it really the god of Jewish scripture?[74] Granted, at least some magical practitioners knew that Iao was the god of the Exodus. Celsus (about 178 CE) observed that "the god of the Hebrews" and "the god who drowned the king of Egypt and the Egyptians in the Red Sea" was a common formula used by exorcists.[75] In a curse tablet buried in a grave near Carthage (first to third century CE), we find reference to Iao who "split the sea," who is also called "Adonai Sabao" (names for Yahweh in biblical Hebrew).[76] Another spell refers to the one who appeared to Israel in a bright pillar (Exod 13:21–22), "who delivered his people from Pharaoh and who inflicted the ten plagues." This "mighty god Sabaoth," made the "Red Sea uncrossable" after "Israel went through" (cf. Exod 14:27).[77]

---

[70] Plutarch, *Isis-Osiris* 359d (τὴν [ψυχὴν] δὲ Τυφῶνος ἄρκτον), with Griffiths, *Iside*, 373 (Seth as Great Bear). *PGM* 4.1331 (ὄνου μέλανος στέαρ).

[71] *PGM* 4.1377 (Σαβαώθ Ἰάω); 1380 (τὸ δὲ ἑκατονταγράμματον τοῦ Τυφῶνος).

[72] *PGM* 4.3257 (ἰαωϊω or ἰαω ϊω).

[73] *PGM* 4.3270. See further Rita Lucarelli, "The Donkey in the Graeco-Egyptian Papyri," in *Languages, Objects, and the Transmission of Rituals: An Interdisciplinary Analysis on Ritual Practices in the Graeco-Egyptian Papyri (PGM)*, ed. Sabina Crippa and Emanuele M. Ciampini (Venice: Cafoscarina, 2017), 89–103; Eleni Pachoumi, *The Concepts of the Divine in the Greek Magical Papyri* (Tübingen: Mohr Siebeck, 2017), 143–50.

[74] See further Morton Smith, "The Jewish Elements in the Magical Papyri," *Studies in the Cult of Yahweh*, ed. Shaye Cohen, 2 vols. (Leiden: Brill, 1996), 2.242–56. Smith suggests that some of what was known of Judaism could go back to the form of Judaism known from Elephantine. See further Gideon Bohak, *Ancient Jewish Magic: A History* (Cambridge: Cambridge University Press, 2008), 194–226.

[75] Origen, *Cels.* 4.34. See further Pieter W. van der Horst, "'The God Who Drowned the King of Egypt': A Short Note on an Exorcistic Formula," in *The Wisdom of Egypt: Jewish, Early Christian, and Gnostic Essays in Honour of Gerhard P. Luttikhuizen* (Leiden: Brill, 2005), 135–39.

[76] Gager, *Curse Tablets*, 67. See further *PGM* 4.3007–86.

[77] *PGM* 4.3033–7; 3052–5 (trans. Granger Cook). See further Cook, *The Interpretation of the Old Testament in Greco-Roman Paganism* (Tübingen: Mohr Siebeck, 2004), 42–48; Wünsch, *Sethianische* 86–118; Procopé-Walter, "Iao," 64–65; Pavlos D. Vasileiadis, "The God Iao and His Connection with the Biblical God, with Special Emphasis on the Manuscript 4QpapLXXLevb," *Vetus Testamentum et Hellas* 4 (2017): 21–51. Jarl Fossum and Brian Glazer, "Seth in Magical Texts," *Zeitschrift für Papyrologie und Epigraphik* 100 (1994): 86–92.

We should also take into consideration certain engraved gems that depict a donkey-headed deity with snake legs and a shield bearing the name IAŌ.[78] The donkey head indicates Seth, the snake legs indicate Typhon, and the name "IAŌ" indicates that Seth-Typhon is also Seth-Yahweh. The carvers of these gems are unknown. In the early twentieth century, Adrien Blanchet traced them back to the "Ophites." But if the donkey image of Seth-Yahweh was widely recognized, a wide variety of persons could be responsible for them.

Other artifacts deserve brief mention. The first is an oval-shaped lead tablet featuring a snake-footed figure with the head of a donkey inscribed with the name IAŌ.[79] The second is an amulet featuring on its obverse a large-headed snake with seven rays on its head. Above it are six stars with the name "IAŌ" inscribed on the left. On the reverse stands a donkey-headed god in a kilt with a short staff and carrying an ankh (Egyptian symbol of life).[80] A third item, a gem from the British Museum, shows the same donkey-headed figure in a kilt carrying an ankh and a scepter (see Figure 1.2). He is labeled "IAŌ" and is surrounded by the names of the four archangels (Uriel, Suriel, Gabriel, and Michael).[81] It seems hard to deny that these donkey-headed figures are images of Seth-Yahweh.

Although we do not know who made them, who used them, and for what purpose they were made, they testify to the recognizability of Seth-Yahweh as a cultural symbol or "meme" recognizable in antiquity.

The Alexamenos Graffito

Probably in the early third century CE, an unknown graffiti artist carved into the plaster of a palace chamber in Rome a donkey-headed deity

---

[78] Adrien Blanchet, "Intailles representant des genies de la secte des Ophites," *Comptes rendus des séances de l'Académie des Inscriptions et Belles-Lettres* 64 (1920): 147–56. For the Christian use of amulets, see *ibid.*, 153, n. 5. For photos, see A. Delatte and Ph. Derchain, *Les Intailles magiques Gréco-Égyptiennes* (Paris: National Library, 1964), 39; cf. 172.

[79] Michel Rostovtsew and M. Prou, eds., *Catalogue des plombs de la antiquité de la Bibliothèque nationale* (Paris: C. Rollin and Feuardent, 1900), 375, no. 820.

[80] Campbell Bonner, "Amulets Chiefly in the British Museum: A Supplementary Article," *Hesperia* 20 (1951): 301–45 and plates 96–100 at 328, with plate 97, fig. 28. This amulet was also published by Erwin Goodenough, *Jewish Symbols in the Greco-Roman Period* (New York: Pantheon, 1953), Vol. 3, fig. 1176, with brief discussion in Vol. 2.280. See further Bonner, *Studies in Magical Amulets Chiefly Graeco-Egyptian* (Ann Arbor: University of Michigan, 1950), 24, 130–32, 238–39.

[81] S. Michel, *Die Magischen Gemmen im Britischen Museum* (London: British Museum Press, 2001), 30, no. 46 (Campbell Bonner Magical Gems Database-425).

Figure 1.2. Gem of Seth-Yahweh in the British Museum. Campbell-Bonner database number 425, found at http://cbd.mfab.hu/cbd/425/?sid=97.

dangling from a cross (see Figure 1.3). At the foot of the cross stands a stumpy, loutish figure with hand raised in adoration. The caption, written in Greek, reads: "Alexamenos worships god." Alexamenos—a slavish buffoon given his posture and dress—is evidently a Christian worshiping the crucified Christ. It just so happens that Christ has the head of an ass.[82]

From where did this image arise? It is possible that a Roman slave or schoolboy who worked in the palace was familiar with a being like Onocoetes, a Christian amulet, or the donkey worship mentioned by Minucius. It is also possible, however, that whoever scratched the crucified donkey into the plaster was familiar with alternative Christian traditions that portrayed the

---

[82] Felicity Harley-McGowan, "The Alexamenos Graffito," in *From Celsus to the Catacombs: Visual, Liturgical, and Non-Christian Receptions of Jesus in the Second and Third Centuries CE*, ed. Chris Keith (London: T&T Clark, 2020), 105–40; John Granger Cook, "Envisioning Crucifixion: Light from Several Inscriptions and the Palatine Graffito," *NovT* 50 (2008): 262–85 at 282–85.

Figure 1.3. Alexamenos Graffito. Reproduced by permission from Felicity Harley-McGowan, "The Alexamenos Graffito," in Christ Keith, ed., *From Celsus to the Catacombs: Visual, Liturgical, and Non-Christian Receptions of Jesus in the Second and Third Centuries CE* (London: T&T Clark, 2020), 105–40, fig. 66.5.

creator or one of his minions as a donkey-headed demon.[83] He would then be invoking the idea of "like father, like son": donkey-headed father god gives birth to donkey-headed son (Jesus).

To more fully understand this option, we must return to Epiphanius's "Phibionites."

---

[83] For this theory, see J. Haupt, "Das Spottkruzifix im Kaiserl. Palaste zu Rome," *Mitteilungen der K. K. Zentral-Kommission Wien* XIII (1868): 150–68; Wünsch, *Sethianische*, 110–15; Erich Dinkler, *Signum Crucis: Aufsätze zum Neuen Testament und zur christlichen Archäologie* (Tübingen: Mohr Siebeck, 1967), 150–53.

"Phibionites"

Reportedly, the Christians called "Phibionites" presented a group of seven demonic rulers who governed the regions outlined by the circles of the planets (see Figure 1.4). The higher the circle, the higher one ascended in the cosmos. The point of ascending was to break out of the universe after bursting through the boundary of what they thought was the highest planetary circle, that of Saturn.

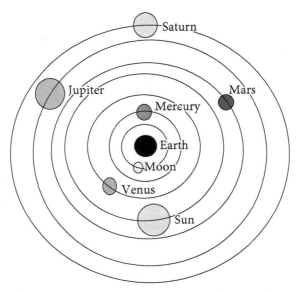

Figure 1.4. The geocentric cosmos.

Knowing the names of the planetary rulers was essential for breaking past them. Most of these rulers had Semitic-sounding names that could be invoked to control them. The names vary, but for the "Phibionites," the first ruler was called Iao, the second Saklas; Seth ruled the third circle, and Davides the fourth. Then there came Eloaeus. Some "Phibionites" said that Yaldabaoth ruled the sixth heaven. Sabaoth—the chief demon associated with Saturn and the Sabbath—ruled the highest circle.[84]

Sabaoth, sometimes identified with Yaldabaoth, was identical to the Judean creator.[85] After the souls of the redeemed depart from this world, they make

[84] Epiphanius, *Panarion* 26.10.1. See further Rasimus, *Paradise*, 103–7, esp. his chart on 104.
[85] Epiphanius, *Panarion* 26.10.1–3. Similar lists of planetary rulers occur in Irenaeus, *Against Heresies (AH)* 1.30.5.

their way past every ruler. The last and most difficult ruler to evade is the creator, who cannot be passed apart from the attainment of full knowledge (*gnosis*).[86]

These Christians believed that Sabaoth had either the shape of a donkey or of a pig.[87] The pig was associated with Seth, as we observed, and Jews were occasionally accused of worshiping a pig-god.[88] Nevertheless, the donkey shape was the more characteristic form of Seth-Yahweh. In short, this Christian group adapted the Seth–Yahweh fusion to portray a hostile cosmic ruler—the creator.

The appearance of the donkey god raises the question: did these Christians conclude that the creator was evil and *then* depict him with the features of Seth, or did they adopt the pre-made negative portrayal of Seth-Yahweh that *already* prompted them to think of the Judean god as evil? It is conceivable— since there were various reasons for considering the Judean creator to be wicked—that depicting him with the features of Seth, with all its negative associations, was secondary.[89]

Nevertheless, since the Seth–Yahweh fusion was already a recognizable meme with considerable symbolic capital, it seems probable that at least *some* of the preestablished negative valence of Seth-Yahweh was adopted by Christian "Phibionites" and then applied to the Judeo-catholic creator. By the early fourth century, and probably earlier, Epiphanius's "Phibionites" dwelt in Egypt where they had access to Egyptian revisionary mythology. They also preserved *The Birth of Mary*, which portrayed the Jewish deity as an ass-headed demon (effectively Seth-Typhon) worshiped in the Jerusalem temple.

The *Secret Book of John*

The "Phibionite" Christians of Epiphanius were not alone in exploiting the Seth-Yahweh tradition. Donkey imagery is attributed to one of the lesser

---

[86] Epiphanius, *Panarion* 26.10.6–7.

[87] Epiphanius, *Panarion* 26.10.6.

[88] Petronius, *Poems* 24: *Iudaeus licet et porcinum numen adoret* (Let a Jew worship even a porkish power).

[89] Rasimus writes that the "theriomorphic imagery was attached to Ialdabaoth only when he was identified as the devil. In fact, the theriomorphism seems to presuppose the demonization, which, as suggested, derives from a controversy over monotheism" (*Paradise*, 186–87, cf. 128). In the Introduction to Part I, I have explained why a controversy over monotheism (advocated by Alan Segal) is inadequate to explain the conception of the evil creator. We cannot conclude that the demonization of Yahweh happened before his animalization (already a kind of demonization). The animal imagery has a distinctively Egyptian flavor, and the Egyptian mythmaking about Seth-Yahweh predates revisionary anti-Yahweh mythology in Sethian Christian texts.

cosmic rulers in the *Secret Book of John*. This work survives in two different versions (longer and shorter), which are attested by four different Coptic manuscripts (three of them in the Nag Hammadi codices). Its earliest Greek version appeared around 150 CE, likely in the context of a small conclave run by a master-teacher in Antioch or Alexandria.[90]

One copy of the shorter version of the *Secret Book* reports that the chief creator Yaldabaoth "had the face of a snake and the face of a lion." In the longer version, he is described as "a lion-faced serpent."[91] These traits were reminiscent of Seth-Typhon's snake heads and lionlike roar—not to mention his eyes, "flashing like fires of lightning."[92] One etymology for Yaldabaoth is "child of chaos" (Aramaic *yalda bahuth*). Even if the etymology is incorrect, it well describes Yaldabaoth's commonality with Seth.

When it comes to donkey features, however, one must attend to Yaldabaoth's offspring. These include the seven planetary rulers. The second of these, called Eloaios, had the face of a donkey.[93] In one manuscript, Eloaios's donkey face is explicitly called "the face of Typhon."[94] The notion of "like father, like son" seems to be implied. Eloaios activated the typhonic potential embedded in the chief creator, Yaldabaoth.

Evidence for this view is Yaldabaoth's shape-shifting character. As a being expressing chaos, he had a "crowd of faces"—innumerable appearances that he could manifest at will.[95] Whenever he desired, apparently, Yaldabaoth could manifest donkey features.[96] Eloaios was the child of the creator, and his donkey visage realized one of Yaldabaoth's many forms.

---

[90] Logan, *Gnostic Truth*, 29–32 (Antioch); Karen L. King, *The Secret Revelation of John* (Cambridge, MA: Harvard University Press, 2006), 11–17 (Alexandria).

[91] For the dual serpent and lion face, see *Secret Book of John* Berlin Gnostic Codex (BG) 37.21. For the "lion-faced serpent," see NHC II,1 10.9 in *Nag Hammadi Codices* 2.61. See further Howard M. Jackson, *The Lion Becomes Man: The Gnostic Leontomorphic Creator and the Platonic Tradition* (Atlanta: Scholars Press, 1985).

[92] Hesiod, *Theogony*, 825–34. Cf. *Secret Book of John* (NHC II,1) 10.10–11. See further J. E. Goehring ("A Classical Influence on the Gnostic Sophia Myth," *Vigiliae Christianae [VC]* 35:1 [1981]: 16–23), who posits other influences from classical myth (note in particular Yaldabaoth and Typhon's asexual birth from a female).

[93] *Secret Book of John* (BG) 41.19–20 (ⲡⲙⲉϩⲥⲛⲁⲩ ⲡⲉ ⲉⲗⲱⲁⲓⲟⲥ ⲫⲟ ⲛ̄ⲉⲓⲱ).

[94] *Secret Book of John* (NHC II,1) 11.28. Other theriomorphic rulers are mentioned in other texts, without specifying which, if any, were onomorphic (*Reality of the Rulers* [NHC II,4] 87.27–29; *Origin of the World* [NHC II,5] 119.16–18). See further Gilhus, *Animals*, 215–17.

[95] The "crowd of faces" (ⲟⲩⲙⲏⲏϣⲉ ⲛ̄ⲡⲣⲟⲥⲱⲡⲟⲛ) comes from *Secret Book of John* (NHC II,1) 11.36–12.1. The innumerable faces (ⲡⲁⲧⲁϣⲏ ⲙⲙⲟⲣⲫⲏ) that appear correspond to the language of BG 42.11–13. See further Bernard Barc, "Samaèl-Saklas-Yaldabaôth: Recherche sur le genèse d'un mythe gnostique," in *Colloque international sur les Textes de Nag Hammadi: Québec 22–25 août 1978* (Leuven: Peeters, 1981), 132–50 at 136–38.

[96] Rasimus remarks: "It is likewise possible that Ialdabaoth is imagined as being able to assume his sons' animal forms at will" (*Paradise*, 119).

The "Ophite" Diagram

A third example of the donkey deity comes from the "Ophite" diagram.[97] This diagram, drawn by Christian theologians sometime in the mid–second century CE, presents yet another list of "ruler angels."[98] These rulers I take to be equivalent to the "ruler demons" later depicted in bestial form.[99] The seventh of these demons manifests a donkey face (*onou . . . prosopon*); he is called Thaphabaoth (aka Thartharaoth), but his more relevant name, for our purposes, is Onoel ("Donkey-god").[100]

The relation of Onoel to a second list of heavenly gatekeepers is contested. One of these lords is donkey shaped (*onoeidē*), so we presume that the ruling demons are also gatekeepers.[101] If so, then an argument can be made for Onoel being another name for Yaldabaoth, the chief creator.[102] The two sets of names are parallel and can be listed in descending order:

7. Onoel	7. Yaldabaoth
6. Erathaoth	6. Iao
5. Thauthabaoth	5. Sabaoth
4. Gabriel	4. Adonai
3. Raphael	3. Astaphaeus
2. Suriel	2. Ailoaeus
1. Michael[103]	1. Horaeus

[97] The relevant description of the diagram can be found in Origen, *Cels.* 6.27–32. See the commentary of Bernd Witte, *Die Ophitendiagramm nach Origenes' Contra Celsum VI,22–38* (Altenberge: Oros, 1993), 98–125.

[98] On the "Ophites," see Pearson, "Ophites," in *DGWE*, 895–98; Rasimus, *Paradise*, 65–282; Fred Ledegang, "The Ophites and the Ophite Diagram in Celsus and Origen," in *Heretics and Heresies in the Ancient Church and in Eastern Christianity: Studies in Honour of Adelbert Davids*, ed. Joseph Verheyden and Herman Teule (Leuven: Peeters, 2011), 51–84.

[99] The ruler angels are mentioned in Origen, *Cels.* 6.27, and the ruler demons appear in 6.30.

[100] Origen, *Cels.* 6.30.

[101] Origen, *Cels.* 7.40.

[102] Origen, *Cels.* 6.27; 6.30; 7.40. A. J. Welburn argued for the identity of Yaldabaoth and Onoel ("Reconstructing the Ophite Diagram," *Novum Testamentum (NovT)* 23:3 [1981]: 261–87 at 263–65). Cf. his "The Identity of the Archons in the 'Apocryphon Johannis,'" *VC* 32 (1978): 241–54 at 244. Other scholars associate Yaldabaoth with Michael because they are in sympathy (τῷ λεοντοειδεῖ ἄρχοντι συμπαθεῖν). Possibly the lists describe two separate groups: the ruling daemones control the sublunar region, while the gatekeepers (planetary rulers) are superlunary (Rasimus, *Paradise*, 112–14).

[103] Michael is explicitly "first" among the ruling demons, and Horaeus is assigned power over "the first gate" (Origen, *Cels.* 6.30–31). Yaldabaoth has control over the seventh gate, which I take to be the highest, and Onoel is called "seventh." Complicating matters is that Yaldabaoth is called "first and seventh" (6.31), but "first" here probably expresses primacy. If Yaldabaoth also represents the planet Saturn, he is said to be in sympathy with the first power Michael (6.31). Sympathy, however, does

The presence of the donkey demon shows that the Christians who drew this diagram (or diagrams) were dipping into the cultural memory of Seth-Yahweh. They too adapted this preestablished meme to identify the creator as an evil ruler. The creator was a hostile deity who sat atop the universe trying to prevent souls from escaping his domain.[104] Although his cosmic place and role are different from what we see in Egyptian lore, his donkey form was already charged with the negative valence of Seth.[105]

Conclusion

It is time to sum up. Briefly put, Seth-Yahweh was a donkey-shaped god of evil established in pre-Christian cultural memory and adapted by alternative Christian groups to express a hostility toward the Judean creator that had been voiced for centuries. This means that so-called Phibionite, Sethian, and Ophite Christians did not have to invent Yahweh as an evil character out of whole cloth. The wicked creator was already available, and his symbolic value was cashed out in new mythmaking practices that could be aimed not (or not only) at Jews but also at other Christian opponents who had adopted the Jewish creator as their chief deity.

The application of the Seth-Yahweh tradition to the creator requires us to rethink the sources of early Christian theology, particularly in Egypt. We cannot assume that Gentile Christians living in second-century Egypt drank solely from the wells of the Septuagint and Philo.[106] Just as Greek and Roman authors learned about the Jewish god from retooled Egyptian cultural memory (Chaeremon and Apion), Gentile Christians living in Egypt learned about the Jewish god from the same traditions featuring Seth-Yahweh. Having Seth-Yahweh in their cultural encyclopedia, many Gentile

---

not mean identity. I disagree with Nicola Denzey (Lewis) that the ruling demons only represent the days of the week ("Stalking Those Elusive Ophites," in *Essays in Honour of Frederik Wisse*, ed. Warren Kappeler [Montreal: ARC, 2005], 89–122 at 100–103).

[104] In the second *Book of Jeu*, in a fragment describing the journey of the soul past the ruler of the middle, the ruler is described as Typhon. He is a donkey-faced, powerful archon who carries off souls by theft (Carl Schmidt, ed., and Violet MacDermot, trans, *The Books of Jeu and the Untitled Text of the Bruce Codex* [Leiden: Brill, 1978], 141). Similarly in *Pistis Sophia*, Typhon—called an assessor of the fourth rank—steals souls and imprisons them for 138 years (Schmidt-MacDermot, *Pistis Sophia* [Leiden: Brill, 1978], 364–65).

[105] This conclusion holds even if Onoel is not, in the end, identical to Yaldabaoth and is only—like Eloaios in the *Secret Book of John*—one of the creator's lower reflections.

[106] Cf. Gruen, *Heritage*, 71–72.

Christians would not have assumed that the Jewish creator was the kindly god and father of Jesus Christ. They would have, rather, imagined him as chaotic and evil—and thus not like Christ at all.

Therefore, if ever there were floodwaters nourishing the thought of the evil creator, it was the preestablished tradition of Seth-Yahweh. Its adaptation by alternative Christian groups in the second century is shown by the donkey-like appearance of the creator or one of his minions in four Christian sources (Epiphanius's report on "Phibionites," the *Secret Book of John*, the Ophite diagram, and the *Birth of Mary*).

This discussion lends credence to the idea that the idea of an evil creator, if not born in Egypt, was in part the result of culturally appropriating polemical Egyptian traditions that originally targeted Egyptian Jews.[107] These traditions were later redeployed against early Christians who worshiped the Judean creator. These other Christians, it was thought, continued to worship the ass god, who—lurking in the smoke of ancient tradition—did not wholly have to *become* evil in the Christian imagination; rather, his wicked nature had long been embedded in the cultural memory of Seth-Yahweh, the onomorphic god of chaos and evil.

---

[107] Cf. Thomas Gaston, "The Egyptian Background of Gnostic Mythology," *Numen* 62:4 (2015): 387–407. Douglas M. Parrott ("Gnosticism and Egyptian Religion," *NovT* 29:1 [1987]: 73–93) cites earlier studies.

2

The Father of the Devil

The lord would not have said, "My father who is in heaven" unless he
had another father, but he would have said simply, "My father."
—Gospel of Philip (NHC II,3) 55.34–36

Introduction

There is a secret lurking in the gospel of John, a secret obscured by virtually
all major English translations on the market today.[1] This secret is buried in
what is perhaps the most anti-Jewish remark in the entire New Testament—
Jesus's daring declaration to the fictional Jews that their father is the devil
(John 8:44). What is not widely recognized is that this verse can be translated
another way, not that the Jews have the devil for a father, but that their father
is the *devil's father*—namely, the father of all, or the creator. This father, as it
turns out, is no better than the devil his son, for he manifests the same murderous and deceptive disposition. In this chapter, we examine how to understand this reading and discuss its implications for the early Christian view of
the evil creator.[2]

---

[1] See note 11 below.

[2] A longer version of this chapter appears in M. David Litwa, "The Father of the Devil (John
8:44): A Christian Exegetical Inspiration for the Evil Creator," *VC (Vigiliae Christianae)* 74.5
(2020): 540–65. I here acknowledge my debts to April D. DeConick, who has argued that Jesus's declaration "you are from the devil's father" is the "clear," "plain," or "literal" reading of John 8:44a ("Why
are the Heavens Closed? The Johannine Revelation of the Father in the Catholic-Gnostic Debate,"
in *John's Gospel and Intimations of Apocalyptic*, ed. Catrin H. Williams and Christopher Rowland
[London: Bloomsbury, 2013], 147–79 at 150, 168). Cf. her *Gnostic New Age*, 142. DeConick's reading
has been countered by Stephen Robert Llewelyn, Alexandra Robinson, and Blake Edward Wassell,
who show that the phrase in Greek is ambiguous ("Does John 8:44 Imply That the Devil Has a Father?
Contesting the Pro-Gnostic Reading," *Novum Testamentum [NovT]* 60 [2018]: 14–23). A general
treatment of John in "gnostic" interpretation can be found in Charles Hill, *The Johannine Corpus
in the Early Church* (Oxford: Oxford University Press, 2004), 205–93. See also Helmut Koester,
"Gnostic Sayings and Controversy Traditions in John 8:12–59," in *Nag Hammadi, Gnosticism & Early
Christianity* (Peabody: Hendrickson, 1986), 97.

The Evil Creator. M. David Litwa, Oxford University Press. © Oxford University Press 2021.
DOI: 10.1093/oso/9780197566428.003.0003

Literary Context

The gospel commonly known today as "John" depicts Jesus's fictional Jewish opponents as unable to accept his identity as the divine Word.[3] Jesus is sent from his divine father to save the world, and he does his father's "works" or miracles (John 10:36–37). His opponents fail to recognize him and despise his works. Jesus accuses them of stubborn spiritual blindness (John 9:41; 12:39–40). Their blindness is naturalized by the practice of genealogizing. These Jews cannot understand Jesus because they are said to have a different father.

Their father is unveiled in a heated speech during the Jewish Feast of Tabernacles (John 7:2). Jesus begins by declaring himself to be "the light of the world" (8:12), a claim that his opponents take as invalid self-testimony. Jesus invokes his "father" as a second witness, a being whom "the Jews," according to Jesus, do not and have not known (8:19, 55). Similarly in John 5:37, Jesus tells the Jews that they have never heard the voice of his father "nor seen his form."[4]

If Jesus's father is taken to be the Jewish deity, Jesus asserts that the Jews do not know their own god—a statement that flies in the face of biblical tradition. What about the revelation at Sinai when Yahweh spoke from the mountain—not to mention the prophetic oracles?[5] Isaiah testified, "I saw the Lord" (6:2), and "the word of the Lord came to me" is a prophetic mantra.[6] One is led to infer that Jesus's father is a different being than the Jewish deity. Only in this way can "the Jews" know their own god yet fail to know Jesus's father.

The Jews of the story claim to be Abraham's children (John 8:33). Jesus seems to acknowledge this point (8:37) but later denies it because they fail to perform Abraham's works (8:39). The patriarch was honored for his hospitality, but Jesus's opponents, though they deny it, seek to murder him (7:1; 8:40; 10:39; 11:55).

---

[3] On John's Ἰουδαῖοι, see R. Hakola, *Identity Matters: John, the Jews and Jewishness* (Leiden: Brill, 2005), 10–15; Adele Reinhartz, *Cast Out of the Covenant: Jews and Anti-Judaism in the Gospel of John* (Lanham: Lexington-Fortress Academic, 2018), 93–108.

[4] Wayne Meeks called this statement "a cavalier denial of a central Jewish belief" ("The Divine Agent and His Counterfeit in Philo and the Fourth Gospel," in *Aspects of Religious Propaganda in Judaism and Early Christianity*, ed. Elizabeth Schüssler Fiorenza [Notre Dame: University of Notre Dame Press, 1976], 43–67 at 58).

[5] Cf. Exod 19:16–25; Deut 4:11–12, 33.

[6] E.g., Mic 1:1; Ezek 20:5: "I [Yahweh] was known by your fathers in the desert" was pointed out by the Marcionite Megethius (*Adamantius* 1.23). See further *Ascension of Isaiah* 3:8–9.

Escalating their defense, the fictional Jews claim god as their father (8:41). Jesus denies that god is their father, for if he were, the Jews would "love" Jesus (8:42). He explicitly says that his opponents are not from god (v. 47), though he well knows that they would identify Jesus's father with their god (v. 54). Jesus himself is not prepared to identify his father with the being these Jews call "god." He implicitly identifies the true and supreme god (*ho theos*) with his father. But he refuses to acknowledge this being as the father of the Jews (8:47). Instead, Jesus claims:

a. You are from the father of the devil [*or*: from the father, the devil][7]
b. And the desires of your father you want to do;
c. He was a murderer from the beginning,
d. And stands not in the truth, since the truth is not in him;
e. Whenever he speaks the lie, he speaks from his own resources
f. Because he is a liar, as well as his father [*or*: the father of it].[8]

As noted by the brackets, ambiguity occurs in two clauses, (a) and (f). In clause (a), Jesus *either* says: "You are from the devil's father" (the relational reading) *or* "You are from your father, the devil" (appositional).[9] In clause (f), one could understand either the devil's father as a liar (possessive), *or* take the devil as the father of the understood antecedent in clause (e), "the lie."[10] These readings have four possible combinations, three of which feature the devil's father:

Appositional possessive	**Relational possessive**
father, devil . . . as his father	*father of the devil . . . as his father*
Appositional antecedent	**Relational antecedent**
father, devil . . . father of it	*father of the devil . . . father of it*

---

[7] ὑμεῖς ἐκ τοῦ πατρὸς τοῦ διαβόλου ἐστὲ.

[8] ὅτι ψεύστης ἐστὶν καὶ ὁ πατὴρ αὐτοῦ.

[9] The appositional reading might be supported by the Hebrew usage of בְּנֵי־בְלִיַּעַל (Deut 13:13; Jud 19:22; 1 Sam 1:16; 2:12; 10:27; 25:17; 2 Sam 16:7; Nah 2:1). 1 Kings 21:13 (Vulgate) even has *filiis diaboli*, "sons of the devil."

[10] Some manuscripts have a καθώς or ὡς in 8:44a, making clear that two persons are spoken of (ψ = 044, 850, 157, Coptic, Syro-Palestinian, and Georgian MSS). Eleven Old Latin witnesses (Vetus Latina 2, 3, 4, 6, 8, 9A*, 9A^c, 11, 14*, 14^c, 15) attest the reading *sicut et pater eius* in 8:44f (http://www.iohannes.com/vetuslatina/edition/index.html). See further W. J. Elliott, D. C. Parker, and Ulrich Schmid, eds., *The New Testament in Greek IV*, 2 vols. (Leiden: Brill, 1995–1997), 2.253; Bart D. Ehrman, Gordon D. Fee, and Michael W. Holmes, *The Text of the Fourth Gospel in the Writings of Origen, Volume One* (Atlanta: Scholars, 1992), 215.

The appositional antecedent reading has been naturalized in modern English translations of John 8:44 ("you are from your father the devil"), but it is problematic.[11] Consider: for Jesus to say that the father of the Jews—whom the Jews claim to be their god (8:41)—is the chief demon (*the* devil) is unprecedented. No previous Jewish tradition identifies Yahweh with the devil. Yet it was Jewish—and early catholic—tradition to say that both the devil and the Jewish people ultimately stem from the creator. All creation—fallen or not—ultimately derives from the biblical god.

Moreover, there is a long tradition of Jews being the children of Yahweh. Yahweh says, "Israel is my son" (Hos 11:1), even "my firstborn son" (Exod 4:22); with Israel responding: "you, Yahweh, are our father" (Isa 63:16).[12] There are thus theological grounds for choosing the relational reading. In this case, the father of the Jews is the father the Jews have always known—the Jewish god. It simply turns out that the Jewish deity is not the father of Jesus, but of "*the* devil"—where "*the*" indicates that we are dealing, not with some lesser minion, but with the chief demon, Satan.

Irenaean "Others"

To be sure, the devil's father is probably an unfamiliar character to most modern readers, but we should not assume he was unfamiliar to the earliest readers of John. For example, in Book 1 Chapter 30 of his work *Against Heresies* (about 180 CE), the early catholic writer Irenaeus of Lyons treated those whom he called "others," whom he considered to be a sect of Christian opponents. After Irenaeus, this group was called "Ophites."[13] According to them, the Jewish deity (called Yaldabaoth) generates a son from matter. This son is called Mind and exists in the form of a serpent.[14] This is the same serpent in paradise who convinced Adam and Eve to eat from the

---

[11] The appositional antecedent reading appears in the NRSV, RSV, ESV, KJV, NKJV, and NIV translations of the English Bible.

[12] Cf. Deut 14:1; Mal 2:10; Jub 1:24–28; 2:20; 19:29–30. See further Marianne Meye Thompson, *The Promise of the Father: Jesus and God in the New Testament* (Louisville: Westminster/John Knox, 2000), 35–55; Hermann Spieckermann, "The 'Father' of the Old Testament and Its History," in *The Divine Father: Religious and Philosophical Concepts of Divine Parenthood in Antiquity*, ed. Felix Albrecht and Reinhard Feldmeier (Leiden: Brill, 2014), 73–84.

[13] The best modern introduction to the Ophites is Rasimus, *Paradise*.

[14] Cf. Epiphanius, *Panarion* 37.4.4 ("Ophites"): Yaldabaoth "sired a power that looked like a snake, which they also call his son"; Pseudo-Tertullian, *Against All Heresies (AAH)* 2.4: *Ialdabaoth . . . ex semetipso edidisse virtutem et similitudinem serpentis* ("Yaldabaoth produced from himself a power, the likeness of a serpent").

tree of knowledge (Gen 3). As a result, this serpent—named devil—was expelled from heaven and from him arose all worldly elements. In brief, Yaldabaoth is depicted as—and directly called—father (*pater*) of this serpentine devil.[15]

Irenaeus never said how this tradition arose. One immediately detects an exegesis of Genesis 1–3 (for there we read of primal light, spirit, waters, humanity's creation, and fall). Yet another passage inspiring the narrative, I argue, was John 8:44. There are several indications of this. First, John 8:44a is the only biblical passage that, in the relational reading, says that the Jewish deity has the devil for a son. Nothing in Genesis would independently suggest this point. Second, even though Yaldabaoth wished to call himself father, this name was stripped from him, "since there was already the incorruptible father" above him.[16] The logic of this theology was suggested by Jesus in John, namely, that the true god is not the father of the fictional Jews. Third, the father of the devil (Yaldabaoth) is depicted as a liar and murderer. He lies by claiming to be the only deity; he murders by killing Adam and Eve.[17] He later tries to drown all of humanity with a flood. His murderous character culminates in his conspiracy to kill Jesus.[18]

I submit that the "others" of Irenaeus mapped the theology of John 8:44 (relational reading) onto their exegesis of Genesis 1–6, such that the devil had a father who is the primal liar and murderer (Figure 2.1). To chart their position:

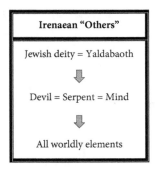

---

[15] Irenaeus, *AH* 1.30.5, 8. That Yaldabaoth is the Judean deity is clear from 1.30.10, where he makes a covenant with Abraham and rescues Abraham's descendants from Egypt.

[16] Irenaeus, *AH* 1.30.7 (*cum esset pater incorruptibilis olim*).

[17] Irenaeus, *AH* 1.30.6–7.

[18] Irenaeus, *AH*, 1.30.10, 13.

Peratai

The Peratai were Christians active probably in the mid-to-late second century CE. Their theology is discussed by the anonymous author of the *Refutation of All Heresies*, head of a Greek-speaking church in Rome who completed his work about 222 CE.[19] This author understood the name "Peratai" to derive from the Greek verb *perasai*, "to traverse."[20] In English, the Peratai are thus the "Traversers."

What did the Peratai traverse? Just as the Israelites of old crossed the Red Sea, the Peratai hoped to traverse the regions of corruption to attain the realm of pure being above the stars. The true exodus was the one out of this world.[21] The exit door for the universe was through the constellation Draco, the revolving snake in the sky taken to be a symbol of Christ.[22] That a snake could symbolize Christ was proved by Moses's bronze snake, the sight of which healed those Israelites who were perishing from snakebites (John 3:14; Num 21:4–9).[23]

The Peratai believed that the son of god, the divine snake, was the mediating link between the unborn father and the corruptible world. The son communicates the powers of incorruption to matter like colors leaking from a rainbow. Thus matter is formed into an ordered whole. Humans strong enough to discern the father's colors in themselves ascend after death to be born into the father's realm.[24]

When Jesus mentioned his heavenly father, he referred to his transcendent father above this cosmos. This father is distinguished from—to quote the Peratai—"Your father [who] murders humans from the beginning" (John 8:44c). They called this father "the ruler and creator of matter."[25] Since the

---

[19] *Refutation of All Heresies (Ref.)* 5.12.1–5.18.1; 10.1. See further M. David Litwa, *Refutation of all Heresies* (Atlanta: SBL, 2016), xxvii–liv. The Peratai are mentioned by Clement of Alexandria (*Stromata [Strom.]* 7.16.108.2), who takes the adjective "Peratic" as a place name (ἀπὸ τόπου).

[20] *Ref.* 5.16.1, 5–6; cf. the pun in 5.18.1.

[21] *Ref.* 5.16.1–7.

[22] *Ref.* 5.16.14–15. Cf. *Ref.* 4.47.2–4. See further Tim Hegedus, *Early Christianity and Ancient Astrology* (New York: Peter Lang, 2007), 291–92; April D. DeConick, "From the Bowels of Hell to Draco: The Mysteries of the Peratics," in *Mystery and Secrecy in the Nag Hammadi Collection and Other Ancient Literature: Studies for Einar Thomassen at Sixty*, ed. Christian H. Bull, Liv Ingeborg Lied, and John Turner (Leiden: Brill, 2012), 3–38, esp. 31–32.

[23] *Ref.* 5.16.8–12.

[24] *Ref.* 5.17.1–6.

[25] τὸν ἄρχοντα καὶ δημιουργὸν τῆς ὕλης (*Ref.* 5.17.7).

devil is not a maker or orderer of matter, this is evidently a reference to the biblical creator.[26]

We can thus chart the Peratic position (Figure 2.2):

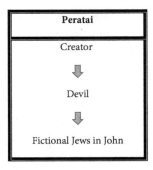

The logic appears to be as follows. The Peratai took a relational reading of John 8:44a ("you [Jews] are from the devil's father") and took the devil's father to be the creator (the biblical father of the Jews). This creator is a murderer (8:44c) in the sense that he makes humans mortal.[27] All creations are mortal because the creator worked with matter, a substance inherently unstable and subject to decay. To call the creator a "murderer" implies a degree of hostility toward him. Given Peratic Christian theology, this hostility is understandable, since their aim was to transcend the world of matter, traverse the stars, and be born anew in the heights of the transcendent father.

Other Christian Groups

While discussing so-called Cainite Christians, Epiphanius mentions other Christian conventicles who, basing themselves on John 8:44, traced the ancestry of the devil to the creator who was seen not as the devil's father, but as his *grand*father. To translate the key passage:

> The other sects, on the basis of this passage [John 8:44], claim that the father of the Jews is the devil, and that he has another father, and that his father has a father in turn . . . Indeed, they trace the devil's family relation to the master

---

[26] Athenagoras calls the devil "the ruler of matter" (ὁ τῆς ὕλης . . . ἀρχών). But the devil is never depicted as creator (*Embassy* 24.5).

[27] *Ref.* 5.17.7.

of all—god of Jews, Christians, and all people—affirming that he is the father of his [the devil's] father. This is the one who gave the law through Moses . . .[28]

These otherwise unidentified sects are significant because they reveal that *several different* Christian groups proposed relational possessive readings of John 8:44, perhaps independently.

Two points in Epiphanius's report surprise. First, even though these Christians supported a relational reading of 8:44a (the devil has a father), they still made the devil the father of the Jews. Technically the reading of 8:44a ought to indicate that the Jews' father is the *devil's* father. Either these sects read the text in multiple ways, or Epiphanius erred. I support the latter view based on this writer's often loose and careless style of reporting.[29]

Second, the creator is made not the devil's father, but his grandfather. April D. DeConick has inferred the interpretive basis of this theology.[30] The devil has a father according to the relational reading of 8:44a: "You are from the devil's father." "He"—referring to the devil's father—"was a murderer from the beginning" (8:44c) and "*his* father" is a liar (8:44f). These Christians, in short, preferred the relational possessive reading of 8:44 and so counted two fathers: the father of the devil, and the father of the father of the devil. The devil's grandfather was identified as the Jewish lawgiver (the creator).[31]

---

[28] Epiphanius, *Panarion* 38.4.3–4 (ὅθεν καὶ αἱ ἄλλαι αἱρέσεις ἀκούουσαι τὸ ῥῆμα τοῦτο πατέρα μὲν τῶν Ἰουδαίων φάσκουσιν εἶναι τὸν διάβολον, ἔχειν δὲ πατέρα ἄλλον καὶ τὸν αὐτοῦ πατέρα πάλιν πατέρα καὶ γὰρ ἐπὶ τὸν πάντων δεσπότην, θεὸν Ἰουδαίων καὶ Χριστιανῶν καὶ πάντων, τὴν συγγένειαν ἐκείνῳ ἀνάγουσι. τοῦτον πατέρα τοῦ ἐκείνου πατρὸς εἶναι λέγοντες. τὸν νομοθετήσαντα διὰ Μωυσέως καὶ τοσαῦτα θαυμάσια πεποιηκότα).

[29] See further Aline Pourkier, *L'hérésiologie chez Épiphane de Salamine* (Paris: Beauchesne, 1992); Young Richard Kim, *Epiphanius of Cyprus: Imagining an Orthodox World* (Ann Arbor: University of Michigan, 2015); Andrew Jacobs, *Epiphanius of Cyprus: A Cultural Biography of Late Antiquity* (Berkeley: University of California Press, 2016).

[30] DeConick, "Why?" 159.

[31] For his part, Epiphanius agreed with the relational possessive reading. In this case, the devil is Judas, according to John 6:70 ("one of you is a devil"); the devil's father is Cain; in turn, Cain's father is *the* devil (Satan). Structurally speaking, then, Epiphanius's understanding mirrors that of "other sects," even though the characters differ (*Panarion* 38.4.5–38.5.3). Reading Cain into John 8:44 was popular among early Christian fathers, with 1 John 3:8 taken as an intertext (Tertullian, *On Patience* 5.15; *Gospel of Philip* [NHC II,3] 60.34–61.12; *Protoevangelium* 13:1; *Secret Book of John* 62.3; see further Nils Alstrup Dahl, "Der Erstgeborene Satans und der Vater des Teufels [Polyk. 7.1 und Joh 8.44]," in *Apophoreta: Festschrift für Ernst Haenchen zu seinem 70. Geburtstag*, ed. Walther Eltester and Franz H. Kettler [Berlin: de Gruyter, 1965], 69–84; Guy Stroumsa, *Another Seed: Studies in Gnostic Mythology* [Leiden: Brill, 1984], 35–70; Kugel, *Traditions of the Bible: A Guide to the Bible As It Was At the Start of the Common Era.* [Cambridge, MA: Harvard University Press, 1998], 78, 100, 121, 123, 147, 157). The problem is that John and 1 John seem to have been written, if not by different authors, then at different times and contexts (see R. Hakola, "The Reception and Development of the Johannine Tradition in 1, 2 and 3 John," in *The Legacy of John: Second-Century Reception of the Fourth Gospel*, ed. T. Rasimus [Leiden: Brill, 2010], 17–47). Besides, if John 8:44 referred to Cain, Jesus would have said "You are from the *son* of the devil" not "the *father* of the devil."

Archontics

The "Archontics" (so Epiphanius) were a Christian group with roots in Palestine but most active in Armenia.[32] They were interested in a reading of Genesis 4 in which the devil sired Cain from Eve. Cain attacked Abel out of jealousy, since they both romantically loved their sister.

In support of their reading, the "Archontics" cited John 8:44. Epiphanius here cited an abbreviated version of 8:44a that favored the appositional reading: "You are from Satan." We should not assume that "Archontic" Christians read 8:44a appositionally, however, since their interpretation as a whole supports a relational understanding:

> From this passage [John 8:44] they say that Cain is [from] the devil, since he [Jesus] has said that he [Cain] was a murderer from the beginning. [They cite it] also to show that his [Cain's] father is the devil, and that the devil's father is the lying ruler whom . . . they say is Sabaoth.[33]

Again we have a relational possessive reading, though tweaked:

<!-- Figure: box labeled "Archontic Christians" with Sabaoth (the creator) → Devil (Satan) → Cain -->

---

[32] See further H.-Ch. Puech, "Archontiker," in *Reallexikon für Antike und Christentum*, ed. Theodor Klauser et al. (Stuttgart: Anton Hiersemann, 1950), Vol. 1, 634–43; van den Broek, "Archontics," in *DGWE*, 89–91.

[33] Epiphanius, *Panarion* 40.3.6–7: δῆθεν εἴπωσι <ἐκ> τοῦ διαβόλου εἶναι τὸν Καῒν ἐπειδὴ εἴρηκεν ὅτι ἀπ' ἀρχῆς ἀνθρωποκτόνος ἦν καὶ ἵνα δείξῃ πατέρα μὲν αὐτοῦ εἶναι τὸν διάβολον, τοῦ δὲ διαβόλου εἶναι πατέρα τὸν ἄρχοντα τὸν ψεύστην ὄν . . . φασιν αὐτὸν εἶναι τὸν Σαβαώθ.

Sabaoth, according to the "Archontics," is the Jewish deity, distinguished from the incomprehensible god whom the "Archontics," perhaps following the logic of Jesus in the gospel of John, called "father."[34]

Severian Christians

Severian Christians also seem to have favored a relational reading of John 8:44. The first mention of Severians occurs in the *Ecclesiastical History* of Eusebius, bishop of Caesarea in Palestine (early fourth century CE).[35] Severus is said to be a follower of Tatian (who flourished in Rome around 170 CE), and to have interpreted scripture (including the gospels).[36]

For his part, Epiphanius made Severus a "successor" to Marcion's student Apelles and related that Severians survived until the late fourth century.[37] According to Epiphanius, Severus posited a good, unnamable god above the creator. The creator, according to Severus, was called Yaldabaoth. He had a son, the devil, a snake later cast to earth.[38]

The idea of the devil as the creator's son probably goes back to John 8:44 for reasons already stated: (1) John 8:44a is the only biblical text that indicates, on the relational reading, that the devil's father is the creator, and (2) John's gospel already suggested that there was a father superior to the Jewish deity.

Epiphanius linked the Severians to the Archontics on the basis of their reputed doctrine that women are the work of Satan.[39] Perhaps they were also linked by their relational reading of John 8:44. If so, the Severians were one of those "other sects" Epiphanius mentioned who supported a relational reading of John 8:44.

---

[34] Epiphanius, *Panarion* 40.2.8.

[35] See further Birger Pearson, "Eusebius and Gnosticism," in *Eusebius, Christianity, and Judaism*, ed. Harold W. Attridge and Gohei Hata (Leiden: Brill, 1992), 291–310; Mary Verdoner, *Narrated Reality: The 'Historia Ecclesiastica' of Eusebius of Caesarea* (Frankfurt am Main: Peter Lang, 2011), esp. 140–6.

[36] Eusebius, *Ecclesiastical History* 4.29.4–5 (χρῶνται . . . εὐαγγελίοις . . . ἰδίως ἑρμηνεύοντες). Cf. Epiphanius, *Panarion* 45.4.1 (ἑτέρως μεταχειρίζονται). Theodoret (*Heretical Fables* 1.21) only adds that Severians are Encratites and that Mousanos, Clement of Alexandria, Apolinarios, and Origen wrote against them.

[37] Epiphanius, *Panarion* 45.1.2; 45.4.9.

[38] Epiphanius, *Panarion* 45.1.2–5.

[39] Epiphanius, *Panarion* 45.2.1.

"Mani"

Mani (about 216 to 277 CE) was a Persian prophet who began a successful version of Christianity that eventually reached from Spain to China.[40] Some sixty years after Mani's death (between 330 and 348 CE), a document appeared claiming to be a transcription of a debate between Mani and a catholic bishop in the city of Carchar (a disputed location in what is now Iraq).[41] The document, which survives complete in Latin, is called the *Acts of Archelaus*. Although in these *Acts* the character Mani is fictional, he still propounds "authentic Manichaean readings of the New Testament."[42]

In the debate, Archelaus invites "Mani" to quote biblical texts "written against the Law." When Mani quotes John 8:44, he presents an appositional possessive reading: "You are from your father the devil . . . he is a liar just as his father."[43]

Archelaus disputes neither Mani's text nor his possessive reading of 8:44f. He concurs that the devil has a father but widely stretches the sense of "father." For Archelaus, a father is anyone who "gives birth" to Satan, and one "gives birth" to Satan simply by doing his works. In this way, the Edenic serpent becomes the devil's father, as did Cain, Pharaoh, Judas (although Judas had an "abortion").[44] Archelaus ends by demonizing Mani himself, suggesting that he, too, is the devil's father.[45]

"Mani" did not approve of Archelaus's reading. For him, the devil's father is the creator. At least this is how Epiphanius understood the text (he read the

---

[40] For an introduction to Mani, see Johannes van Oort, "The Paraclete Mani as the Apostle of Jesus Christ and the Origins of a New Church," in *The Apostolic Age in Patristic Thought*, ed. Anthony Hilhorst (Leiden: Brill, 2004), 140–57; Albert Viciano, "The Life and Works of Mani and the Expansion of Manichaeism (216–276)," in *Handbook of Patristic Exegesis*, ed. Charles Kannengiesser (Leiden: Brill, 2004), 647–69; Iain Gardner, *The Founder of Manichaeism: Rethinking the Life of Mani. The Jordan Letters in Comparative Religion, School of Oriental and African Studies, University of London May 30–June 2 2016* (Cambridge: Cambridge University Press, 2020).

[41] Samuel N. C. Lieu, *Hegemonius: Acta Archelai (The Acts of Archelaus)* (Turnhout: Brepols, 2001), 1–32; Jason BeDuhn and Paul Mirecki, eds., *Frontiers of Faith: The Christian Encounter with Manichaeism in the Acts of Archelaus* (Leiden: Brill, 2007), 9–14. Latin text edited by Charles Henry Beeson, *Hegemonius. Acta Archelai* (Leipzig: Hinrichs, 1906).

[42] BeDuhn and Mirecki, *Frontiers* 98. On John 8:44, see Kevin Kaatz, "The Light and the Darkness," in ibid., 115–16.

[43] *Acts of Archelaus* 33.1–2, 46: *vos ex patre diabolo estis . . . mendax est sicut et pater eius.* The English translation by Mark Vermes does not bring out the possessive reading of John 8:44f. He translates this phrase in 33:2: "[the devil is] a liar and also the father of a lie" (*Acta Archelai*, 88), but the *sicut* shows that this rendering is incorrect, as does the reference to "the devil's father" in 15.6. Adimantus the Manichean believed that John 8:44a ("Jews" as devil's children) contradicted Gen 1:26 (humans as image of god; Augustine, *Against Adimantus* 5.1).

[44] *Acts of Archelaus* 37.1–15.

[45] *Acts of Archelaus* 37.12.

Acts of Archelaus in Greek). After quoting Mani's reading of 8:44, Epiphanius reported that Mani meant that "the creator of heaven and earth is father of the devil."[46]

The reason why Jesus spoke the words of John 8:44, according to "Mani," is "because whatever the ruler of this world wished and desired, he wrote through Moses and gave to humans as acts that must be performed."[47] "Mani's" mention of the "ruler of this world" hints at a wider knowledge of John (12:31; 14:11; 16:30).[48] For "Mani," the ruler of this world is the creator and lawgiver, Satan's father.

From this data, it is evident that "Mani" knew: (1) the devil had a father based on John 8:44f, (2) this father was in league with the devil mentioned in 8:44a, and (3) the devil's father is the wicked creator.[49]

Results

These six witnesses (Irenaeus's "others," the Peratai, Epiphanius's "other sects," the Archontics, Severians, and "Mani") indicate that several Christian groups saw the devil's father in John 8:44. It would be tendentious, I think, to dismiss their readings as secondary supports for preconceived notions about an evil creator. John 8:44—a scriptural text putatively reporting the direct words of Jesus—was a generative source for their theologies, as it was for virtually all other Christians.

The creator, in the relational reading, is wicked, as is proved by the context of John 8:44. The Jews wish to do the desires of the devil's father (the Jewish god, Yahweh). What are Yahweh's desires? In this case, we can only infer his desires from the similar desires of his children. The fictional Jews covertly wish to kill Jesus (John 18:31; 19:6, 15). The implication is that the creator also (secretly) wants to murder him—a point made explicitly by Irenaeus's "others."[50]

---

[46] Epiphanius, *Panarion* 66.63.2: ὑμεῖς υἱοὶ τοῦ διαβόλου ἐστέ . . . ὅτι ὁ πατὴρ αὐτοῦ ψεύστης ἦν. Βούλεται [Μανής] λέγειν τὸν ποιητὴν οὐρανοῦ καὶ γῆς πατέρα εἶναι τοῦ διαβόλου.

[47] Beeson, *Hegemonius. Acta Archelai* (Leipzig: Hinrichs, 1906), 46.

[48] Epiphanius indicated that Manicheans read John 12:31 and 14:30 together with 2 Cor 4:4 to refer to the creator (*Panarion* 66.66.1). Mani's wider knowledge of John is indicated by his claim to be the paraclete promised in John 14:16, 26. See also Iain Gardner, ed., *The Kephalaia of the Teacher: The Edited Coptic Manichaean Texts in Translation with Commentary* (Leiden: Brill, 1995), 307.

[49] The *Acts of Thomas* 32 also seems to assume that the devil has a father. The serpent who speaks describes himself as Satan and remarks that he is "a baleful son of a baleful father" (trans. Elliott, *Apocryphal New Testament* 460; cf. *Acts of Thomas* 76).

[50] Irenaeus, *AH*, 1.30.10, 13.

In the Johannine gospel, Jesus opposes "the ruler of this world" (John 12:31; 14:30). This figure could be Satan, but he could also be Satan's father (the creator).[51] Given that lying and murdering ran in the family, the choices are not mutually exclusive. In later reception history, the ruler of this world is the Jewish deity Yaldabaoth.[52] The *Secret Book of John*, designed as a kind of continuation to John's gospel, presents Yaldabaoth in the position of world ruler, a position he earns by virtue of creating the world.[53] One cannot but think that the author of the *Secret Book* understood the Johannine "ruler of this world" to refer to the creator. Peratic Christians apparently made the same deduction from 8:44 itself: the devil's father is "the creator and ruler of matter."

Assuming that the ruler of this world is the creator, then the creator attacks Jesus directly before the crucifixion. "The ruler of the world is coming," says Jesus in John 14:30. Even though the world ruler has no cause against the sinless Jesus, he succeeds in having him crucified. But if the creator succeeded in killing Jesus, then he is not the true god, but—as Jesus himself said—a liar and a murderer. He is a liar because he posed as the true god, and the fictional Jews accepted him as such (John 8:54); he is a murderer because he killed Christ and effectively all other people by making their bodies frail and subject to death.

Conclusion

I conclude that it was possible, from the words of Jesus in John 8:44, for early Christians to make five deductions—some direct, some by inference:

1. That the devil has a father (by the relational and/or possessive reading)
2. This father is also the father of the fictional Jews (8:44a)
3. This father of the fictional Jews is the Jewish deity (based on traditional Jewish theology)
4. That the Jewish deity and the devil are liars and murderers (stated directly given the relational reading)

---

[51] Beliar is called the "ruler of this world" and the "king of the world" in *Ascension of Isaiah* 2:4; 4:2 (Ethiopic).

[52] *Secret Book of John* (NHC II,2) 10.19–13.13, *passim*.

[53] John D. Turner, "The Johannine Legacy: The Gospel and *Apocryphon* of John," in *Legacy of John: Second-century Reception of the Fourth Gospel*, ed. Rasimus (Leiden: Brill, 2010), 105–44.

5. That the Jewish deity had a hand in murdering Jesus (if "the Jews" do the same works as their father, according to John 8:41)

The reception history of this verse indicates that many if not all of these deductions were made by some early Christian groups. These groups represented the Jewish deity as an evil being in league with the devil his child. The devil's father, the ruler of this world, worked behind the scenes to murder Jesus. For Christians who took this reading, then, the Jewish deity unmistakably exhibited his evil nature. This deduction gave some early Christian groups license to rewrite stories about the wicked actions of the creator in Genesis and beyond (as evidenced in the *Secret Book of John* and the *Reality of the Rulers*, among other early Christian texts). This investigation indicates that the idea of an evil creator emerged from second-century Christian readings of a distinctly Christian text, namely, the words of Jesus in John 8:44.

PART II

MARCIONITE APPROACHES TO THE EVIL CREATOR

Introduction to Marcion

If the gods do something foul, they are not gods.[1]

—Euripides.

Marcion of Pontus is the major focus of Part II and thus merits a brief introduction here.[2] This early Christian theologian was born in the late first century CE in Pontus (north-central Turkey), immediately south of the Black Sea. Although most of his early history recorded by his opponents is unreliable, it is relatively secure that he became a shipowner who managed an affluent shipping business. He was wealthy enough, at least, to make a large donation to a church in Rome when he settled there sometime in the late 130s CE.[3]

In Rome, Marcion met Cerdo from the Roman province of Syria. The report of Cerdo's teachings and the extent of his influence on Marcion are unclear.[4] Apparently both men distinguished the Judean creator from the good and true deity revealed in and through Jesus Christ.[5]

---

[1] Euripides as quoted by Plutarch, *Stoic Self-Contradictions* 1049f (Εἰ θεοί τι δρῶσι φαῦλον, οὐκ εἰσὶν θεοί); cf. Origen, *Cels.* 5.23.

[2] For recent treatments of Marcion, see Peter Lampe, *From Paul to Valentinus: Christians at Rome in the First Two Centuries*, trans. Michael Steinhauser; ed. Marshall D. Johnson (Minneapolis: Fortress, 2003), 241–56; Andrew McGowan, "Marcion's Love of Creation," *Journal of Early Christian Studies* 9:3 (2001): 295–311; Sebastian Moll, *The Arch-heretic Marcion* (Tübingen: Mohr Siebeck, 2010), 25–47; Heikki Räisänen, "Marcion," in *The Blackwell Companion to Paul*, ed. Stephen Westerholm (Malden: John Wiley & Sons, 2011), 301–15; Judith Lieu, *Marcion and the Making of a Heretic: God and Scripture in the Second Century* (Cambridge: Cambridge University Press, 2015); Stephen G. Wilson, "Marcion and Boundaries," in *Crossing Boundaries in Early Judaism and Christianity: Ambiguities, Complexities, and Half-forgotten Adversaries*, ed. Kimberley Stratton and Andrea Lieber (Leiden: Brill, 2016), 200–220; David E. Wilhite, "Was Marcion a Docetist? The Body of Evidence vs. Tertullian's Argument," *Vigiliae Christianae (VC)* 71 (2017): 1–36; Markus Vinzent, ed., *Marcion of Sinope as Religious Entrepreneur* (Leuven: Peeters, 2018).

[3] Tertullian, *Prescription* 30.1. See further Lampe, *From Paul*, 241–46; Moll, *Arch-heretic*, 30.

[4] This unclarity need not lead to a skepticism that would deny Cerdo's existence, *pace* David W. Deakle, "Harnack and Cerdo: A Reexamination of the Patristic Evidence for Marcion's Mentor," in *Markion und seine kirchengeschichtliche Wirkung*, ed. Gerhard May and Katharina Greschat (Berlin: de Gruyter, 2002), 177–90.

[5] Cerdo was said to distinguish a just and good god (Irenaeus, *AH* 1.27.1; affirmed in *Ref.* 7.37.1; contradicted in 10.19.1), whereas Marcion distinguished a good god and an evil creator. Pseudo-Tertullian, however, said that Cerdo distinguished a good and "savage" (*saevum*) god (*AAH* 6.1), and

The Evil Creator. M. David Litwa, Oxford University Press. © Oxford University Press 2021.
DOI: 10.1093/oso/9780197566428.003.0004

Likely, however, Marcion already made this distinction before coming to Rome.[6]

At the time, Roman Christian movements formed a loosely connected network of churches run by individual leaders called presbyters. Individual presbyters jostled for preeminence with no undisputed leader. Claims about a succession of single bishops suggesting a unified organization appeared only later (in the 160s CE).[7]

After some years laboring within established ecclesial networks, there was an opportunity for Marcion to present his views to a group of presbyters. A meeting—we do not know how official or how large—was convened. It became clear on this occasion that Marcion's conception of an evil creator, although based on a biblical principle—that good character cannot come from evil actions (Luke 5:36–37; 6:43)—was not supported by the majority.

Marcion was not excommunicated.[8] He left the established networks of his own accord. Probably using the cash of his previous donation (dutifully returned to him), Marcion organized his own ecclesial movement in Rome.[9] From Rome, he began an ambitious mission to establish his form of Christianity in other parts of the empire.

Marcionite Scriptures

By Marcion's time, there was already an edition of Paul's letters known where he grew up in Pontus.[10] Marcion republished an edited version of these letters

---

Epiphanius said he distinguished a good and wicked (πονηρός) god (*Panarion* 41.1.6). On Cerdo, see further G. May, "Marcion und der Gnostiker Kerdon," in *Evangelischer Glaube und Geschichte, Grete Mecenseffy zum 85. Geburtstag*, ed. A. Raddatz and K. Lüthi (Vienna: Oberkirchenrat, 1984), 233–48.

[6] Clement of Alexandria, *Stromata* 7.17.106.4–7.17.107.1 (Marcion appeared with his teaching in the reign of Hadrian, 117–138 CE). Barbara Aland thought that Marcion's theology could be understood against the backdrop of "gnostic" notions of an evil creator ("Marcion: Versuch einer neuen Interpretation," *Zeitschrift für Theologie und Kirche* 70 [1973]: 420–47 at 445). I agree that Marcionite and Sethian Christians shared notes on the topic, even if both derived their notions independently from scriptural interpretations. See further R. Joseph Hoffman, *Marcion: On the Restitution of Christianity: An Essay on the Development of Radical Paulinist Theology in the Second Century* (Missoula: Scholars Press, 1984), 155–84.

[7] Hegesippus in Eusebius, *Ecclesiastical History (EH)* 4.22. See further Lampe, *From Paul*, 397–408.

[8] *Pace* Moll, *Arch-heretic*, 44.

[9] A skewed account of this event can be found in Epiphanius, *Panarion* 42.2.1–8; cf. Pseudo-Tertullian, *AAH* 6.2; Filastrius, *Diverse Heresies* 45. See the comments of Lampe, *From Paul*, 393; Einar Thomassen, "Orthodoxy and Heresy at Second-century Rome," *Harvard Theological Review* 97:3 (2004): 241–56 at 243.

[10] Harry Y. Gamble, *Books and Readers in the Early Church: A History of Early Christian Texts* (New Haven: Yale University Press, 1995), 58–63.

(the Apostolikon). To it he attached a single gospel, called the Evangelion, evidently an early form of the gospel now referred to as Luke.[11] Marcion also published a prefatory tract called *Antitheses* (or *Oppositions*), which I will introduce in Chapter 3.

Marcion had several leading disciples (Lucanus, Potitus, Basilicus, Syneros, Apelles, and Prepon are named in the sources). In these sources, it is often hard to distinguish their teaching from the master's. To highlight this confluence (and ambiguity), I will often use the descriptor "Marcion(ites)."

When Marcion died and under what circumstances are unknown, but his church movement lasted several centuries, notably in the eastern Mediterranean. Epiphanius said that in his day (about 375 CE), Marcionites existed in Rome, Italy, Egypt, Palestine, Arabia, Syria, Cyprus, Persia— among other places.[12] A Syrian bishop (about 450 CE) spoke of converting over a thousand Marcionites in a Syrian town and mentions eight other entirely Marcionite villages in his area.[13] Evidently Marcion's message proved compelling to many, and in some areas Marcionite Christianity was the most widely known form.[14] An inscription found in Damascus refers to a Marcionite congregation (*synagogē*) and dates from 318 to 319 CE.[15] In the mid–fourth century, Cyril of Jerusalem advised Christians that, if they arrive in a new town, always to ask for the *catholic* church, lest someone lead them to the Marcionite counterpart.[16] To Marcionites themselves, their Christian

[11] The debate rages as to whether Marcion modified what is now canonical Luke or used an earlier version that was later revised to become canonical Luke. See, e.g., Andrew Gregory, *The Reception of Luke and Acts in the Period Before Irenaeus: Looking for Luke in the Second Century* (Tübingen: Mohr Siebeck, 2003), 173–210; Joseph B. Tyson, *Marcion and Luke-Acts: A Defining Struggle* (Columbia: University of South Carolina Press, 2006), 24–49; Jason D. BeDuhn, *The First New Testament: Marcion's Scriptural Canon* (Salem, OR: Polebridge, 2013), 25–98; Markus Vinzent, *Tertullian's Preface to Marcion's Gospel* (Leuven: Peeters, 2016), 255–348; Dieter Roth, "The Link Between Luke and Marcion's Gospel: Prolegomena and Initial Considerations," in *Luke on Jesus, Paul and Christianity: What Did He Really Know?*, ed. Joseph Verheyden and John S. Kloppenborg (Leuven: Peeters, 2017), 59–80; Daniel A. Smith, "Marcion's Gospel and the Synoptics," in *Gospels and Gospel Traditions in the Second Century: Experiments in Reception*, ed. Jens Schröter, Tobias Nicklas, and Joseph Verheyden (Berlin: de Gruyter, 2019), 129–73; Matthias Klinghardt, *The Oldest Gospel and the Formation of the Canonical Gospels* (Leuven: Peeters, 2021).

[12] Epiphanius, *Panarion* 42.1.2.

[13] Theodoret, *Letter* 113; *Letter* 81. See further Adolf von Harnack, *Marcion: The Gospel of the Alien God*, trans. John E. Steely and Lyle D. Bierma (Durham: Labyrinth, 1990), 102–3; Edwin Cyril Blackman, *Marcion and His Influence* (London: SPCK, 1948), 3–5; Lieu, *Marcion*, 179–80.

[14] Walter Bauer, *Orthodoxy and Heresy in Earliest Christianity* (Philadelphia: Fortress, 1971), 22–32.

[15] Philippe Le Bas and William Henry Waddington, *Inscriptions grecques et Latin de la Syrie* (Rome: L'Erma, 1968), Vol. 3, 582, no. 2558.

[16] Cyril of Jerusalem, *Catechetical Lectures* 18.26, translated by John Henry Parker (London: Rivington, 1845).

identity was not in doubt, and their movement produced not a few martyrs who died confessing the name of Christ.[17]

Marcion's Teachings

I follow the current consensus that Marcion's intellectual project was not so much the separation of Law ("Old Testament") and gospel ("New Testament") as it was the distinction between two superhuman entities competing for the hearts and minds of human beings.[18] Marcion compared two scriptural anthologies (now called the Old and New Testaments) to show that they were inspired by two different superhuman figures with two opposing characters.

Under the influence of the famous church historian Adolf von Harnack, older scholarship maintained that Marcion opposed a *good* god and a *just* creator. More recent interpreters, however, understand that he contrasted a *good* god with an *evil* creator.[19] Although later Marcionites came up with a range of theological positions (causing confusion in the sources), Marcion's own position, it seems, was that the creator was evil.[20]

Marcion and Philosophy

Based on his literary activity, scholars infer that Marcion had a solid education in grammar, though he probably lacked formal philosophical training.[21]

---

[17] Eusebius, *EH* 4.15.46; 7.12.1; *History of the Martyrs of Palestine* 10. Cf. Clement, *Stromata* 4.4.17.1–2.

[18] Lieu, *Marcion*, 256, 400; Matthew J. Thomas, *Paul's "Works of the Law" in the Perspective of Second Century Reception* (Tübingen: Mohr Siebeck, 2018), 141–42.

[19] Irenaeus, *AH* 3.12.12 (*alterum quidem bonum, alterum autem malum*); *Ref.* 7.29.1 (ἀγαθὸν τινα λέγων καὶ τὸν ἕτερον πονηρόν), 7.30.2 (δημιουργὸν φῇς εἶναι τοῦ κόσμου πονηρόν). See further Winrich Löhr, "Did Markion Distinguish Between a Just God and a Good God?" in *Marcion*, ed. May and Greschat, 131–46; Moll, *Arch-heretic*, 47–76, 161. Dieter Roth, although he agrees that for Marcion the creator is evil, sees Marcion as setting up a more varied set of contrasts between the creator and the superior deity ("Evil in Marcion's Conception of the Old Testament God," in *Evil in Second Temple*, ed. Keith and Stuckenbruck, 340–55 at 354–55).

[20] Lieu maintains that for Marcion the creator is not evil but the source of evils (*Marcion*, 347–49). Nevertheless, if she admits that for Marcion the creator makes evils, that he is jealous and is therefore characterized by "ignorant hubris" (340), that he is "severe, ignorant . . . capricious . . . petty, a lover of war" (347), that he is "angry, jealous, proud, and angry" (as in Tertullian *AM* 2.16.3), and if these adjectives describe the creator's *character* (in accordance with Lieu's subtitle and discussion beginning on her *Marcion*, 337), then it is hard to see how the creator, for Marcion, is not wicked. Lieu avoids asserting that for Marcion the creator is evil because she is concerned that such an assertion will make Marcion "a principled dualist" (348). Yet Marcion was hardly a "principled dualist" if, as I argue, the creator was not considered to be a true deity.

[21] See further Lampe, *From Paul*, 252–56.

At the same time, popular philosophical ideas had long dyed the wool of Marcion's mind, forming his sense of what was theologically appropriate.[22]

Christian scripture teaches that god alone is good (Luke 18:19). Marcion, following Plato, went further by his assumption that god, to be god, must be good—in fact *the* Good and source of all good for all beings. This Platonized Christian divinity was immensely powerful but had one limitation: he could not do evil.[23] Indeed, it was sacrilegious to say that god did anything morally base.[24]

By Marcion's time, belief in god's exclusive goodness had become cultural common coin. The idea appears in Philo, Plutarch, Alcinous, Numenius, and Apuleius—all leading Middle Platonists of the period.[25] The *Chaldean Oracles* scold the ignorant: "you do not know that every god is good, you drudges. Sober up!"[26] Bellerophon, a character in one of Euripides's famous plays, declared "If the gods do something bad, they are not gods."[27] The idea that god(s) must be good was widespread. In essence, then, all Marcion had to show was that the actions and character of the Judean creator were not—or not exclusively—good. Marcion could thereby show that the Judean god was no god at, but rather an imposter.

Two Gods?

It is often stated that Marcion believed in two gods, but this formulation is not correct.[28] Marcion would not have described himself as a ditheist (a

---

[22] Ugo Bianchi, "Marcion théologien biblique ou docteur gnostique?" *VC* 21 (1967): 141–49; John G. Gager, "Marcion and Philosophy," *VC* 26:1 (1972): 53–59. In the opinion of Enrico Norelli, Marcion faced the great philosophical problems of his day but answered them in an anti-philosophical way ("Marcion: ein christlicher Philosoph oder ein Christ gegen die Philosophie?" in *Marcion*, ed. May and Greschat, 113–30 at 128).

[23] Plato, *Republic* 379b–c; cf. 509b. Cf. Philo: "God is the cause of good things only and of nothing at all that is bad" (*Confusion of Tongues* 180).

[24] Plato, *Timaeus* 29e; *Republic* 379b–c; 380b–c; 391e1–2; *Laws* 672b; 899b; 900d; 941b.

[25] Philo, *Decalogue* 176; Diogenes Laertius, *Lives of Philosophers* 7.147; Plutarch, *Decline of Oracles* 423d; Plutarch, *Epicurus Makes a Pleasant Life Impossible* 1102d; Alcinous, *Handbook on Platonism* 10.3; Numenius, frag. 2, 16, 19 (Des Places); Apuleius, *On Plato and His Doctrine* 5. See further Oskar Dreyer, *Untersuchungen zum Begriff des Gottgeziemenden in der Antike mit besonderer Berücksichtigung Philons von Alexandrien* (Hildesheim: Georg Olms, 1970), 68–151; David Runia, *Creation of the Cosmos According to Moses* (Atlanta: SBL Press, 2005), 236–44; Claudio Moreschini, *Apuleius and the Metamorphosis of Platonism* (Turnout: Brepols, 2014), 45–47.

[26] Ruth Majercik, ed., *The Chaldean Oracles: Text, Translation and Commentary* (Leiden: Brill, 1989), 55, frag. 15 (translation hers).

[27] Euripides as quoted by Plutarch, *Stoic Self-Contradictions* 1049f.

[28] See further M. David Litwa, "Did Marcion Call the Creator 'God'?" *Journal of Theological Studies*, forthcoming autumn 2021.

kind of polytheist). He maintained that there was another god superior to the creator, without affirming the creator's deity in an absolute sense.[29] Marcion's distinctive term for the "god" of Jewish scripture was the "creator" or "cosmocrator" ("world governor").[30]

Marcion's most thoroughgoing opponent, Tertullian, called both Marcion's supreme deity and the creator "gods" in a polemical attempt to portray Marcion as a polytheist. Indeed, Tertullian opened his description of Marcion's theology with the claim that Marcion "presents two gods."[31] Tertullian made this charge even though he largely adopted Marcion's way of referring to the Jewish deity as "the creator."[32]

Tertullian well knew that for Marcion the creator was wicked, or at least not good. The creator, as Tertullian's Marcion observed, was known to become enraged, grow jealous, exalt himself, become irritated, and so on.[33] Marcion called him "severe, ignorant . . . capricious . . . petty, a lover of war," and "most pitiless."[34] Whoever Marcion's creator was, therefore, he was not good; and a being who lacked goodness, no matter how powerful, could not be god.[35]

Superhuman beings overcome by nasty emotions and who stirred up trouble for humanity shared a common designation in Christian thought: they were demons. It is nowhere attested that Marcion called the creator a demon, though one early writer—a theologian named Ptolemy— indicated that for Marcion the creator was the devil.[36] In our description of Marcion's theology, we cannot blindly follow Ptolemy, but neither should we follow heresy hunters in calling Marcion's creator "god," since Marcion himself demonstrably preferred other terms.

---

[29] Justin, *1 Apology* 26.5 (ἄλλον τινὰ νομίζειν μείζονα τοῦ δημιουργοῦ θεόν). The Refutator said that Marcion "posited two principles in the universe" (*Ref.* 7.29.1, δύο ἀρχὰς). In this case, only the good principle is explicitly called god (7.30.3). When the Refutator introduces the other principle as "evil" (πονηρός), he did not add the noun "god."

[30] Irenaeus, *AH* 1.27.2.

[31] Tertullian, *Against Marcion (AM)* 1.2.1 (cf. 1.3.1; 1.6.1), likely following Irenaeus, *AH* 3.12.12.

[32] Lieu observes: "Tertullian probably owes the term Creator to Marcion," citing René Braun (*Deus Christianorum: Recherches sur le vocabulaire doctrinal de Tertullian* [Paris: Études Augustiniennes, 1977], 374–75), who notes that 763 of the 800 occurrences of the word *creator* in Tertullian are found in *AM*. See further E. P. Meijering, *Tertullian contra Marcion: Gotteslehre in der Polemic* (Leiden: Brill, 1977), 23–24. Ephrem, when he attacked Marcion, predominately refers to "the Maker" (*S. Ephraim's Prose Refutations: Mani, Marcion and Bardaisan*, trans. C. W. Mitchell, 2 vols. [Piscataway: Gorgias Press, 2008], 1.lii–liii).

[33] Tertullian, *AM* 2.16.3.

[34] Tertullian, *AM* 3.4.2. Further references in Lieu, *Marcion*, 347.

[35] Irenaeus, *AH* 3.25.3.

[36] Ptolemy, *Letter to Flora* 3.2.

For Marcion one could reasonably say that the creator *looks more like* what most early Christians called a demon than a god. Christians since the days of Paul had been demonizing competing gods (on the basis of Ps 96:5). The idea that Marcion demonized the creator fits this trend, especially since some of the very criticisms that early Christian apologists hurled against Greco-Roman gods were launched, by Marcion, against the Judean creator.[37] Although Marcion recognized the creator's power and his control over this world, he complained of his wicked character and refused to worship him as god.[38] When compared with the supremely good Father, the creator was one of those falsely named "gods" who, to adapt a Pauline phrase, are "by nature not gods" (Gal 4:8).[39]

Biblical Interpretation

If Marcion's assumptions were informed by philosophy, the springs of his thinking were biblical through and through. He had his own canon, the Evangelion and Apostolikon. Marcion also used the Jewish Bible as a source for his thinking, though not as scripture. It would be a mistake to think that Marcion's depiction of the evil creator is based "completely on Old Testament testimony."[40] For Marcion, the Law and the Prophets told the true (if partial) story of a false god. Yet the wicked character of the creator was equally—if not more so—exposed in Marcion's "New" Testament.

---

[37] Aristides accused the god Ares of being πολεμιστής (warlike) and ζηλωτής (jealous) (*Apology* 10.7). He also criticized Apollo for being a θεὸν ζηλωτήν (a jealous god) (11.1) in J. Rendel Harris and J. Armitage Robinson, eds., *The Apology of Aristides on Behalf of the Christians* (Cambridge: Cambridge University Press, 1891), 106. Plutarch accused Typhon of doing terrible things through envy (φθόνος) and ill-will (δυσμενείας) (*Isis-Osiris* 361d).

[38] Tertullian's question for Marcion—"Certainly you confess that the creator is a god?" (2.16.5; cf. 1.13.2)—belies certainty. Marcion's disciple Apelles thought of the creator as an angel of the higher god (Tertullian, *Prescription* 34.4). The Manichean Adimantus referred to Yahweh as the "Jewish daimon," not a god (Augustine, *Against Faustus* 18.2).

[39] φύσει μὴ οὖσιν θεοῖς, attested in Tertullian, *AM* 5.4.5-6. See further Hans J. W. Drijvers, "Marcion's Reading of Gal 4:8. Philosophical Background and Influence on Manichaeism," in *A Green Leaf. Papers in Honour of Jes. P. Amussen*, ed. W. Sundermann (Leiden: Brill, 1988), 339-48.

[40] Moll, *Arch-heretic*, 58. In his attempt to undercut Harnack's views, Moll is prone to over-statement. For instance: "Marcion's system was so radically different from the one of Paul that it seems unlikely to assume any substantial influence of the Apostle on the arch-heretic" (85–86). See further Todd D. Still, "Shadow and Light: Marcion's (Mis)Construal of the Apostle Paul," in *Paul and the Second Century*, ed. Michael F. Bird and Joseph R. Dodson (London: T&T Clark, 2011), 91–107 at 106-7.

Only by contrasting the god revealed in Christ did the evil of the creator shine through.[41]

The task of exploring the logic of Marcionite biblical interpretation is complicated because hostile reporting has obscured Marcion's interpretive decisions. Heresy hunters generally presented Marcion's teaching as daring doctrine with little or no discussion of its biblical background or logic. Fortunately, there are careful scholarly reconstructions of Marcion's scriptures that provide the basis of his interpretations.[42]

We also possess reliable editions of the chief anti-Marcionite tracts. The longest of these, a Latin work by the aforementioned Tertullian, was composed in North Africa (its third edition dated to 207 CE).[43] Another useful work is the *Adamantius*, a late third or fourth century dialogue featuring two different Marcionite speakers (Markus and Megethius).[44] Finally, there is the ample report on Marcion made by Epiphanius, a bishop and heresy hunter whom we have already had occasion to meet.[45]

Roadmap

To summarize our itinerary for Part II, then: Chapter 3 studies Marcion(ite) interpretations of Jewish scripture whence derived the evil creator idea. Of

---

[41] According to Moll, "*Marcion did not understand the Old Testament in light of the New, he interpreted the New Testament in light of the Old*" (*Arch-heretic*, 82, repeated on 106, italics original). This is a false opposition; both were understood in light of each other.

[42] Ulrich Schmid, *Marcion und sein Apostolos: Rekonstruktion und historische Einordnung der Marcionitischen Paulusbriefausgabe* (Berlin: de Gruyter, 1995); Dieter Roth, *The Text of Marcion's Gospel* (Leiden: Brill, 2015); Matthias Klinghardt, *Das älteste Evangelium und die Entstehung der kanonischen Evangelien*, 2 vols. (Tübingen: Francke, 2015); Klinghardt, *The Oldest Gospel*. See also BeDuhn's reconstruction, translated into English as *The First New Testament*.

[43] Followed here is the five-volume Sources Chrétiennes (SC) edition edited by René Braun and Claudio Moreschini: Tertullian, *Contre Marcion*. 5 vols. (Paris: Cerf, 1990-2004). See the English translation by Ernst Evans, ed., *Tertullian: Adversus Marcionem*, 2 vols. (Oxford: Clarendon, 1972).

[44] Traditionally this work has been dated between 280 and 313 CE, but Kenji Tsutsui moves the date range to between 350 and 360/378 CE, with Syria or perhaps Asia Minor as the place of composition (*Die Auseinandersetzung mit den Markioniten im Adamantios-Dialog: Ein Kommentar zu den Büchern I-II* [Berlin: de Gruyter, 2004], 108-9). See also Gregor Emmenegger, "Adamantius et le De recta Fide," in *Histoire de la littérature grecque chrétienne des origenes à 451*, ed. Bernard Pouderon (Paris: Belles Lettres, 2017), 393-98. For the Greek edition, we must still depend on W. H. van de Sande Bakhuyzen, ed., *Der Dialog des Adamantius ΠΕΡΙ ΤΗΣ ΕΙΣ ΘΕΟΝ ΟΡΘΗΣ ΠΙΣΤΕΩΣ* (Leipzig: Hinrichs, 1901). This edition is deficient because Bakhuyzen assumed the priority of Rufinus's Latin translation, as, unfortunately, did the English translator Robert A. Pretty, *Adamantius: Dialogue on the True Faith in God* (Leuven: Peeters, 1997).

[45] For Epiphanius, see further Pourkier, *L'hérésiologie* esp. 29-52; Kim, *Epiphanius* esp. 17-43; Jacobs, *Epiphanius*; Todd S. Berzon, *Classifying Christians: Ethnography, Heresiology, and the Limits of Knowledge in Late Antiquity* (Berkeley: University of California Press, 2016), esp. 130-44, 186-217. Further sources for Marcionite Christianity are discussed by Lieu, *Marcion*, 15-176.

chief importance was Isaiah 45:7, where the creator confessed to making "evils." The creator also admitted to being jealous and enraged (Exod 20:5; Isa 5:25). Marcion's special talent was contrasting the divine character deduced from Jewish scripture with the divine character of Christ. For example: (1) the creator's command to despoil the Egyptians with Christ's exhortation to voluntary poverty, (2) the creator's directive to punish "eye for eye" with Christ's principle of non-retaliation, (3) the creator's genocidal violence with Christ's call to be free from anger.

Chapter 4 treats the Marcionite interpretation of 2 Corinthians 4:4. Marcion(ites) understood "the god of this world" (2 Cor 4:4), to be the creator because (1) this is one of the creator's known scriptural titles, (2) it accords with his well-known function (ruling creation), and (3) it concurs with his past actions (cognitive incapacitation). According to Marcion, "the god of this world" joined forces with the blind "rulers of this world" who crucified Christ (1 Cor 2:8). This wicked alliance encouraged the idea that the creator was evil.

Chapter 5 examines the Marcionite reception of Ephesians 2:15 (Christ "destroyed the Law of commandments by [his] teachings"). If Christ destroyed the Law by his teachings, the Law could not be good. Paul called the Law "good" in the sense of "just" (Rom 7:12). For Marcion, however, the creator's justice was only a cover for his savagery. From his perspective, the Law revealed sin and thus enslaved people to the creator. Christ came to abolish this Law to free humanity from slavery. Since Christ came as destroyer of the creator's Law, he proved that the Law was evil. If the Law was evil, so was the Lawgiver.

Chapter 6, in turn, shows how Christ "destroyed" the Law from stories in Marcion's Evangelion. After treating Evangelion 23:2 (Jewish leaders accuse Christ of "destroying the Law"), the discussion focuses on Jesus's concrete violations of the Law. For example, Christ touched lepers in violation of the Law and healed them apart from the Law's purification rites. Moreover, Christ controverted the Law to honor parents by requiring a would-be disciple not to bury his father, and in general by urging his disciples to abandon their families. Finally, Christ, according to Marcion(ites), violated Sabbath laws on numerous occasions, even claiming to be lord of—effectively over—the Sabbath.

Chapter 7, finally, examines the Marcionite interpretation of Galatians 3:13. In this verse, Christ "becomes" a curse on the cross. As the source text (Deut 21:23) shows, Jesus was cursed specifically by the creator. The creator's curse against Christ, despite its presumed salvific benefit, was an act of harm incompatible with the view that a divine being cannot inflict evil. Marcionite Christians understood the creator's curse against Christ as incriminating the creator's character. Whatever good resulted from the curse was not planned by the creator and could not exculpate him. A being who cursed the sinless savior was not only lacking goodness from a Marcionite perspective, he was also evil.

Finally, a word about method—here also reminding readers of what was said in the Introduction to Part I. In what follows, I will try to reconstruct how Marcion read or would have read certain scriptural texts as productive of the evil creator idea. This is my primary aim. To achieve that aim, I will appeal to the grammar and context of the text that we think Marcion was interpreting. In no case, however, am I trying to determine what the text "actually" or "originally" meant. I will also occasionally invoke interpreters roughly contemporary with Marcion to get a better idea of what might have been plausible to Marcion or indicative of his logic. In rare cases, I will invoke modern interpreters who read biblical texts in a way analogous to Marcion. All this data is gathered to support and reconstruct what I think was the *Marcionite* reading of a particular text. I make no claim whatsoever to ex-egete texts in a way that covers their entire biblical context or that engages with all the recent scholarly literature (most of which is miles apart from a Marcionite mentality). My endeavor is, through and through, to understand texts as Marcion(ites) would.

3

Creator of Evils

Whenever we read the obscene stories, the voluptuous debaucheries, the cruel and torturous executions, the unrelenting vindictiveness, with which more than half the Bible is filled, it would be more consistent that we call it the word of a demon rather than the word of God.

—Thomas Paine[1]

Introduction

Irenaeus accused Marcion of "impudent blasphemy" for saying that the god proclaimed in Jewish scripture was "the maker of evils."[2] Yet Marcion was a student of these same scriptures. He pointed out that in the book of the prophet Isaiah, the creator announced: "I am he who creates evils" (*kitizōn kaka*, 45:7).[3]

These "evils" are sometimes translated by the word "woe," an archaic term still featured in the New Revised Standard Version (1989). Other English translations opt for "calamity" (New King James, English Standard Version, New American Standard). The original Hebrew term *rā'* includes disasters like famine, pestilence, and war, but it also includes morally perverse actions. Translators bring out this moral sense of the term when they refer to the tree of the knowledge of good *and evil* (*rā'*) (Gen 2:17). This same ambiguity between moral and physical evil is present in the Greek translation *kaka* (Isa 45:7).[4] The Lord who creates *kaka* could be interpreted *not only* as the creator

---

[1] Paine, *The Age of Reason* (Newburyport: Open Road Media: 2017), 16 (Part I, chap. 7).
[2] Irenaeus, *AH* 1.27.2. Cf. Plutarch, who accused Typhon of filling land and sea with evils (κακῶν) (*Isis-Osiris* 361d).
[3] Joseph Ziegler, ed. *Isaias*, 3rd ed. (Göttingen: Vandenhoeck & Ruprecht, 1983), 291. Cf. 4 Ezra 15:5–11; Tertullian, *AM* 1.2.2; 2.14.1; 2.24.4; Augustine, *Against Adimantus* 27; *Enemy of the Law* 1.48–49. See further Andrew Davies, *Double Standards in Isaiah: Re-evaluating Prophetic Ethics and Divine Justice* (Leiden: Brill, 2000), 193–99; Stoyanov, *Other God*, 56–59.
[4] See further Thomas Römer, "The Origin and the Status of Evil according to the Hebrew Bible," in *Die Wurzel allen Übels: Über die Herkunft des Bösen und Schlechten in der Philosophie und Religion*

The Evil Creator. M. David Litwa, Oxford University Press. © Oxford University Press 2021.
DOI: 10.1093/oso/9780197566428.003.0005

of pestilence and plague, but also of moral vices like jealousy, rage, and bloodlust.

Isaiah 45:7 was not the only verse Marcion(ites) used to associate the creator with evil.[5] In Jeremiah 18:11, the creator announced to his own people, "behold I fashion evils (*kaka*) against you"; in Micah 1:12 it is said that "evils (*kaka*) have descended from the Lord against the gates of Jerusalem,"[6] and in Amos 3:6, the prophet asks: "will there be evil (*kakia*) in the city which the Lord has not caused?"[7] It is instructive also to note that the creator sends "an evil spirit" against his anointed king Saul in order to choke him (1 Sam 18:10).[8]

From the Jewish deity's production of "evils," Marcionites deduced an evil creator. Their mode of thinking, I propose, was shaped by their reading of their gospel. They recalled and often repeated the saying of Jesus that a bad tree produces bad fruit (Evangelion 6:43). The principle is simple: evil doings emerge from an evil character.[9]

In this chapter, I focus on the creator's malign character with evidence from Marcionite readings of Jewish scripture. Throughout this discussion, I remain open to the idea that texts from the Hebrew scriptures were formative in Marcionite conceptions of the creator, not just secondarily applied as proof texts. I take for granted that Marcion and his followers did not read these scriptures in a vacuum but understood them in terms of philosophical conceptions regarding exclusive divine goodness. These conceptions, however, were not the driving force generating the idea of an evil creator. Rather, they provided an interpretive framework for discovering the evil creator in Jewish scripture.

---

des 1.– 4. Jahrhunderts, ed. Fabienne Jourdan and Rainer Hirsch-Luipold (Tübingen: Mohr Siebeck, 2015), 53–66 at 63–65.

[5] Origen, *First Principles* 4.2.1.

[6] Jerome, *Commentary on Micah* 1:12: "Both the Marcionites and the Manicheans use this scripture to show that the god of the Law is the creator of evil things" (trans. Thomas P. Scheck, *Ancient Christian Texts: Commentaries on the Twelve Prophets. Vol. 1: Jerome* [Downers Grove: IVP Academic, 2016], 74).

[7] This verse is also cited by Adimantus in Augustine, *Against Adimantus* 26.

[8] 1 Sam 18:10 is roughly equivalent to 1 Kingdoms 15:14 LXX, a verse noted by Origen, *Cels.* 6.55; Cf. the "angel of the Lord" trying to kill Moses on his way back to Egypt (Exod 4:24). See further Heikki Räisänen, *The Idea of Divine Hardening: A Comparative Study of the Notion of Divine Hardening, Leading Astray and Inciting to Evil in the Bible and the Quran* (Helsinki: Finnish Exegetical Society, 1976), 47–52.

[9] Tertullian, *AM* 1.2.1; Origen, *First Principles* 2.5.4; *Adamantius* 1.28; 2.20.

The Vain Claim

The Jewish scriptures, according to Marcion, did not tell the story of a good creator. In the very same chapter of Isaiah in which the creator confessed to making "evils," he declared: "I am the master, the god, and there is no other god besides me . . . I am the god and there is no other" (45:5, 22). The Greek practice of using a definite article (*the* god) was a way of signifying that the creator claimed to be the chief god—and in this case, the only god. Perhaps in their original setting, these declarations sounded with a ring of comfort. Isaiah's creator cradled the world in his hands, invisibly tugging the strings of global politics. But to Marcion(ites), the creator's words sounded presumptuous. Any Gentile in the ancient Mediterranean could look around and observe that Yahweh was hardly the only god; he was barely even heard of outside the confines of the province of Judea. Yahweh was in every way a particular deity, dyed in local color, showing open favoritism for his own nation. To the average Greek or Roman, there was nothing particularly unique about this deity except perhaps his claim to be so.[10]

Marcion—who was probably of Greek or Anatolian heritage—did not assume the creator's uniqueness. To be sure, he believed, like other Christians, in a transcendent, loving Father revealed by Jesus. But the creator's particularity and malice showed that he was not that transcendent, good deity. Marcion and his followers were thus led to interpret the creator's *claim* to be singular as ignorant.[11] The creator was simply unaware of the true deity existing above him, so he foolishly declared that he alone was god.

Yet foolishness and ignorance were not the creator's only flaws. His trumpeted uniqueness sounded to Marcion's ears like arrogance—widely considered to be a vice in antiquity. The Epicurean philosopher Philodemus (about 110–40 BCE), for instance, studied arrogance in his work *On Vices*. In it, he defined arrogance as a disposition involving a sense of superiority and the haughty scorn of perceived competitors.[12] The competitors of the creator were the other deities worshiped by the nations (e.g., Exod 20:3; 34:14).

---

[10] E.g., Numenius, frag. 56 (des Places): the Jewish god "considers no one worthy to share his honor."

[11] Tertullian, *AM* 1.11.9. Cf. Tertullian, *Flesh of Christ* 24.1–2. Cf. Ephrem in Mitchell, *Prose Refutations* 2.xxviii; cf. 2.xliv.

[12] Philodemus, "On Arrogance," 2.27, with Voula Tsouna, *The Ethics of Philodemus* (Oxford: Oxford University Press, 2007), 145. See further Tsouna, "Aristo on Blends of Arrogance," in *Aristo of Ceos: Text, Translation and Discussion*, ed. William Fortenbaugh (London: Routledge, 2017), 279–92.

A sign of the creator's arrogance, according to Marcion(ites), was the fact that he swore by himself (Isa 45:22–23: "I am god; there is no other, I swear by myself").[13] In effect, the creator lacked evidence for his uniqueness, so he appealed to his own authority, employing a kind of self-authenticating and self-deifying rhetoric.[14]

Jewish scripture typically presented self-deifiers as horrible sinners suffering a swift demise. For instance, the personified city of Babylon proclaimed: "I am, and there is no other!" (Isa 47:10). Yahweh himself responded to this proclamation with heated words: "Destruction shall seize you, though you don't anticipate it; there will be a pit into which you fall" (Isa 47:11). A similar oracle was addressed to Lucifer the morning star: "You said in your heart, 'I will ascend to heaven . . . I will be like the Most High,' but now you go down into hell!" (Isa 14:12–14; cf. Ezek 28:1–10).

The most open and stubborn form of self-deification, however, was not perpetrated by Lucifer or Babylon. The most patent self-deifier in Jewish scripture was the creator himself, who repeatedly announced, "I am god and there is no other!" (Isa 45:22); "I am god, there is no one like me!" (Isa 46:9); "Behold, behold that I am, and there is no god except me!" (Deut 32:39).[15]

When Marcionite Christians encountered these apparent boasts, they made a logical conclusion: this god was not simply asserting his authority and control over world history; he was infected with the vices of ignorance and arrogance.[16] He did not know that the Father revealed in Christ—the true god who performed no evil—was far superior.

---

[13] Tertullian, *AM* 1.11.9: "How is it that the creator, ignorant—as the Marcionites allege—that another deity exists above him, even states on oath that he is alone . . . ?" Cf. 2.26.1 and Eznik of Kolb, *On God* 358: "Marcion says that when the god of the Law, who was lord of the world, saw that Adam was genteel and worthy for service, he contrived how he might be able to steal him from matter and join him to his own side. Having taken him to one side, he said, 'Adam, I am god, and there is no other, and apart from me there is no other god for you'" (trans. Blanchard and Young [modified], *A Treatise on God Written in Armenian by Eznik of Kolb [floruit c.430–c.450]: An English Translation, with Introduction and Notes* [Leuven: Peeters, 1998], cf. §370).

[14] M. David Litwa, *Desiring Divinity: Self-deification in Ancient Jewish and Christian Mythmaking* (Oxford: Oxford University Press, 2016), 47–65.

[15] Note also Isa 43:10; 44:6; 45:5–7, 18, 21–22.

[16] For other Christians who accused the creator of boasting, consult *Secret Book of John* (NHC II,1) 11.20–21; 13.8–9; *Reality of the Rulers* (NHC II,4) 86.30–31; *Origin of the World* (NHC II.5) 103.11–12; Irenaeus, *AH* 1.29.4; 1.30.6; *Ref.* 6.33; 7.25.3; Ps.-Clement, *Recognitions* 2.57.3; *Second Discourse of Great Seth* (NHC VII,2) 64.20–26. See further Dahl, "Arrogant Archon," in *Rediscovery of Gnosticism* 2.689–712 at 692–706; Steve Johnston, "Le mythe gnostique du blasphème de l'Archonte," in *Les textes de Nag Hammadi: Histoire des religions et approches contemporaines. Actes du colloque international réuni à Paris*, ed. M. Jean-Pierre Mahé, M. Paul-Hubert Poirier, and Madeleine Scopello (Paris: AIBL, 2010), 177–201.

Evil in Eden

For a number of early Christians, the vice of the creator was showcased in the very first law legislated for humanity. Yahweh commanded Adam not to eat from the tree of the knowledge of good and evil (Gen 2:17). This unexplained rule seemed to many an arbitrary obstacle to humanity's education and growth. To quote the famous line from the *Testimony of Truth* (NHC IX,3): "What kind of god is this? First, he begrudged Adam's eating from the tree of knowledge . . . He has certainly shown himself to be a malicious envier."[17]

Marcion's disciple Apelles helped to bring out the logic of this accusation. Apelles inferred that the creator himself knew good and evil. He reasoned that if it was good for the creator to know good and evil, then it was good for humanity as well.[18] Nevertheless, the creator prohibited human beings from sharing this knowledge. The prohibition indicated that the creator begrudged humanity a positive good.[19]

What struck Marcion(ites), in addition, was that the creator commanded a law he knew the first humans would transgress. It was as if the creator foreknew that humans would run headlong off a cliff but still set them playing like children on the edge of a precipice.[20] This precipice, moreover, was not

---

[17] *Testimony of Truth* (NHC IX,3) 47.14–48.4. See furtherWillem Cornelis van Unnik, "Der Neid in der Paradiesgeschichte nach einigen gnostischen Texten," in *Essays on the Nag Hammadi Texts in Honour of Alexander Böhlig*, ed. M. Krause (Leiden: Brill, 1972), 120–32; Miriam von Nordheim-Diehl, "Der Neid Gottes, des Teufels und der Menschen—eine motivgeschichtliche Skizze," in *Emotions from Ben Sira to Paul*, ed. Renate Egger-Wenzel and Jeremey Corley (Berlin: de Gruyter, 2012), 431–50.

[18] See further Meike Willing, "Die neue Frage des Marcionschülers Apelles—zur Rezeption marcionitischen Gedankenguts," in May and Greschat, *Marcion*, 221–31. Cf. Augustine, who addressed the claim that humanity's "maker kept the people he had made from a great good, when he wanted humankind to be like an animal without discernment of good and evil" (*Enemy of the Law* 1.19).

[19] Apelles in Ambrose, *Paradise* 6.30. See further Katharina Greschat, *Apelles und Hermogenes: Zwei theologische Lehrer des zweiten Jahrhunderts* (Leiden: Brill, 2000), 54–56. Theophilus of Antioch may have opposed Apelles (or other Marcionite opponents) when he claimed: "god did not envy Adam, as some suppose, by ordering not to eat from the [tree] of knowledge" (*Autolycus* 2.25–26). Cf. Irenaeus: "god did not envy him the tree of life, as some dare to declare" (*AH* 3.23.6). Cf. *Life of Adam and Eve* (J. Tromp, ed., *The Life of Adam and Eve in Greek: A Critical Edition*. [Leiden: Brill, 2005]) 18:4 (the serpent speaking): "god knew that you would be like him, envied you and said not to eat from it." See further Gerhard May, "Marcions Genesisauslegung und die 'Antithesen,'" in *Die Weltlichkeit des Glaubens in der Alten Kirche. Festschrift für Ulrich Wickert*, ed. Dietmar Wyrwa (Berlin: de Gruyter, 1997), 189–98; Williams, *Rethinking*, 68–72; Luttikhuizen, *Gnostic Revisions*, 72–82; Lautaro Roig Lanzillotta, "The Envy of God in the Paradise Story According to the Greek *Life of Adam and Eve*," in *Flores Florentino: Dead Sea Scrolls and Other Early Jewish Studies in Honour of Florentino García Martínez*, ed. Anthony Hilhorst et al. (Leiden: Brill, 2007), 537–50.

[20] The precipice image comes from Tertullian, *AM* 4.38.1. On the basis of *AM* 2.4.5–6 it can be gathered that Marcion(ites) cited Gen 2:17 to undermine the goodness of the creator.

some necessary evil, but the creator's own design. He deliberately crafted an object—a beautiful tree with ripe and seductive fruit—and himself decreed the lethal punishment for eating from it (Gen 2:17). Given this data, Marcion(ites) accused the creator not simply of carelessness, but of malice.

We can again trace this argument through Apelles, whose comments are likely reflected in the early Christian novel *Recognitions*.[21] Apelles asked why the creator forbade Adam to know good and evil so that Adam could knowingly avoid evil and choose the good. Then, because Adam tasted of the tree and realized what was good, the creator condemned him to death. But if humanity was bound to be harmed by the tree, why did the creator plant it at all?[22]

Earlier we saw how Apelles criticized the creator for keeping the first humans ignorant. He also argued that in Eden the creator led Adam into death either because the creator was too weak to prevent it or because he was cruel.[23] We find a similar argument in the *Recognitions*: the uncorrected evils of the world show either that the creator is weak or, if he is capable, that he is evil because he does not will to remove evils.[24]

With this argument we can compare another attributed to Marcion himself:

If god is good and knows the future and is able to prevent evil, why did he allow humanity, his own image and likeness—even his own substance on account of the soul[25]—to fall from obedience to the Law into death, outwitted by the devil? For, given the fact that god is good, he would not have wanted such a horror to occur, and given the fact that he foreknows, he would not be ignorant of what was to come, and given the fact that he is powerful, he would be able to prevent it. Therefore what cannot occur under these three conditions of divine majesty could by no means have

---

[21] This novel uses the character of Simon as a mouthpiece for Apelles, as argued by F. Stanley Jones, "Marcionism in the Pseudo-Clementines," in *Poussières de christianisme et de judaïsme antiques*, ed. Albert Frey and Rémi Gounelle (Lausanne: Zèbre, 2007), 225–44. See further Harnack, *Marcion*, 113–22; Greschat, *Apelles*, 17–136.

[22] Pseudo-Clement, *Recognitions* 2.53.4–7. From Ambrose (*Paradise* 8.38) we know that Apelles believed that the creator commanded something superfluous (Gen 2:17) because he knowingly bid Adam to follow a rule that would be broken. Apelles undermined the goodness of the creator's command (*Paradise* 8.40). See further Greschat, *Apelles*, 60–61. On divine evil in the garden of Eden, see David Penchansky, *What Rough Beast? Images of God in the Hebrew Bible* (Louisville: Westminster John Knox, 1999), 5–20.

[23] Apelles in Ambrose, *Paradise* 7.35 with the comments of Greschat, *Apelles*, 58–60.

[24] Pseudo-Clement, *Recognitions* 2.54.5.

[25] *Adamantius* 2.7: "The soul is the infused breath (ἐμφύσημα) of the creator."

happened. But given that it [the fall into evil] did happen, we must conclude that god is neither good, foreknowing, or powerful.[26]

Here we focus on the creator's lack of goodness. As was pointed out by Skeptic (Pyrrhonic) philosophers in antiquity, the goodness of god is threatened if (1) god foresees evil, (2) is able to prevent it, but (3) proves unwilling to do so.[27] Marcion(ites) assumed that the creator could foresee evil and that he was strong enough to prevent it. Given the actual presence of evil in the world, however, the only other option was that the creator lacked the will to prevent it. Ergo, the creator could not be good.[28]

In response, opponents of Marcion appealed to human freedom. In their view, the creator did not want to prevent evil because that would undermine humanity's free will. But this argument had been undercut at least a century before Christianity. Philosophers of the Skeptical Academy accused the creator of a simple design flaw. If god is all powerful and all good, he should have designed human rationality so as to preserve *both* freedom and goodness. The fault does not lie with human vices, but with the designing deity who should have given humans a rational faculty that precluded vice and blame.[29]

There were additional problems. Even if the creator "did not create evil himself," as Tertullian put it, "he still allowed its creation by some author or from some source."[30] Evil, in short, must be traced back to the creator. If the creator is the creator of all, that includes evil, even if it emerges indirectly through the will of his creatures. The creator is indirectly the maker of evil,

---

[26] Tertullian, *AM* 2.5.1–2. See further E. P. Meijering, *Tertullian contra Marcion: Gotteslehre in der Polemik Adversus Marcionem I–II* (Leiden: Brill, 1977), 100–101; Lieu, *Marcion*, 66–69, 285–88.

[27] Sextus Empiricus, *Outlines of Pyrrhonism* 3.11: if he is able to foresee everything but not willing, he [god] would have to be regarded as malevolent (βάσκανος)." Cf. Lactantius, *Wrath of God* 13.20–21: "if he is able but will not, he is envious/hostile (*invidus*)." Tertullian was aware of this argument (*Hermogenes* 10): "If he was able and yet unwilling, he was evil, as having favored evil." See further Victor Naumann, "Das Problem des Bösen in Tertullians zweitem Buch gegen Marcion," *Zeitschrift Katholische Theologie* 58 (1934): 311–63 at 337–38; Gager, "Marcion and Philosophy," 56–58; Lampe, *From Paul*, 254–55; Volker Lukas, *Rhetorik und literarischer "Kampf": Tertullians Streitschrift gegen Marcion als Paradigma der Selbstvergewisserung der Orthodoxie gegenüber der Häresie* (Frankfurt am Main: Peter Lang, 2008), 517–18.

[28] Cf. Apelles in Ambrose, *Paradise* 8.40: "if you say that god knew humankind would sin but impressed on him the common notions of good and evil so that by the admixture of evils humanity could not keep eternal life . . . then in this respect you do not seem to display a good god." See further Greschat, *Apelles*, 61–62. Cf. Augustine, *Enemy of the Law* 1.28.

[29] Cicero, *Nature of the Gods* 3.31.76. Cf. *Life of Abercius* 33; Augustine, *Enemy of the Law* 1.20.

[30] Tertullian, *Against Hermogenes* 10.1: *nullus omnino deus liberetur ista quaestione, ut non auctor mali videri proinde possit quisquis ille est, qui malum, etsi non ipse fecit, tamen a quocumque et unde-unde passus est fieri.*

since it would not have existed apart from his creation. By creating, he favored the advent of evil, became its enabler, thereby proving to Marcionite interpreters that "he was himself evil."[31]

Jealousy

Plato famously wrote that, "There is no jealousy in the divine choir."[32] Aristotle (384–322 BCE) made the same point more prosaically: "the divine is not susceptible to jealousy."[33] To be sure, Aristotle could distinguish zeal (*zēlos*) from jealousy (*phthonos*).[34] Both jealousy and zeal are desires to attain certain perceived goods and the feeling of distress when those desires are not fulfilled. Zeal is a kind of competitive spiritedness useful as a motivator for anyone striving to be the best they can. Jealousy, however, tends to denigrate a competing party.[35] The jealous lover, for instance, becomes enflamed when a third party obtains the affections and favors of the beloved. Jealousy is thus associated with anger, which is often fierce.[36]

---

[31] Tertullian, *Against Hermogenes* 10.3. In the immediate context Tertullian mentioned "heretics," who, discovering the evil of the creator, concluded that there was "another supremely good god"— the trademark of Marcion(ites).

[32] Plato, *Phaedrus* 247a (φθόνος γὰρ ἔξω θείου χοροῦ ἵσταται). Cf. *Timaeus* 29e; Musonius Rufus, *Discourses* 17; Celsus in Origen, *Cels.* 8.21; *Corpus Hermeticum* 4.3; Alexander of Lycopolis, *Against the Manicheans* 10. See further Ernst Milobenski, *Der Neid in der griechischen Philosophie* (Wiesbaden: Harrassowitz, 1964), 21–58; Thomas Rakoczy, *Böser Blick, Macht des Auges und Neid der Götter: Eine Untersuchung zur Kraft des Blickes in der griechischen Literatur* (Tübingen: Gunter Narr, 1996), 247–70; F. G. Herrmann, "φθόνος in the World of Plato's *Timaeus*," in *Envy, Spite and Jealousy: The Rivalrous Emotions in Ancient Greece*, ed. David Konstan and N. Keith Rutter (Edinburgh: Edinburgh University Press, 2003), 53–84; Esther Eidinow, "Popular Theologies: The Gift of Divine Envy," in *Theologies of Ancient Greek Religions*, ed. Eidinow et al. (Cambridge: Cambridge University Press, 2016), 205–32.

[33] Aristotle, *Metaphysics* 982a (οὔτε τὸ θεὸν φθονερὸν ἐνδέχεται εἶναι). See further Michael J. Mills, "ΦΘΟΝΟΣ and Its Related ΠΑΘΗ in Plato and Aristotle," *Phronesis* 30:1 (1985): 1–12.

[34] Aristotle, *Rhetoric* 2.11, 1388a35b6. Aristotle defined φθόνος as "having to do with what people compete for and seek prestige for in activities or possessions or fame, or any chance good, and especially things which they think they need to have so that, with more, they rise in status; and with less, they lack."

[35] Chrysippus defined φθόνος as "pain felt due to the goods of others with the wish to denigrate a third party so that one dominates" (H. von Arnim, *Stoicorum veterum fragmenta*, 4 vols. [Leipzig: Teubner, 1903], 3.418). Cicero defined it as "distress arising from the fact that another person has gained possession of what oneself desires" (*Tusculan Disputations* 4.17).

[36] Although Aristotelians saw a place for anger, Stoics considered it slavish, a sign of weakness (e.g., Marcus Aurelius, *Meditations* 11.18.5). For various philosophical and popular conceptions of jealousy and anger, see William V. Harris, *Restraining Rage: The Ideology of Anger Control in Classical Antiquity* (Cambridge, MA: Harvard University Press, 2002), esp. 88–128; David Konstan, *The Emotions of the Ancient Greeks: Studies in Aristotle and Classical Literature* (Toronto: University of Toronto Press, 2006), 41–76, 111–28, 219–43.

By Marcion's day, a (true) god could not be jealous.[37] Genuine deity desires nothing for the simple reason that it *lacks* nothing. Jealousy assumes a degree of insecurity and emotional fluctuation. But god, according to Platonic theology, does not change.[38] Deity is already perfect, complete, and self-sufficient.[39] Thus it is impossible for god to feel jealousy, or in fact to feel any negative emotions ("passions") at all.[40]

This enlightened conception of god created a major stumbling block for early Christians and Jews. A famous passage in the Jewish scriptures has the creator declare himself to be a "jealous god." This declaration was memorable given its place at the opening of the Ten Commandments (Exod 20:5; cf. Deut 5:9). It was emotionally loaded because in context, the creator promised to punish the children of sinful fathers as far as the fourth generation.[41]

The creator's jealousy was not a passing mood, but a defining attribute. His very name was "Jealous," as recorded in Exodus: "Do not worship another god, for the Lord god, whose name is Jealous, is a jealous god" (34:14).[42] Modern Hebrew Bible experts concur that jealousy is a key trait of the Hebrew deity. It is "the very center of his self-revelation,"[43] "the essential

---

[37] Philo (about 20 BCE–45 CE) rooted out all jealousy from his conception of god, refusing to refer to the creator as a "jealous god" (*Special Laws* 2.249; *Every Good Person Is Free* 13; *On the Creation* 21, 77; *Cherubim* 127; *Allegorical Interpretation* 1.80; 3.164, 203; *Questions on Genesis* 1.55). See further David T. Runia, *Philo of Alexandria and the* Timaeus *of Plato* (Leiden: Brill, 1986), 136; Lieu, *Marcion*, 338. In the Septuagint (LXX) , jealousy (φθόνος) was already a negative attribute. See Tob 4:7, 16; 1 Macc 8:16; 3 Macc 6:7; Wisd 2:24; 6:23; 7:13; Sir 14:10. Irenaeus agreed that "jealousy is alien to god" (*AH* 5.24.2). Cf. Clement, *Stromata* 7.2.7.2; 5.4.24.1.

[38] Plato, *Republic* 380d–382a.

[39] Alcinous, *Handbook of Platonism* 10.3: "The primary god is self-perfect (that is, deficient in no respect), ever-perfect (that is, always perfect), and all-perfect (that is, perfect in all respects)"; Apuleius, *Plato and His Teaching* 1.5: god "needs nothing" (*nihil indigens*).

[40] Marcion openly represented this point of view. In the words of Tertullian: "Marcion denies that his god is disturbed," that is, by passions (*AM* 4.31.5, *negat Marcion moveri deum suum*). Cf. 5.4.14: "the God of Marcion knows neither how to get angry nor take revenge." Cf. Alcinous, *Handbook* 10.4: the primary god "never moves anything, nor is he himself moved." See further Herbert Frohnhofen, *Apatheia tou Theou: Über die Affektlosigkeit Gottes in der griechischen Antike und be den griechischsprachigen Kirchenvätern bis zu Gregorios Thamaturgos* (Frankfurt am Main: Peter Lang, 1987), 143–57, 221–31; Anthony Ellis, "The Jealous God of Ancient Greece: Interpreting the Classical Greek Notion of Φθόνος Θεῶν Between Renaissance Humanism and Altertumswissenschaft," *Erudition and the Republic of Letters* 2 (2017): 1–55.

[41] Marcion criticized multigenerational punishment as a travesty of justice (Tertullian, *AM* 2.15.1–2; cf. 4.27.8). Tertullian treated the topic of jealousy against Marcion on numerous occasions. See, e.g., *AM* 1.28.1; 2.29.3; 3.23.7; 4.21.10; 4.25.2–3; 4.27.8; 4.39.18; 4.42.2; 5.5.8; 5.7.13; 5.16.6.

[42] Adimantus noted this passage according to Augustine, *Against Adimantus* 11. Adimantus believed, perhaps following Marcion, that a jealous god could not be just.

[43] Christoph Dohmen, "Eifersüchtiger ist sein Name (Ex 34,14). Ursprung und Bedeutung der alttestamentlichen Rede von Gottes Eifersucht," *Theologisches Zeitschrift* 46:4 (1990): 289–304 at 290.

description of God,"[44] and "the foundational component of the entire Old Testament understanding of God."[45]

The creator's jealousy was linked with rage. For at the same time he announced himself to be jealous, he warned the Israelites that—if they worship other gods—he will flare with anger and wipe them from the face of the earth (Deut 6:15). When the Israelites did enflame the creator's jealousy, the creator confessed to wrath and vowed to pay them back by favoring another nation (Deut 32:21).[46]

Given the ambiguity of the Greek phrase *theos zēlōtēs* ("jealous god" *or* "zealous god") one might argue that the creator simply felt a sense of rivalry. Yet this is doubtful. First, there is the linguistic consideration that the meanings of *zēlos* and *phthonos* had blended by the second century CE, as can be seen in both Jewish and Christian texts.[47] Second, the biblical creator was threatened by and aimed to undermine other beings called "gods" (Exod 20:3; cf. Ps 82:1). These beings competed for the affections and worship of the Israelites and on many occasions these Israelites seemed to have favored them. Evidently, the creator yearned for human love and worship, which indicated a need or lack.

In the second century, Marcionites were known for exposing the creator's jealousy.[48] Jealousy indicated that the creator was somehow deficient, subject to change and so to corruption. If the creator was subject to corruption, then he could and would perish with every other being in the universe bound by the laws of decay.[49] Marcion(ites) probably adapted this argument from

---

[44] E. Reuter, "*qn*'" in *Theologisches Wörterbuch zum Alten Testament*, ed. G. Johannes Botterweck and Helmer Ringgren, Vol. 7 (Stuttgart: Kohlhammer, 1993), 51–62 at 57, 60.

[45] Walther Eichrodt, *Theologie des Alten Testaments Volume 1*, 5th ed. (Stuttgart: Ehrenfried Klotz, 1957), 133, n.15 (*die Grundkomponente des ganzen alttestamentlichen Gottesbegriffs anerkannt werden*). I owe the references in this and the two previous notes to Rik Peels, "Can God Be Jealous?" *Heythrop Journal* 59:1 (2018): 1–15.

[46] Deuteronomy 32:20–21 is quoted by Tertullian in *AM* 4.31.6. See further R. Miggelbrink, *Der zornige Gott. Die Bedeutung einer anstössigen biblischen Tradition* (Darmstadt: Wissenschaftliche, 2002); S. Joo, *Provocation and Punishment. The Anger of God in the Book of Jeremiah and Deuteronomistic Theology* (Berlin: de Gruyter, 2006); J. Jeremias, *Der Zorn Gottes im Alten Testament. Das biblische Israel zwischen Verwerfung und Erwählung* (Neukirche-Vluyn: Neukirchener, 2009).

[47] 1 Macc 8:16; 1 Clement 3.2; 4.7; 5.2. This point was made by Lieu, *Marcion*, 340.

[48] Tertullian, *AM* 4.27.8 (*zelotes, qualem arguunt Marcionitae*). Marcionites were not alone in underscoring the creator's jealousy. See, e.g., Irenaeus, *AH* 1.30.7; *Secret Book of John* (NHC II) 13,5–13; *Reality of the Rulers* (NHC II,4) 96.3–6. The creator proclaims his jealousy in Irenaeus *AH* 1.29.4; *Gospel of the Egyptians* (NHC III,2) 58.25–26. Note also Julian, *Against the Galileans* 155c–e. See further A. H. B. Logan, "The Jealousy of God: Exod 20,5 in Gnostic and Rabbinic Theology," *Studia Biblica* 1 (1978): 197–203; Ekkehard Muehlenberg, "Marcion's Jealous God," in *Disciplina Nostra: Essays in Memory of Robert F. Evans*, ed. Donald F. Winslow (Philadelphia: Patristic Foundation, 1979), 93–114.

[49] Tertullian, *AM* 2.16.3.

Skeptical philosophers: if god experiences any kind of distress, he is incomplete, and if he is incomplete, he desires change, and if he is changeable, he is also perishable, but a god cannot perish.[50] A god who can change and perish—such as the creator—is not god.[51]

Antitheses

Marcion's special talent was contrasting information gleaned from the Hebrew scriptures with knowledge gained from his own "New Testament." He collected his contrasts into a work called *Antitheses*. The *Antitheses* was an introductory tract that Marcion attached as a kind of preface to his scriptures.[52] Although the *Antitheses* does not survive today, reports and reminiscences of it indicate that it belonged to a well-known genre in the ancient world called the introductory text (*eisagōgē*). These kinds of texts were designed to initiate new trainees into a discipline and to reinforce the essentials for those already familiar with the topic.[53] In Marcion's case, the *Antitheses* shaped the minds of his readers to interpret Jewish and Christian texts in his own way.[54]

The primary purpose of the *Antitheses* was not to show the separation of Law (Jewish scriptures) and gospel (Christian scriptures).[55] Proving the fundamental difference between these two "testaments" was only instrumental. The chief end was to prove that these two anthologies described the character of two different beings: the true god revealed by Jesus, and a local godling wrongfully claiming to be the most high.[56] Stated briefly, Marcion's *Antitheses* compared the characters of two different superhuman beings by

---

[50] Sextus Empiricus, *Against the Physicists* 1.157, 170. Carneades and Panaetius concluded that "what receives suffering must also accept death" (Cicero, *Nature of the Gods* 3.32; *Tusculan Disputations* 1.79).

[51] Jealousy was associated with the devil (Wisd 2:23). For the death of daimones, see Plutarch, *Decline of Oracles* 17, with Philippe Borgeaud, "The Death of the Great Pan: Problems of Interpretation," *History of Religions* 22:3 (1983): 254–83.

[52] Tertullian's longest description of the *Antitheses* occurs at the opening of book 4 of *AM*. Other references can be found in Eric W. Scherbenske, "Marcion's *Antitheses* and the Isagogic Genre," *Vigiliae Christianae (VC)* 64:3 (2010): 255–79 at 257, n.5.

[53] Scherbenske, "Marcion's *Antitheses*," 258.

[54] On this point see Eric W. Scherbenske, "Marcionite Paratexts, Pretexts, and Edition of the Corpus Paulinum," in *Canonizing Paul: Ancient Editorial Practice and the Corpus Paulinum* (Oxford: Oxford University Press, 2013), 71–115. See also Moll, *Arch-heretic*, 107–14; Lieu, *Marcion*, 272–89; Markus Vinzent, *Tertullian's Preface*, 267–92; Roth, "Evil," 352–53; Tsutsui, *Auseinandersetzung*, 148–52.

[55] Tertullian, *AM* 1.19.4; cf. 4.1.1.

[56] For daimones claiming to be the highest deity, see Porphyry, *Abstinence* 2.42.2.

describing their traits based on their recorded practices—or those of their human representatives.[57]

I make no claim here to reconstruct any of Marcion's original antitheses. Discussed are some oppositions made in the anti-Marcionite literature that could go back to the *Antitheses*. Of these, I focus only on those seeking to underline the creator's evil character. Other contrasts that highlighted his ignorance, self-contradiction, and favoritism will be left aside.[58]

Despoiling Egypt

We begin with a story in Exodus. We have already sketched Exodus lore in Chapter 1, so there is no need to repeat the storyline here. What bothered Marcion about the Exodus was not so much that the creator inflicted devastating plagues upon the Egyptian populace, but that he twice commanded the Hebrews to gather from them gold, silver, and fine clothing.

The creator's stated purpose was to "despoil" or "pillage" the Egyptians (Exod 3:22; 11:2; 12:36). The Greek verb operative here is *skuleuō*—which could be used of stripping valuables off the body of a slain enemy. The word indicates that the creator did not demand wage compensation for the Israelites (as was often alleged), but military spoils.[59] Marcion used the creator's demand for spoils to illustrate his bellicosity and greed.[60]

The following is a version of the Marcionite antithesis as recorded in the *Adamantius:*

> The god of generation ordered Moses as he left the land of Egypt, saying,
> "Be prepared! Have your loins girded, your sandals tied, your staffs in your

---

[57] Tertullian, *AM* 1.19.4. Tertullian understood that Marcionites "prove the difference between the gods by the difference of the two documents' propositions" (*ex diversitate sententiarum utriusque instrumenti diversitatem quoque argumententur deorum*). Tertullian indicates that the focus of Marcion's attention in his *Antitheses* was the *ingenium* (character) of the two gods as revealed by their laws (*leges*) and powerful deeds (*virtutes*) (*AM* 2.29.1). See further Löhr, "Did Marcion?," in May, and Greschat, *Marcion*, 145.

[58] In the early twentieth century, Harnack provided a reconstruction of the *Antitheses* based on ancient sources (*Marcion*, 60–63) found in Appendix V of his German edition (*Marcion: Das Evangelium vom fremden Gott: eine Monographie zur Geschichte der Grundlegung der katholischen Kirche* [Leipzig: Hinrichs, 1921], 256–314).

[59] The wage compensation argument occurs, e.g., in Irenaeus, *AH* 4.30.1–3; Tertullian, *AM* 2.20; Epiphanius, *Ancoratus* 111.1–3. Manicheans also complained about the creator ordering "the Jews to take the Egyptians' clothing" (Epiphanius, *Panarion* 66.70.3; cf. 66.83.2).

[60] The attempt to deflect criticism based on the spoliation can already be detected in Philo, *Life of Moses* 1.140–42; Josephus, *Antiquities* 2.314; Jub 48:18; Wisd 10.17.

hands and your wallets attached! Cart off from the Egyptians gold, silver and everything else!" But our Lord [Jesus], the good, when he sent out his disciples into the world, says, "Don't have shoes on your feet, nor wallets, nor two shirts, nor cheap coins in your belts."[61]

In other words, Marcion(ites) contrasted the creator's demand to despoil with Christ's command to his disciples not to carry extra supplies with them on their missionary journeys (Evangelion 9:1–3).[62]

Although the contexts of the commands are different, Marcionites thought them worthy of contrast. They assumed, like other Christians, that if the testaments came from a single deity, there should be a theological continuity between them. If Jesus was the Christ of the creator, their instructions for advancing the kingdom should have agreed.

Yet this was not the case. In the one passage, Jesus invited his disciples to accept voluntary poverty and full dependence upon god as they sought to inaugurate the kingdom. In Exodus, by contrast, the creator ordered the Hebrews to weigh themselves down with gold, silver, and clothing so they could decorate his tabernacle in the desert. Marcionites concluded that the creator's kingdom is material, based on worldly wealth, whereas Christ's was immaterial, based on almsgiving and voluntary self-limitation.

But it was not the materialism of the creator that bothered Marcion(ites) as much as the command openly to defraud the Egyptians. In short, the creator commanded his people to get rich off the spoils of their enemies—many of whom had perished in the preceding plagues. Taking such spoils, even if they were given "voluntarily" and on the spur of the moment, was a form of robbery typical of plundering.[63] An element of deceit is highlighted by the fact that Moses spoke with the Israelites "in secret," urging them to ask their neighbors for expensive items (Exod 11:2). Little did these neighbors know that what was "borrowed" would never be returned.

Marcion's chief criticism was that the creator "commanded the theft (*fraudem*) of silver and gold."[64] This command contradicted one of the Ten Commandments ("do not steal," Exod 20:15), widely taken to exemplify

---

[61] *Adamantius* 1.10. Cf. Tertullian, *AM* 4.24.1–2; *Acts of Archelaus* 44.8.

[62] Cf. Augustine, *Against Adimantus* 20.1.

[63] The late first-century BCE historian Pompeius Trogus (Justin, *Epitome* 2.12–13) believed that Moses carried off the sacred vessels of the Egyptian by stealth (*sacra Aegyptiorum furto abstulit*) in Stern, *Greek and Latin Authors*, 1.335. See further J. Allen, "Ezekiel the Tragedian and the Despoliation of Egypt," *Journal for the Study of the Pseudepigrapha* 17.1 (2007): 3–19.

[64] Tertullian, *AM* 2.28.2; cf. 5.13.6.

basic morality even today. Far from upholding this morality, the creator ordered his servants to engage in serious robbery—what amounted to pillage. These were immoral acts, and the creator who ordered them could only have, according to Marcion, a corrupt character.

Retaliation

"An eye for an eye" is still a well-known saying today. It refers to a law of the Jewish scriptures called the *ius talionis* or "law of retaliation." The creator commanded the Israelites: "Show no pity: eye for eye, tooth for tooth, foot for foot" (Deut 19:21; cf. Exod 21:24; Lev 24:20). The order to "show no pity" indicates that the creator was not speaking metaphorically. He actually demanded that, if someone knocked out a person's eye or tooth, then that same act had to be performed on the perpetrator. It was a brutal logic in which punishment quite literally fit the crime.

By the second century CE, this law of retaliation was not assumed to be just, especially by Christians familiar with Jesus's sayings. A Marcionite in the *Adamantius* contrasted the retaliation principle with Christ's words in the gospel: "It says in the Law, 'An eye for an eye and a tooth for a tooth', but the Lord, because he is good, says in the gospel, 'If anyone slaps you on the cheek, turn the other one to him.'"[65]

In other words, Marcion(ites) understood Christ's command to engage in self-sacrificial submission as a rejection of retaliation. They assumed a proposition articulated by Justin Martyr: "a law placed against another law abrogates the earlier one."[66] Even Tertullian agreed that the retaliation principle "has been cancelled" and "abolished." "For the old Law used to . . . gouge out eye for eye and would pay back injury with revenge. However, the new Law [of Christ] ordained clemency."[67]

---

[65] *Adamantius* 1.15: ἐν τῷ νόμῳ λέγει ὀφθαλμὸν ἀντὶ ὀφθαλμοῦ καὶ ὀδόντα ἀντὶ ὀδόντος, ὁ δὲ κύριος ἀγαθὸς ὤν, λέγει ἐν τῷ εὐαγγελίῳ ἐὰν τίς σε ῥαπίσῃ εἰς τὴν σιαγόνα, παράθες αὐτῷ καὶ τὴν ἄλλην. The statement is virtually a quotation of Matthew 5:38–39; cf. Evangelion 6:29. See further Tertullian, *AM* 2.18.1; 4.16.4–6; Origen, *Cels.* 7.25; *Acts of Archelaus* 44.9; Augustine, *Against Adimantus* 8.

[66] Justin, *Dialogue with Trypho* 11.2: νόμος δὲ κατὰ νόμου τεθεὶς τὸν πρὸ αὐτοῦ ἔπαυσε.

[67] Tertullian, *Against the Jews* 3.10. Geoffrey D. Dunn, who dates this work to 195–96 CE, considers the work to be authentic and to be addressed to a primarily Christian audience (*Tertullian's Adversus Iudaeos: A Rhetorical Analysis* [Washington, DC: Catholic University of America Press, 2003], 173–82).

For Marcion(ites), Christ rejected the creator's law of retaliation not only because it was unkind, but because it was unjust. This was not simply a disagreement of law but of principle. Christ forbade retaliation, while the creator enforced it. The moral character of the Christ who rejected retaliation was therefore significantly different from the creator who commanded it.

If the creator was "just," Marcion(ites) thought, his justice was a mask for cruelty. The creator's justice really meant severity, harshness, and savagery, which could hardly be described as good.[68] A justice without goodness was no justice at all but, rather, a travesty of justice emerging from a depraved character.

Child Murder

Another antithesis recorded in the *Adamantius* went as follows: "The prophet of the god of generation told a bear to come out of a thicket and devour the children who met him, but the good Lord says, 'Let the children come to me, for of such is the kingdom of heaven'" (Evangelion 18:16).[69] Tertullian also recorded this contrast: "Christ loves the little children, teaching that those who always wish to be great should become such as these. But the creator launched bears against young boys, taking vengeance for their insult suffered by the prophet Elisha."[70]

To explain: Marcion(ites) appealed to the story in Jewish scripture where Elisha the prophet, while traveling to the city of Bethel, was met by young children who mocked his baldness. The prophet responded by cursing the children in the name of the creator. The creator immediately fulfilled the curse by sending two bears against the children who were immediately mauled (2 Kings 2:23–24).

---

[68] The "just" god is in effect the savage god, e.g., in Tertullian, *AM* 4.8.7: "The god who is a judge wants to be feared, and he has the traits that inspire fear: wrath, savageness, vindictive judgment, condemnation." Although I agree with Harnack in distinguishing justice and goodness, his attempt to distinguish the creator's justice from his *wicked* nature (e.g., *Marcion*, 69–70, 75–76) fails. Yet even Harnack allowed that, for Marcion, the justice of the creator "turns into wickedness" (*Marcion*, 87). See further Löhr, "Did Marcion Distinguish," in May, and Greschat, *Marcion*, 131–46; Lieu, *Marcion*, 343–49.

[69] *Adamantius* 1.16: ὁ προφήτης τοῦ θεοῦ τῆς γενέσεως ἄρκτῳ εἶπειν ἐξελθεῖν ἐκ δρυμοῦ καὶ καταφαγεῖν τοὺς ἀπαντήσαντας αὐτῷ παῖδας. ὁ δὲ ἀγαθὸς κύριος «ἄφετε,» φησίν «τὰς παιδίας ἔρχεσθαι πρὸς με, τῶν γὰρ τοιούτων ἐστὶν ἡ βασιλεία τῶν οὐρανῶν.» Cf. Matt 19:14; Mark 10:14.

[70] Tertullian, *AM* 4.23.4: *Sed ecce Christus diligit parvulos, tales docens esse debere qui semper maiores velint esse, creator autem ursos pueris immisit, ulciscens Helisaeum Propheten convicia ab eis passum.*

It is tempting to soft-peddle the troubling details of this story. According to the Septuagint, Elisha cursed not wily teenage toughs, but "small children" (*paidaria mikra*). He cursed not just two or three of these children but "forty-two" of them—all of whom were gored. He cursed them not for a repeated offense, but for a single occurrence of jesting, and for a relatively minor infraction—for exposing the prophet's baldness. Consequently, Elisha's cursing of the children indicates serious moral flaws in both his character and the character of the being he represented—the creator.

There were, of course, attempts to mitigate the morally problematic nature of the story. One ancient commentator blamed the parents of the children for bad childrearing, but this hardly makes up for child murder.[71] Attempts are made in the modern period to make the children's insult more cutting—to say that baldness was a sign of Elisha's prophetic office or indicative of leprosy.[72] But even if these speculations proved convincing, Elisha's curse still lies beyond the moral pale.

For Marcion(ites), the angry, cursing prophet represented the character of the one who sent him—the creator. The anger of the creator and his jealous need to retaliate has already been discussed. In the bear attack episode, it was the creator who perpetrated the crime, for it is he who sent the bears against the children.

These bears quite literally tore the children apart. The Greek verb at play (*anerrēxan*) expresses incredible violence. It can be used to describe breaking through a wall, or of a lion ripping open a carcass. Etymologically, the verb means "break up," and one can almost hear the sound of the children's bones cracked by the bears' teeth—though their screams go unmentioned. Far from showing any compassion, the cursing prophet continued his journey as if nothing had even happened.[73]

Such, for Marcion(ites), was the justice of the creator. The crime committed was petty; its punishment was swift, cruel, deadly. The creator's prophet was

---

[71] Ephrem, whose comments are translated in Marco Conti, ed., *Ancient Christian Commentary on Scripture V: 1–2 Kings, 1–2 Chronicles, Ezra, Nehemiah, Esther* (Downers Grove: InterVarsity, 2008), 149. On the same page, Caesarius of Arles is quoted as saying that Elisha's purpose in having the children "torn to pieces" was not revenge but their "amendment."

[72] Bernard P. Robinson opted for the baldness as a religious tonsure ("II Kings 2:23–25: Elisha and the She-Bears," *Scripture Bulletin* 14:1 [1983]: 2–3). Richard G. Messner ("Elisha and the Bears," *Grace Journal* 3 [1962]: 12–24 at 18) cited arguments for baldness signifying leprosy.

[73] John Gray comments: "The supposition that Elisha invoked the name of Yahweh to curse the boys, with such terrible consequences . . . borders on blasphemy" (*I and II Kings: A Commentary,* 3rd ed. [London: SCM, 1977], 480). See further Penchansky, *What Rough Beast?* 81–90; Brian P. Irwin, "The Curious Incident of the Boys and the Bears: 2 Kings 2 and the Prophetic Authority of Elisha," *Tyndale Bulletin* 67:1 (2016): 23–35.

quick to curse, and the creator who mirrored his character proved hasty to fulfill it. Elisha cursed in the name of the creator. This is significant, for as we shall see in Chapter 7, the creator is characterized by cursing. A curse in his name is duly effective. Indeed, the creator had already warned the Israelites by adding curses to his covenant. If Israel did not follow his laws, the creator would send "wild animals" against them who would bereave them of family members by devouring them (Lev 26:22). As the creator himself put it: "I will send the teeth of beasts!" (Deut 32:24).

Marcion opposed the curse against the children to what occurs in the gospel. Votaries of Jesus brought infants and small children to him so that he could bless them. When his disciples tried to prevent this, Jesus invited the young to approach, saying: "Let the little children come to me and do not hinder them, for the kingdom of heaven is made up of their kind" (Luke 18:15–17).[74] In short, Jesus transmitted the blessings of the true god to the children, whereas Elisha effectively destroyed kids by the curse of the creator.

One can argue here that the two scenes are fundamentally different. The children of the gospel, after all, do not mock Jesus. If they did, perhaps his response would have been different. But we have little reason to think so, for when Jesus was rejected and refused hospitality by the (adult) Samaritans, he did not curse them. When his disciples suggested they call down fire from heaven like the prophet Elijah (2 Kings 1:9–13), Jesus rebuked them as if they were raving mad (Evangelion 9:54–55).[75] For Marcion(ites), Jesus was on a different wavelength than the prophets of the creator. He did not represent their character. He certainly did not replicate the character of the creator, whose "justice" was exposed as cruel, even murderous.

Violent in War

The Marcionites in the *Adamantius* presented three more significant contrasts:

The prophet of the god of generation [Moses], when a battle commenced against his people, climbed to the top of a mountain and extended his hands

---

[74] The full passage is not attested in Marcion's Evangelion, so I cite the Lukan text.

[75] Tertullian specifically mentioned this as a point made by Marcion(ites) (*AM* 4.23.8: "The creator, at Elijah's demand, brings down a plague of fire upon that false prophet. I grant the judge's severity, and by contrast Christ's gentleness when reproving the disciples as they call for the same punishment upon that village of the Samaritans"). See further Lieu, *Marcion*, 280.

to his god in order to slaughter masses of people in the battle (Exod 17:8–9). But our Lord [Jesus], since he is good, stretched out his hands [on the cross] not to slaughter human beings but to save them.[76]

The prophet of the god of generation, in order to kill as many as possible in battle, had the sun stand still that it might not go down until the adversaries of the people were utterly annihilated (Joshua 10); but the Lord, since he is good, says, "Let not the sun set on your rage." (Eph 4:26)[77]

The prophet of the god of generation says, "My bows are taut and my arrows are sharpened" (Isa 5:28; Deut 32:23), but the apostle says, "Put on the full armor of god, that you may be able to quench the fiery arrows of the evil one." (Eph 6:11, 16)[78]

To understand these contrasts, we must examine the biblical contexts.

Amalekites

We begin with the first, namely, Exodus 17:8–15, which can here be summarized. In an apparent attempt to protect their borders, a tribe called the Amalekites drew up its battle lines against Israel.[79] According to Exodus, over half a million armed Israelite men had recently marched from Egypt and were moving up toward the desert of the Negev (modern-day southern Israel). This was the homeland of the Amalekites, a people stemming from the grandson of Israel's brother Esau (Gen 36:12). According to this family tree, Amalekites and Israelites were cousins. Yet family ties could not prevent the clash of war.

Moses immediately ordered his military lieutenant Joshua to choose his best troops to array themselves against the Amalekites. For his part, Moses climbed a nearby hill to oversee the battle. Whenever Moses lifted his hands,

---

[76] *Adamantius* 1.11: ὁ προφήτης τοῦ θεοῦ τῆς γενέσεως, πολέμου συστάντος πρὸς τὸν λαόν, ἀναβὰς ἐπὶ τὴν κορυφὴν τοῦ ὄρους ἐξέτεινε τὰς χεῖρας αὐτοῦ πρὸς τὸν θεόν, ἵνα πολλοὺς τῷ πολέμῳ ἀνέλῃ. ὁ δὲ κύριος ἡμῶν ἀγαθὸς ὤν, ἐξέτεινε τὰς χεῖρας αὐτοῦ οὐχὶ τοῦ ἀνελεῖν τοὺς ἀνθρώπους ἀλλὰ τοῦ σῶσαι.

[77] *Adamantius* 1.13: ὁ προφήτης τοῦ θεοῦ τῆς γενέσεως, ἵνα πολεμῶν πλείονας ἀνέλῃ, ἔστησεν τὸν ἥλιον τοῦ μὴ δῦσαι μέχρι συντελέσῃ ἀναιρῶν τοὺς πολεμοῦντας πρὸς τὸν λαόν. ὁ δὲ κύριος ἀγαθὸς ὤν λέγει «ὁ ἥλιος μὴ ἐπιδυέτω ἐπὶ τῷ παροργισμῷ ὑμῶν.»

[78] *Adamantius* 1.19: ὁ προφήτης τοῦ θεοῦ τῆς γενέσεως λέγει «τὰ τόξα μου ἐντεταμένα καὶ τὰ βέλη μου ἠκονημένα,» ὁ δ' ἀπόστολος φησιν «ἐνδύσασθε τὴν πανοπλίαν τοῦ θεοῦ πρὸς τὸ δύνασθαι τὰ βέλη τοῦ πονηροῦ τὰ πεπυρωμένα σβέσαι.»

[79] Philo wrote that the king of Amalek feared being pillaged by the incoming Israelites (πόρθησιν εὐλαβηθείς, *Life of Moses* 1.215).

the Israelite troops cut down their enemies. But when his arms lowered in exhaustion, the Amalekites rallied. Realizing this, Moses's companions sat him down and supported each of his arms until the Israelites completely slaughtered—not just the Amalekite army—but its civilian population with the edge of the sword.[80] The creator then sent Moses a dispatch that he would "utterly wipe out the memory of Amalek from under heaven."[81]

Yet it was the Israelites themselves who did the dirty work, for Moses later commanded them to "wipe out the name [that is, existence] of Amalek from under heaven" with the heated warning "Do not forget!" (Deut 25:19). "This command," in the words of a recent interpreter, was meant "to return Amalek to a state of non-existence, i.e., Amalek is to be drummed out of the world order."[82]

The creator himself did not let the command to slaughter slip away from his mind. Four hundred years later, he informed his anointed king Saul: "I will take vengeance because of what Amalek did to Israel . . . . Now, advance and strike Amalek . . . and utterly destroy it by dedicating it to me, all that belongs to it. Do not spare anything; kill man and woman, infant and suckling child, calf and sheep, camel and donkey" (1 Kingdoms 15:3 LXX). When Saul spared—not the women and children—but the choice animals of the Amalekites, the creator regretted making Saul king and vowed to dethrone him (15:9–35).

What interested Marcion in this story was the contrast in divine character, a contrast he illustrated by a posture dear to Christians—the outstretched hands. Contemporaneous Christian writers had already interpreted Moses's outstretched hands as a foreshadowing of Christ's arms extended on the cross.[83] For Christians, the open arms were a sign of sacrificial love and

---

[80] ἐτρέψατο Ἰησοῦς τὸν Ἀμαληκ *καὶ πάντα τὸν λαὸν αὐτοῦ ἐν φόνῳ μαχαίρας* (Exod 17:13, emphasis added), in John William Wevers, ed., *Exodus* (Göttingen: Vandenhoeck & Ruprecht, 1991), 220–22.

[81] Ἀλοιφῇ ἐξαλείψω τὸ μνημόσυνον Ἀμαλῆκ ἐκ τῆς ὑπὸ τὸν οὐρανόν (Exod 17:14). Philo, although he acknowledged the slaughter of the Amalekites, omitted any mention that god told Moses he would erase Amalek's memory (*Life of Moses* 1.214–19). The same is true of Josephus, who added that the Israelites, after slaughtering the Amalekites, inspired great terror and gained great wealth (*Antiquities* 3.56–57). See further Avi Sagi, "The Punishment of Amalek in Jewish Tradition: Coping with the Moral Problem," *Harvard Theological Review* 87:3 (1994): 323–46; Louis H. Feldman, *"Remember Amalek!" Vengeance, Zealotry, and Group Destruction in the Bible According to Philo, Pseudo-Philo, and Josephus* (Cincinnati: Hebrew Union College Press, 2004), 19–21, 29–37.

[82] Feldman, *"Remember Amalek!"* 10.

[83] *Epistle of Barnabas* 12.2; Justin, *Dialogue with Trypho* 90.4; Irenaeus, *AH* 4.21.1; *Sibylline Oracles* 8.251–52; *Acts of Archelaus* 51.7.

forgiveness. For Marcion, however, Moses's outstretched hands signaled the opposite—war and bloodlust, the slashing of swords, and the (attempted) annihilation of a whole tribe.

Such was the character of the creator, who held a grudge against Amalek—not simply for four generations but for four hundred years—secretly warring against them (Exod 17:16) until he could annihilate every man, woman, child, and animal. There was simply no similarity, for Marcionites, between the outstretched hands of Moses and Christ. "What is the likeness here?" cried out the Marcionite in the *Adamantius*. "The one by stretching out his hands slaughters, while the other saves!"[84]

Stopping the Sun

The second Marcionite contrast refers to a story in the book of Joshua (10:1–15). To set the scene: Moses had recently died. The Israelites invaded Canaan (modern Israel) under the command of Joshua. Their armies annihilated several towns west of the Jordan River, but one of the cities guilefully signed a peace treaty with Israel. A coalition of Canaanite kings then attacked that city. When Joshua's army came to its defense, his soldiers proceeded to slaughter their opponents to a man. Realizing that there was not enough time in a day to kill them all, Joshua commanded the sun to stand still to provide sufficient light to cut them down.

Marcion(ites) contrasted this halting of the sun—caused by none other than the sun's creator—with the biblical saying not to let the sun set on one's rage. This particular directive comes from "the Lord" in a broad sense, since it is found in a Pauline letter (Eph 4:26). But Marcionites understood the original Pauline epistles as inspired by the true deity. The contrast highlighted a difference in character. The creator interfered with the physical laws of the universe to make time for Joshua to finish spilling human blood in the Judean hills. The creator thereby showed himself to be bellicose—determined to wipe out his enemies to support a program of invasion.

By contrast, the lord known to Paul was not even willing for his servants to stay angry overnight before reconciling. The creator, in support of a bloody battle, cut short the night; the true god, however, commanded that anger cease before nightfall.

---

[84] *Adamantius* 1.11: Τί οὖν ὅμοιον; ὁ μὲν διὰ τῆς ἐκτάσεως τῶν χειρῶν ἀναίρει, ὁ δὲ σώζει. See further Tsutsui, *Auseinandersetzung*, 161–62; Lieu, *Marcion*, 288–89.

Arrows of the Evil One

The final Marcionite contrast quoted a verse from the prophet Isaiah. In context, the prophet had just finished an oracle condemning Israelites for buying up too many properties, for being excessively drunk at parties, and for acquitting people who accepted bribes (Isa 5:8– 23). He then launched this speech:

> The lord of armies was enraged with wrath against his people; he pressed his hand against them and struck them. The mountains shuddered; their bodies became like dung on the street. Yet with all this, his anger did not abate, his hand remained high. And so, he will raise a signal to the nations far away and will whistle for them from the height of earth—swiftly they will come. They will not labor nor grow tired; they will not doze nor sleep; they will not loose their belts or untie their sandals—their arrows are sharp and their bows are taut. (Isa 5:25–28)

The Marcionite quotation reads as if the creator spoke it in the first person: "*My* bows are taut and *my* arrows are sharpened." This may be a simple deduction: since it is the creator who organized the attack on his people, effectively he is the one who bent the bows and launched the arrows.

Yet Marcion(ites) may have blended in their memory of Deuteronomy 32:23, 42 where the creator said against his people, "I will gather evils against them and expend all my arrows against them . . . I will make my arrows drunk with blood" (cf. 4 Ezra 16:13). Whatever the case may be, the creator was ultimately responsible for declaring war against his own people. To Marcion(ites), the creator seemed hostile, warlike, and unstable—all traits indicating a vicious character.

The contrast Marcion(ites) drew in this instance is unlike anything we have seen before. It comes from a Pauline letter that invites Christians to don the armor of god. The armor is spiritual because, as the author points out, "our battle is not against flesh and blood but . . . against the spiritual forces of evil" (Eph 6:12). Thus the call to arms is not a call to literal war and bloodshed. It is a call for defense against spirit beings, and specifically against "all the fiery arrows of the evil one" (Eph 6:16).

But the only arrows of which Isaiah 5:28 and Deut 32:23 speak are the arrows of the creator. We are to deduce, then, that the "arrows of the evil one" are in fact arrows of the creator. The creator, for Marcion(ites), *was* the evil one.

This interpretation is daring to be sure, but not arbitrary. Even apart from the intertextual connections, the evil of the creator had already been established elsewhere in the "Old" Testament. Marcionites knew that the creator was a being who—using human armies to be sure—fought and killed his own people, leaving their bodies like dung on the streets.

This is not the action of a good deity. The creator's abandonment and killing of his own people—though it might be "just" from the perspective of the scriptural author—is yet another example of his desire for vengeance and jealous hostility when his people fail. For Marcion(ites), to be sure, one could hardly force oneself to love this being. The only appropriate action was to take defensive measures against him in an attempt to quench the flames of his demon-like attack.[85]

Conclusion

Marcionites were, like all readers of the Bible, selective (perhaps culpably so). Yet whereas most Christians today read Jewish scripture to emphasize the creator's goodness, Marcionite Christians underscored precisely the opposite—his wicked character. As it turned out, they hardly lacked material. Indeed, we have barely scratched the surface of the texts they treated, hindered as we are by the loss of the *Antitheses* and the selective reporting of Marcion's views. We have only discussed the creator as maker of evils, ignorantly boasting, designing evil in Eden, jealous of other gods, commanding pillage, issuing brutal punishments, murdering children, and savage in war.

We know from various lists, however, that Marcion(ites) underscored other offenses of the creator. According to Tertullian, Marcion(ites) emphasized the creator's wiping out of humanity with a flood, his firebombing the cities of Sodom and Gomorrah, his plagues against Egypt, his hardening of Pharaoh's heart, and his killing of the Israelites in the desert.[86] In the report of

---

[85] For the Hebrew creator and violence, see further Bernhard Lang, *The Hebrew God: Portrait of an Ancient Deity* (New Haven: Yale University Press, 2002), 45–74; David Penchansky and Paul L. Reddit, *Shall Not the Judge of All the Earth Do Right? Studies on the Nature of God in Tribute to James L. Crenshaw* (University Park: Pennsylvania State University Press, 1999), esp. 1–42; Eryl W. Davies, *The Immoral Bible: Approaches to Biblical Ethics* (London: Bloomsbury, 2010); M. Carroll, R. Daniel, and J. Blair Wilgus, *Wrestling with the Violence of God: Soundings in the Old Testament* (Winona Lake: Eisenbrauns, 2015); Terrence Fretheim, *What Kind of God? Collected Essays of Terrence E. Fretheim*, ed. Michael J. Chan and Brent A. Strawn (Pennsylvania State University Press, 2015), esp. 129–58.

[86] All these episodes are mentioned by Tertullian, *AM* 2.14.4. Origen added the killing of the Israelites in the desert (*First Principles* 2.5.1). Cf. Jerome, *Commentary on Micah* 1.9: "But if he [the

Irenaeus, the creator "makes evils, is lustful for war, is inconstant in his judgments, and contradicts himself."[87]

Two additional sin lists (combined here) from the Pseudoclementine *Homilies* (a fourth-century CE novel related to the *Recognitions*) sum up the Marcionite critique of the creator from the Jewish scriptures: the creator lies, tempts people while playing dumb, flies into fits of anger, changes his mind, becomes jealous, hardens hearts, blinds people, makes them deaf, counsels people to pillage, mocks them, shows weakness, creates evils, delights in war, shows no familial affection, and is not faithful to fulfill his promises.[88] For Marcion(ites), such a being could not be described as good.

In their minds, Marcionites did not invent the evil creator. Rather, they exposed him from his own scriptures. Despite the accusation of anti-Marcionite reports, Marcionites did not simply proof-text scriptural documents. Rather, they performed serious exegetical and comparative work to display the creator's wicked character. They were innovative and poignant in the art of contrast, showing how the character of Jesus and the god revealed by him was incompatible with the character of the creator.

Marcion's enemies did their best to show how the two characters were in fact compatible, with the creator, for instance, altering his salvific program in response to human maturation. But the enormity of the anti-Marcionite response from the second to the fifth centuries CE shows just how powerful and enduring Marcionite arguments were perceived to be.[89] Marcion strongly argued from the creator's own scriptures that the creator's justice was a form of cruelty, and that his repeatedly evil actions—which he himself confessed (Isa 45:7)—proved that he was malign.

creator] seems to us to be cruel, harsh and bloodthirsty, since he obliterated the human race in the flood, rained fire and brimstone upon Sodom and Gomorrah, drowned the Egyptians in the waters and made the corpses of the Israelites fall in the desert . . ." (trans. Thomas P. Scheck).

[87] Irenaeus, *AH* 1.27.2.

[88] Pseudo-Clement, *Homilies*, 43–44: ψεύδεται . . . πειράζει ὡς ἀγνοῶν . . . ἐνθυμεῖται καὶ μεταμελεῖται . . . ζηλοῖ . . . σκληρύνει καρδίας . . . τυφλοῖ καὶ κωφοῖ . . . ἀποστερεῖν συμβουλεύει . . . ἐνπάιζει . . . ἀδυνατεῖ . . . ἀδικεῖ . . . κακὰ κτίζει . . . πολέμους αὐτὸς ἀγαπᾷ . . . τὰ κακὰ κτίζει . . . ἄστοργος αὐτός . . . πιστὸς οὐκ ἔστιν περὶ ὧν ὑπισχνεῖται. See further *Homilies* 3.38, where the creator is "without foreknowledge, imperfect, needy, not good, and a slave to countless horrid passions." Tertullian, addressing Marcion, listed some of the creator's passions: he becomes enraged (*irascitur*) and jealous (*aemulatur*), exalts himself (*extollitur*), and becomes irritated (*exacerbatur*) (*AM* 2.16.3); he is also "most pitiless/bitter (*acerbissimus*)" (3.4.2).

[89] For the enormity of the anti-Marcionite response, see Harnack, *Marcion*, 99–103; Lampe, *From Paul*, 250–51.

4

The God of This World

Who comes to the road that seduces, to the beginning of the two
poison roads (and) to the gate of hell? It is . . . the one who worships
the devil and addresses him as god.

—Manichean Confession[1]

Introduction

Marcion was famous chiefly as an interpreter, not of Jewish scriptures, but of
Pauline texts. For Marcion, the Pauline epistles were the favored mine from
which he chiseled out the ore of his theology. If the Jewish scriptures could be
used to prove the wicked, spiteful, and jealous character of the creator, it was
Paul who gave Marcion the eyes to behold him. One of the most important
Pauline texts in this regard was 2 Corinthians 4:4.

What does this text say in context? In 2 Corinthians 3:14, Paul claimed that
a veil lies over the hearts of the Jews whenever they read Jewish Law. Yet although Paul promoted himself as a minister of a superior covenant (2 Cor
3:1–6), he admitted that sometimes his message about Christ was also veiled.
It was veiled to those "who are being destroyed." They are being destroyed, in
part, because "the god of this world blinded their minds so that they do not
behold the brilliance of the gospel of the glory of Christ" (2 Cor 4:4).[2]

In this chapter, I explore the Marcionite reception of this verse with a
view to understanding how Marcionites derived their conception of the
wicked creator.[3] Before delving straight in, however, I will lay out some of the

---

[1] Translated by Jes P. Asmussen, *Manichean Literature: Representative Texts Chiefly from Middle
Persian and Parthian Writings* (Delmar: Scholars' Facsimiles, 1975), 72.

[2] ὁ θεὸς τοῦ αἰῶνος τούτου ἐτύφλωσεν τὰ νοήματα τῶν ἀπίστων εἰς τὸ μὴ αὐγάσαι τὸν φωτισμὸν
τοῦ εὐαγγελίου τῆς δόξης τοῦ Χριστοῦ. The words in bold are attested in Marcion's Apostolikon
(Tertullian, *AM* 5.11.9). See Schmid, *Marcion*, 329.

[3] Long ago, Andreas Lindemann recognized the importance of 2 Corinthians 4:4 for Marcion
but left the issue unexplored (*Paulus im ältesten Christentum: Das Bild des Apostels und die
Rezeption der paulinischen Theologie in der frühchristlichen Literatur bis Marcion* [Tübingen: Mohr
Siebeck, 1979], 384).

The Evil Creator. M. David Litwa, Oxford University Press. © Oxford University Press 2021.
DOI: 10.1093/oso/9780197566428.003.0006

interpretive groundwork of the verse with an eye to how it might have been interpreted by a second-century reader. These readers, just like readers today, were challenged to answer key questions. We can isolate three inquiries here. First, who is "the god of this world"? What are his deeds and character in both the larger biblical context and in the context of 2 Corinthians? Finally, is "the god of this world" a good or an evil being?

Terminology

First, a word about the "world" in the phrase "the god of this world."[4] The Greek term at play here (*aiōn*) can also be translated as "age." (Tertullian, for instance, took it in this sense.) My translation "world" already fits a particular trajectory of reception. Today, it is common to say that Paul was an apocalyptic thinker who assumed a present age overlapped by an age to come.[5] But to those removed from an apocalyptic worldview, Paul's language of *aiōn* could be taken in a spatial sense to refer to our cosmic realm.[6]

Paul referred not just to *a* god of this world but to "*the* god" (*ho theos*)— designating a definite deity, evidently the one who controls the world. There was some cause to take this being as the creator since early Christians generally assumed that there was no other god who ruled this world. He ruled the world, to state it most simply, because he created it.[7]

To support this understanding, early Christians had only to recall their own scriptural or para-scriptural texts. The book of Tobit records that all the nations will one day bless "the god of the world" in righteousness (14:7).[8] Daniel 5:4 (LXX) censures those who bless idols and not "the god of the

---

[4] According to Victor Paul Furnish, Paul's phrase ὁ αἰών οὗτός (1 Cor 1:20; 2:6, 8; 3:18; Rom 12:22) is not essentially different from his references to ὁ κόσμος οὗτός (1 Cor 3:19; 5:10; 7:31) (*II Corinthians Translated with Introduction, Notes, and Commentary* [New York: Doubleday, 1984], 220).

[5] E.g., Clinton Arnold, *Powers of Darkness* (Downers Grove: InterVarsity, 1992), 102. See in general Barry R. Matlock, *Unveiling the Apocalyptic Paul: Paul's Interpreters and the Rhetoric of Criticism* (London: Bloomsbury, 1996).

[6] For the spatial sense of αἰών, see Wisd 13:9; 14:6; 18:4; Heb 1:2; 11:3.

[7] Tertullian remarked: "the ages (saecula = αἰῶνες) belong to the creator" (*AM* 5.6.3). Interestingly, Tertullian referred to the creator as *princeps potestatis saeculorum* ("prince of the power of the ages"), semantically close to the *deus huius saeculi* of 2 Corinthians 4:4 (*AM* 5.17.7).

[8] τὸν θεὸν τοῦ αἰῶνος in Robert Hanhart, ed., *Tobit* (Göttingen: Vandenhoeck & Ruprecht, 1983), 179–80, from Codex Sinaiticus (ℵ). Most other MSS have, instead of τὸν θεὸν τοῦ αἰῶνος, simply τὸν κύριον.

world" who holds power over their breath.[9] The Greek version of I Enoch 1:4 identifies "the god of the world" with the god of Exodus who treads upon Mount Sinai.[10] In all three passages, "the god of the world" is the Jewish deity, creator of heaven and earth.

The God Who Blinds

The fact that "the god of this world" blinded people (2 Cor 4:4) might sound repellent today, but it is not out of character for the deity known from Jewish scripture. The creator repeatedly hardened the heart of Pharaoh (Exod 4:21; 7:3–4; 9:12, 35), ordained that life-saving advice be refused (2 Sam 17:14), and incited a wicked spirit to speak lies in the royal court (1 Kings 22:20–24). Yahweh also hardened the heart of his people (Isa 63:17), threatened to inflict them with blindness (Deut 28:28), and sealed the eyes of Israel's prophets (Isa 29:10, cf. 14).

The phenomenon of divine blinding and mental incapacitation is not restricted to Jewish scripture. According to Paul in Romans 1:28, god "gave up" people who worship the divine through images "to a debased mind" so that they would perform shameful acts. In 2 Thessalonians, god "sends the operation of deceit" so that unbelievers accept "the lie" of the "man of lawlessness" (2:11). If this god is not himself a deceiver, he is not above sending agents of deceit or performing operations that result in blinding people from the truth.

In the second century, a paradigm proof text for the god who blinds was Isaiah 6:10. In the Hebrew version of this verse, Yahweh commanded Isaiah to dull (literally "fatten") the hearts of his people, to close (literally "make heavy") their ears, and to blind (or "smear something over") their eyes.

Septuagintal versions of Isaiah attempted to avoid the fact that Yahweh commanded blindness to afflict his own people. It said that the heart of the Israelites "became stupid; they heard poorly with their ears and they closed their eyes so that they do not see with their eyes." The word "stupid" could more literally be translated "thick," "fat," or "dense." It represents a passive

---

[9] τὸν θεὸν τοῦ αἰῶνος in Joseph Ziegler and Olivier Munnich, eds., *Susanna, Daniel, Bel et Draco. Editio secunda versionis iuxta LXX interpretes textum plane novum constituit* (Göttingen: Vandenhoeck & Ruprecht, 1999), 310.

[10] ὁ θεὸς τοῦ αἰῶνος in M. Black, ed., *Apocalypsis Henochi Graece* (Leiden: Brill, 1970), 19.

In a Christian spell (K. Preisendanz and A. Henrichs , eds., *Papyri Graecae magicae*, 3 vols., 2nd ed. [Stuttgart: Teubner, 2001], 2.221 = §13.8) Christ himself who came from the father's right hand is called "the god of this world" (ὁ θεός τοῦ αἰῶνος).

verb, often taken to be a divine passive (*epachunthē*). The creator, in other words, is likely the one who incites the stupidity, an interpretation in accord with the previous verse, where the creator orders Isaiah: "Go and say to this people, 'With hearing you will hear and certainly not understand; seeing you will see and certainly not perceive."[11] The statement is worded like a prediction. But the certainty of Yahweh indicates that he willed the prediction to come true and apparently played a role in realizing it. As we learn from the context (6:11), Yahweh had already sealed Israel's fate: the people would be exiled and their country destroyed.[12]

A similar logic of divine incapacitation appears in late first-century citations of Isaiah 6:10. In John 12:40, the narrator understands Isaiah 6:10 as a prophecy explaining the fictional Jews' refusal to believe in Jesus. For them, the creator "has blinded their eyes and hardened their heart *so that (hina)* they do not see with their eyes and understand with their heart and convert" (emphasis added). This purpose clause (also attested in Mark 4:12 and Luke 8:10) brings out the idea that the creator actually *intended* to blind his own people from seeing the light of Christ.[13]

Sources from the Nag Hammadi codices present a heightened vilification of the creator buttressed by Isaiah 6:10. According to the *Secret Book of John* (the earliest version dated to the mid–second century CE), the creator induced a slumber in Adam. The main text adapted is Genesis 2:21–22, but the creator's bestowal of a "spirit of stupefaction" (Isa 29:10) lurks in the background, for Adam's sleep is interpreted as an intellectual numbing. The creator made Adam "heavy," Jesus explains, "with senselessness."[14] Jesus then recalls Isaiah 6:10 to illustrate the stupefying behavior: the creator "will make the ears of their hearts heavy so that they do not understand and see."[15]

The *Testimony of Truth* (NHC IX,3) also questions the creator's behavior in Eden. The creator gives an arbitrary command. When Adam disobeys it, the creator cannot locate Adam and does not know who instructed him to disobey. He begrudged Adam both the gift of knowledge and that of eternal life. To support this negative portrayal of the Hebrew deity, the author quoted

---

[11] Isa 6:9–10 in Ziegler, ed., *Isaias*, 143–44. See further Räisänen, *Hardening*, 60–66, 88–93.

[12] Later reflections of Isaiah 6:10 emphasize the guilt of Israel (Isa 42:20; 43:8; Jer 5:21–23; Ezek 12:2–3). C. A. Evans shows that later versions of Isaiah 6:10 (LXX, Targums, and Peshitta) soften the theme of divinely inflicted obduracy (*To See and Not Perceive: Isa 6.9–10 in Early Jewish and Christian Interpretation* [London: Bloomsbury, 2009], 61–80, 164).

[13] Evans, *To See*, 91–136.

[14] *Secret Book of John* (BG) 58.20–59.1 (ⲁϥⲉⲣϣ̅ⲟⳓ ⲉ̅ⲛ̅ ⲧⲁⲛⲁⲓⲥⲑⲏⲥⲓⲁ).

[15] *Secret Book of John* (BG) 59.3–4; compare the longer version (NHC II,1) 22.26–28.

a version of Isaiah 6:10: "I will make their heart thick, and I will cause their minds to become blind, that they might not understand or comprehend the things that are said." The creator in this rendering is quite clearly the cause of his people's blindness.[16]

In all likelihood, Marcion cited Isaiah 6:10 in his *Antitheses*. Whereas the creator tells his own people, "Hear but do not understand" (Isa 6:10), Christ says, "The one who has ears to hear, let him hear" (Luke 8:8).[17] The contrast in character was clear to Marcion: Jesus invited his disciples to understand, whereas the creator darkened his people's minds. The opposed actions of these reputedly divine figures indicate their conflicting characters.

The shorter version of the *Secret Book of John* suggests yet another inspiration for understanding the creator's work of cognitive incapacitation. Before citing Isaiah 6:10, Jesus says that Yaldabaoth (the creator) "veiled" Adam's "perception with a veil."[18] The veiling languages echo Paul's in 2 Corinthians 3:14–4:3.[19] Quite possibly, then, 2 Corinthians 3–4 was also an intertext in this passage of the *Secret Book*.

In 2 Corinthians 3:14, Paul noted that the minds of the Jews were hardened (*epōrōthē*, probably another divine passive). He used the same verb to refer to the Jews in Romans 11:7–8: "But the rest were hardened." He then quoted a mixture of Isaiah 29:10, where the creator gave his people "a spirit of stupefaction," and Deuteronomy 29:3, where he treated his people like he treated his enemy Pharaoh, refusing to grant them "a heart to know, eyes to see, and ears to hear."

This is exactly the sort of incapacitation imposed by "the god of this world" (2 Cor 4:4): he blinds minds. The analogous action reinforces the idea that when Paul referred to "the god of this world," he spoke of the creator, with his long track record of dulling human senses. Based on this track record, it was possible and even plausible, for Marcion(ites), to identify "the god of this world" with the creator.

---

[16] *Testimony of Truth* (IX,3) 48.8–14; 29.6–9. For other allusions to Isaiah 6:10, see *Secret Book of John* (NHC II,1) 30.9–11; *Gospel of Thomas* (NHC II,2) 28.3; *Second Revelation of James* (NHC V,4) 60.5–10; *Revelation of Peter* (NHC VII,3) 73.11–16. See further Evans, *To See*, 160–61.

[17] Harnack, *Marcion*, 61. The Marcionite use of Isaiah 6:9–10 can be gleaned from Irenaeus, *AH* 4.29.1 (which seems to follow the Hebrew text); Tertullian, *AM* 3.6.5; 4.19.2; 5.11.9. The contrast between Luke 8:8 and Isa 6:10 derives from Tertullian, *AM* 4.19.2: "from difference [of characters], Christ permits a hearing which the creator removes."

[18] The word used for veil in the *Secret Book* (BG) 58.18–20 (ⲚⲦⲀϤ ϨⲰⲂⲤ̄ ⲈⲂⲞⲖ ⲈⲕⲚ̄ⲚⲈϤⲀⲓⲤⲐⲎⲤⲓⲤ ϨⲚ ⲞⲨ ϨⲂⲤ̄) is the same word used in the Coptic version of 2 Corinthians to translate Paul's language of veiling.

[19] 2 Cor 3:14 (ⲠⲒϨⲂⲤ̄); 2 Cor 4:3 (ⲈϢϪⲈ ⲠⲈⲚⲔⲈⲈⲨⲀⲅⲅⲈⲖⲒⲞⲚ ϨⲞⲂⲤ̄) in G. W. Horner, *Sahidic New Testament in the Southern Dialect* (Piscataway: Gorgias, 2010).

Inflicting cognitive dysfunction on people collided head-on with Greek philosophical conceptions of deity in the early second century CE. Basic to Platonic philosophy (but not limited to Platonism) is the idea that "god is good and in no way promotes falsehood, neither through ignorance of the truth nor through any deceit."[20]

This doctrine is based on the passage in Plato's *Republic* where Socrates asks: "Would a god want to be false, either in word or deed, by presenting an illusion?" After discovering no morally satisfactory motivation for a deity to do so, Socrates concludes that the divine is "in every way free from falsehood."[21] Any person who upheld this rule (that deity does not deceive) while simultaneously believing that the blinding "god" of 2 Corinthians 4:4 refers to the creator could not assert that the creator was (the true) god. The logic was simple: a deceitful creator was not good, and if he was not good, then he was not (the true) god.

Satan?

Understandably, some early Christians balked at the idea that the creator would blind people from seeing the light of Christ, so they understood "the god of this world" to refer to Satan.[22] Modern scholars are so accustomed to this reading that it is even inscribed in the pages of a leading dictionary of New Testament Greek.[23] But is this the most plausible reading for someone

---

[20] *Anonymous Prolegomena to Platonic Philosophy*, trans. L. G. Westerink (Wiltshire: Prometheus, 2011), 15 = §7.23.

[21] Plato, Republic 382a, e: ψεύδεσθαι θεὸς ἐθέλοι ἂν ἢ λόγῳ ἢ ἔργῳ φάντασμα προτείνων; ... Πάντῃ ἄρα ἀψευδὲς τὸ δαιμόνιόν τε καὶ τὸ θεῖον. Cf. Plato's Laws: "Truth leads the list of goods for gods and people alike" (730c). This Platonic sentiment had a long afterlife. According to Philo, for instance, to make god a witness to a lie is the most impious thing imaginable (*Decalogue* 86). Peter in the Pseudo-Clementine Homilies remarks that if the creator lies, "who tells the truth?" (2.43.1); "if he makes blind and deaf, who has given sight and hearing?"

[22] E.g., Tertullian, *AM* 5.11.13—though he presents the "god of this world = Satan" reading as secondary. See further Origen, *Commentary on Matthew* 13.8–9. Modern commentators generally take "the god of this world" to be Satan. See, e.g., Ralph P. Martin, 2 Corinthians, 2nd ed. (Grand Rapids: Zondervan, 2014), 222–23; Mark A. Seifrid, *The Second Letter to the Corinthians* (Grand Rapids: Eerdmans, 2014), 196; Frank J. Matera, *II Corinthians: A Commentary* (Louisville: Westminster/John Knox, 2003), 101–2. The most recent extensive defense of Satan as the referent in 2 Cor 4:4 is that of Derek Brown, *The God of This Age: Satan in the Churches and Letters of the Apostle Paul* (Tübingen: Mohr Siebeck, 2015), 130–51.

[23] Frederick William Danker, *A Greek-English Lexicon of the New Testament and Other Early Christian Literature*, 3rd ed. (Chicago: University of Chicago Press, 2000), 452; s.v. θεός, under definition 5, informs us that the ὁ θεὸς τοῦ αἰῶνος τούτου in 2 Cor 4:4 refers to the devil.

in the second century? Would they have thought that Paul referred to Satan as "the god of this world"?

Presumably they would have known that calling Satan "the god of this world" is without parallel in Paul's writings. True, Paul criticized his opponents by calling their god their "belly" (Phil 3:19). But this instance of invective differs from the apparently sober point expressed in 2 Corinthians 4:4. It is Paul who refers to and believes in "the god of this world" as a real and powerful entity in the cosmos.

A "god" as defined in Mediterranean antiquity was a being with immortality and superhuman power.[24] "The god of this world" is presumably a being with power over the entire world. For Jews and early Christians, the implication would be that a god with control over the entire world had such power because he created the world. Yet Paul's Satan never had power over the cosmos genuinely to master it, let alone create it.

It is true that in the gospel called Luke, the devil is given authority over the kingdoms of the inhabited world (4:5–6). But Luke's devil is not a god, as is indicated by Jesus's refusal to worship him. Beginning in the late second century, Johannine texts were invoked to prove that Satan ruled the world. These texts refer to the "ruler of this world" (John 12:31; 14:30; 16:11) who—though expelled and judged—remains powerful.[25]

One should not, however, assume that for an early Christian reader, the "ruler of this world" was automatically viewed as the devil. The "ruler of this world" could be the devil's father (John 8:44), as noted in Chapter 2. The father of the devil is also the father of the Jews. This father is evidently the biblical deity, whom the Jews claim for themselves (John 8:41).[26]

Even apart from these intertexts, it would be difficult simply to assume that Paul's Satan merited the title "god." At most, Tertullian argued, Satan "filled

---

[24] Albert Henrichs, "What Is a Greek God?," in *The Gods of Ancient Greece: Identities and Transformations*, ed. Jan N. Bremmer and Andrew Erskine (Edinburgh: Edinburgh University Press, 2010), 19–39; David Levene, "Defining the Divine in Rome," *Transactions of the American Philological Association* 142 (2012): 41–81; M. David Litwa, *We Are Being Transformed: Deification in Paul's Soteriology* (Berlin: de Gruyter, 2012), 37–57, esp. 55–56.

[25] Ignatius employs a Johannine turn of phrase in his references to ὁ ἄρχων τοῦ αἰῶνος τούτου (Eph 17:1; 19:1; IgnMagn 1:2; IgnTrall 4:2; Rom 7:1; Phila 6:2). This is evidently his title for the devil. Ascension of Isaiah 2:4 (Ethiopic) also uses "ruler of this world" to refer to Beliar. Beliar later hangs Christ on a tree (9:14–15; cf. 4:4–13). Neither text uses "the god of this world" to refer to Satan or Beliar.

[26] Segal believed that "within the [Johannine] conception of the Lord of the World lies the clue to the negative portrayal of the demiurge in Gnosticism." Yet he wrongly assumed that "the Lord of the World is not yet the gnostic demiurge, for he is not the creator of the world" ("Ruler of This World," 262). Segal's statement is in tension with his earlier observation that "ruler of this world" is "clearly a normal epithet for the Hebrew God [= the creator]" (250).

the whole world with his lying pretense of deity."[27] If he only ruled the hearts of unbelievers, his kingdom was meager to be sure. Patristic authors conceded to him control over the air (following Eph 2:2), but anything higher than the moon was a no-fly zone for demonic lords.[28] Granting Satan the title "the *god* of this world" thus seems grandiose, even if metaphorical. Paul never even called Christ a god—at least without ambiguity.[29] Would he have bestowed this title upon the one who—at best—can masquerade as a luminous angel (2 Cor 11:14)?

The devil may have ruled the cosmos in the past, but he did not do so after Christ's advent.[30] His power, in the early Christian imagination, had been broken. In 2 Corinthians 4:4, however, Paul was not referring to a past "god of this world" but to a *present* one who hinders Christian enlightenment. If this god's blinding activity occurred in the past, its consequences continued in the "new creation" (2 Cor 5:17).[31]

The strongest argument that "the god of this world" is not Satan, however, comes from the literary context of 2 Corinthians 4:4. Eight verses earlier (2 Cor 3:14), Paul observed, following the logic of Isaiah 6:10, that the minds of the Jews "were hardened." By who? Here Marcion, among others, could have seen a divine passive: the hardener was the creator.[32] Thus when in 2 Corinthians 4:4, Paul wrote that "the god of this world" blinded unbelievers, this is the same god assumed in 3:14. One "god" hardens minds, the other "god" blinds them. It is in fact the same activity stemming from the same creator.[33]

---

[27] Tertullian, *AM* 5.17.9.

[28] Tertullian observed: "Nor can he who is the prince of the power of the ages [that is, god] be described as the prince of the power of the air" (*AM* 5.17.7, quoting Eph 2:2).

[29] Murray J. Harris, *Jesus as God: The New Testament Use of Theos in Reference to Jesus* (Grand Rapids: Baker Book House, 1992), esp. 143–72.

[30] This is the interpretation of Per Bilde, "2 Cor. 4,4: The View of Satan and the Created World in Paul," in *Apocryphon Severini*, ed. Per Bilde et al. (Aarhus: Aarhus University Press, 1993), 29–41.

[31] The aorist ἐτύφλωσεν (2 Cor 4:4) is probably ingressive, denoting the inception of an ongoing condition.

[32] Cf. Margaret Thrall, *The Second Epistle to the Corinthians*, 2 vols. (London: T&T Clark, 1994), 1.262; Furnish, *II Corinthians*, 207–8.

[33] After about 150 CE, patristic interpreters who understood "the god of this world" to be Satan were probably already responding to an earlier Christian (Marcionite) interpretation that took this god to refer to the creator (e.g., Tertullian, *AM* 5.11.9–13). Nevertheless, even in the fourth and fifth centuries CE, some patristic readers still took "the god of this world" (2 Cor 4:4) to refer to the creator. See, e.g., Epiphanius, *Panarion* 66.68.9; Cyril of Jerusalem, *Catechetical Lectures* 6.28–29; Adamantius 2.21; Augustine, *Against Faustus* 21.2; cf. Augustine, *Enemy of the Law* 2.7.29; John Chrysostom, *Homilies on Second Corinthians* 8.2 (*Patrologia Graeca* [*PG*] 61.455). Chrysostom's interpretation inspired Frances M. Young and David Ford, *Meaning and Truth in 2 Corinthians* (London: SPCK, 1987), 115–17. Other modern scholars who doubt that Satan is "the god of this world" include Jerome Murphy-O'Connor, *The Theology of the Second Letter to the Corinthians* (Cambridge: Cambridge

Two Gods?

"The god of *this* world," according to Marcion(ites), implied a god of *another* world.[34] If there was "this world" or cosmic space, then presumably there were other worlds or cosmic spaces not ruled by the god who blinds.[35] If the god of *this* world blinds people from seeing Christ's brilliance, there is *another* god who does precisely the opposite. This other god is the one referred to in 2 Corinthians 4:6: the one who shines the light of the knowledge of Christ into human hearts.[36] In the space of three verses, Paul contrasted two beings whom he, at least rhetorically, called "gods." These beings are starkly opposed:

---

2 Cor 4:4	2 Cor 4:6
"the god of this world"	"the god who said, 'From darkness, light will shine.'"

Modern interpreters often conclude that the god who made light shine from darkness is the creator. Most detect an allusion to Genesis 1:3 ("god said: 'let there be light!'").[37] Nonetheless, we cannot assume that the allusion was recognized by readers in the second century. Strictly speaking, 2 Corinthians 4:6 combines parts of two other verses: Isaiah 9:1 LXX ("light will shine") and Job 37:15 LXX ("from darkness").

Even if we grant the allusion to Genesis 1:3, we cannot presume that the light referred to in "let there be light!" was physical light.[38] Other early second-century readings, for instance, indicate that the light designated

---

University Press, 1991), 42; B. J. Oropeza, *Exploring Second Corinthians: Death and Life, Hardship and Rivalry* (Atlanta: SBL Press, 2016), 263. Cf. Thrall, *Second Epistle*, 1.307.

[34] Tertullian, *AM* 5.11.9: "By reading '. . . the god of this age,' Marcion . . . suggested a different god of another age."

[35] Paul mentioned a "third heaven" in 2 Cor 12:2.

[36] ὃς ἔλαμψεν ἐν ταῖς καρδίαις ἡμῶν πρὸς φωτισμὸν τῆς γνώσεως τῆς δόξης τοῦ θεοῦ ἐν προσώπῳ Χριστοῦ. Marcion's Apostolikon apparently replaced τοῦ θεοῦ with αὐτοῦ (Schmid, *Marcion*, 329).

[37] E.g., Furnish, *II Corinthians*, 223; George W. MacRae, *Studies in New Testament and Gnosticism*, ed. Daniel J. Harrington and Stanley B. Marrow (Wilmington: Michael Glazier, 1987), 258.

[38] Philo, for his part, clearly distinguished between perceptible light (αἰσθητὸν φῶς) and the light that god used for himself before creation (ἑώρα δὲ ὁ θεὸς καὶ πρὸ γενέσεως φωτὶ χρώμενος ἑαυτῷ) (*God Is Unchanging*, 58).

the primal Man. This idea is rooted in the linguistic ambiguity between "light" and one of the Greek words for "man" (both *phōs* in Greek, though with a different accent). In a first-century Enochic text (now called 2 Enoch), the Light Man was Adoil, an angel involved in creation.[39] For second-century Christians, the Light Man became Christ, the father's perfect Image (2 Cor 4:4). In the Gospel of Thomas, Jesus says: "I am the Light above them all," and John 1:9 calls Christ the true Light.[40] All this is to say is that if "the god of this world" (2 Cor 4:4) refers to the creator, the god who unveils the primal Light (namely Christ, 2 Cor 4:4) is not necessarily the same being.[41]

Paul opposed the deities of 2 Corinthians 4:4 and 6 in terms of their actions. The first god blinds people's minds from seeing Christ's light; the second performs the opposite by shining the same light into human hearts. The first god is effectively Christ's opponent, the second, his revealer.

Patristic evidence testifies that Marcionites saw two opposed figures in 2 Corinthians 4:4-6, namely, the creator and the true god. After citing 4:4, Irenaeus writes: "there is one god of this world, they [Irenaeus's opponents] say, but another who is over every principality and rule and power (Eph 1:21; Col 1:16)."[42] Tertullian, making the same point, reveals the precise target: "Marcion aimed at this when he read 'In whom the god of this age,' so that by pointing to the creator as the god of this age he might suggest the idea of a *different* god of a *different* age."[43] Markus, a Marcionite speaker in the *Adamantius*, observed: "I cite the clear voice of the apostle which shows that there is *another* god of the universe."[44] The text cited was 2 Corinthians 4:4.

---

[39] 2 Enoch 11 with the comments of Jarl Fossum, *The Name of God and Angel of the Lord* (Leiden: Brill, 1985), 289–91; Andrei A. Orlov, "Adoil Outside the Cosmos," in *Histories of the Hidden God: Concealment and Revelation in Western Gnostic, Esoteric, and Mystical Traditions*, ed. April D. DeConick and Grant Adamson (London: Acumen, 2016), 30–57. Compare god as φώς (man) in Ezekiel the Tragedian, *Exagoge* 70, with Andrei A. Orlov, *Enoch-Metatron Tradition* (Tübingen: Mohr Siebeck, 2005), 197–200.

[40] *Gospel of Thomas* (NHC II,2), logion 77 Among the "others" reported by Irenaeus (*AH* 1.30.1), the incorruptible light of Christ (called the Third Man) is produced from Spirit (invoking Gen 1:2–3). See further Elaine Pagels, "Exegesis of Genesis 1 in the Gospels of Thomas and John," *Journal of Biblical Literature (JBL)* 118 (1999): 477–96 at 483–84; Rasimus, *Paradise*, 168, 175–80.

[41] This is a point missed by George MacRae ("Anti-Dualist Polemic in 2 Cor 4,6?," in *Studia Evangelica IV*, ed. F. L. Cross [Berlin: Akademie, 1968], 420–31), although he observed: "The Jewish god could not effectively had said, 'Let there be light,' for he belonged essentially to the realms of darkness" (424).

[42] Irenaeus, *AH* 3.7.1–2.

[43] Tertullian, *AM* 5.11.9, my emphasis.

[44] *Adamantius* 2.2, emphasis added.

Rules of Grammar

It was this implication of another god—the true revealer of Christ—that some patristic authors strove hard to undercut. They were willing to go to great lengths, even to the point of forcing Paul's grammar. Beginning with Irenaeus, they took the qualifier "of this world," which immediately follows "god," and mentally moved it to modify another noun five words away, namely, "unbelievers."[45] In this reading, "god" blinded "the unbelievers of this world."

Yet such a reading tortures the Greek and has little to vouch for it semantically. In antiquity, Didymus of Alexandria (313–398 CE) already pointed out the major problem: "unbelievers of this world" is redundant—what *other* world would they belong to?[46]

The weakness of the Irenaean reading helps to gauge the perceived threat of the Marcionite interpretation. Patristic writers were willing to make implausible grammatical choices to undermine an alternative Christian reading (the creator blinds people, including Jews and perhaps some Christians). In the end, however, grammar did not resolve the problem of two "gods" with two opposed actions in 2 Corinthians 4:4–6.

One God?

The "two gods" interpretation opens up a larger interpretive question: how could a reader of Paul, a man who asserted that for him god was one (1 Cor

---

[45] Irenaeus, *AH* 3.7; Tertullian, *AM* 5.11.10 (*reading ita __non__ huius aevi deus sed infidelium huius aevi excaecat cor* with Norbert Brox, "Non huius aevi deus (Zu Tertullian adv. Marc. V 11,10," *Zeitschrift für die neutestamentliche Wissenschaft (ZNW)* 59 [1968]: 259–61); Adamantius 2.21 with the discussion of Paul-Hubert Poirier, "Exégèse manichéenne et antimanichéenne de II Corinthiens 4,4 chez Titus de Bostra (Contre les Manichéens IV, 108)," in *Gnose et Manichéisme. Entre les oasis d'Egypte et la Route de la Soie: Hommage à Jean-Daniel Dubois*, ed. A. van den Kerchove and L. G. Soares Santoprete (Turnhout: Brepols, 2017), 273–86 at 276–81. Patristic authors appealed to the grammatical technique of hyperbaton, but a pure concern for grammar was not their driving motive. Cf. John Calvin: "If everyone read Paul's words [in 2 Cor 4:4] with a composed mind, no one would intend to twist them into a forced meaning, but because their enemies pressed them, they were more anxious to repel them than to inquire into Paul's mind" (quoted by Alfred Plummer, *Second Epistle of St. Paul to the Corinthians* [Edinburgh: T&T Clark, 1915], 116, emphasis added).

[46] Didymus: "If there are unbelievers of this world, other unbelievers will be found not of this world; for every unbeliever is of this world" (πᾶς γὰρ ἄπιστός ἐστι τούτου τοῦ αἰῶνος) in Staab, *Pauluskommentar aus der griechischen Kirche aus Katenenhandschriften gesammelt.* (Münster: Aschendorff, 1933), 23. See further BeDuhn, *First New Testament*, 181.

8:6), conceive of two gods? Two worlds or two ages is possible, but two gods seem too much.

For a second-century reader, however, two considerations must be kept in mind. It is easy to call Paul a monotheist (a term created in the sixteenth century), but Paul did not proclaim the univocal unity of god.[47] Instead, in the context of the passage just cited, he proclaimed *one god* and *one lord*—two manifestly different beings (1 Cor 8:6).[48] Paul evidently saw these two distinct beings as one in power, but they were still two. Of these beings, Christ is consistently depicted as subordinate to his father, both now and in the future (1 Cor 15:28).[49]

The second consideration is that proclaiming a deity to be "one" in the ancient world had less to do with quantity than with asserting mastery and greatness.[50] In the Roman imperial era, "There is one god!" generally meant *not* that "My god is mathematically one," but that "My god has supreme power."[51]

---

[47] On the problems of the category monotheism applied to ancient texts, see Nathan MacDonald, *Deuteronomy and the Meaning of "Monotheism"* (Tübingen: Mohr Siebeck, 2012), 5–58; Litwa, *We Are Being Transformed*, 229–57.

[48] Harris, *Jesus as God*, 47. The fact that Paul was reworking the Shema does not detract from this argument. Claudio Moreschini notes that "For the whole of the 3d-century Christian theology had been binitarian in nature, wherein the Father was God in the fullest sense, and the Son, while still God, was nevertheless considered inferior to the Father" ("Tertullian's Adversus Marcionem and Middle Platonism," *Zeitschrift für Antikes Christentum [ZAC]* 21:1 [2017]: 140–63 at 152).

[49] The subordination is maintained by Justin in the second century (*Dialogue with Trypho* 56.3–4). In the third century, Tertullian vouched for divine monarchy (*Against Praxeas* 3.2) since monarchy allowed for multiple divine agents (Father, Son, and Spirit). See further Peter Hayman, "Monotheism—a Misused Word in Jewish Studies?" *Journal of Jewish Studies* 42 (1991): 1–15 at 15.

[50] Erik Peterson and Christoph Markschies, *Heis Theos: Epigraphische, formgeschichtliche und religionsgeschichtliche Untersuchungen: Nachdruck der Ausgabe von Erik Peterson mit Ergänzungen und Kommentaren* (Würzburg: Echter, 2012). Examples: Isis as *numen unicum* in Apuleius, *Metamorphoses* 11.5; Asclepius as unique in Aristides, *Orations* 42; Nero as "one and alone" (εἷς καὶ μόνος) (Christoph Auffarth, "Herrscherkult und Christuskult," in *Die Praxis der Herrscherverehrung in Rom und seinen Provinzen*, ed. Hubert Cancik and Konrad Hitzl [Tübingen: Mohr Siebeck, 2003], 283–318 at 294–306). See also Christoph Markschies, "Heis Theos-Ein Gott? Der monotheimus und das antike Christentum," in *Polytheismus und Monotheismus in den Religionen des Vorderen Orients*, ed. M. Krebernik and J. van Oorschot (Münster: Ugarit, 2002), 209–34; Nicole Belayche, "Deus deum ... summorum maximus (Apuleius): Ritual Expressions of Distinction in the Divine World in the Imperial Period," in *One God: Pagan Monotheism in The Roman Empire*, ed. Stephen Mitchell and Peter van Nuffelen (Cambridge: Cambridge University Press, 2010), 141–66.

[51] Suzanne Nicholson, *Dynamic Oneness: The Significance and Flexibility of Paul's One-God Language* (Cambridge: James Clark, 2010), 59; Paul A. Rainbow, "Monotheism and Christology in 1 Corinthians 8:4–6" (D.Phil. thesis, Oxford University, 1987), 105–46; Oskar Skarsaune, "Is Christianity Monotheistic? Patristic Perspectives on a Jewish/Christian Debate," *Studia Patristica* 29 (1997): 340–63, esp. 355–61; Bert Jan Lietaert Peerbolte, "Jewish Monotheism and Christian Origins," in *Empsychoi Logoi—Religious Innovations in Antiquity: Studies in Honour of Pieter Willem van der Horst*, ed. Alberdina Houtman et al. (Leiden: Brill, 2008), 227–46; M. V. Ceruti, "'Pagan Monotheism?' Towards a Historical Typology," in *Monotheism Between Pagans and Christians in Late Antiquity*, ed. Stephen Mitchell and Peter van Nuffelen (Leuven: Peeters, 2010), 15–32.

All this being said, Marcion probably did not think that "the god of this world" was a true deity. This being only *claimed* godhead, like the creator who ignorantly claimed: "I am god and there is no other!" (Isa 45:5). In short, the "god" of this world is called "god" because he controls and creates the world, not because he is the true, transcendent god.

Of This World

To sum up the Marcionite argument so far: there are two superhuman beings in 2 Corinthians 4:4–6: one of *this* world, and one of *another* world. But what did it mean to be "of this world," and what did this imply about the character of the so-called god of this world?

We know that there is "both the god of this world" (2 Cor 4:4) and "rulers of this world" (1 Cor 2:8) who killed Christ because they failed to know divine wisdom.[52] To quote the key text from Marcion's Apostolikon:

> We speak wisdom among those who are initiated, (but not the wisdom of this world nor that) of the rulers of this world, who are being destroyed. (Rather), we speak god's hidden wisdom in a mystery, which god foreordained before the worlds for our glory, which none of the rulers of this world knew; for if they had known, they would not have crucified the lord of glory. (1 Cor 2:6–8)[53]

Common to both "the god" (2 Cor 4:4) and the "rulers" (1 Cor 2:8) here is the qualifier "of this world." The identical qualifier hints that "the god" and "rulers" of this world are somehow aligned.[54] At least this is how some

---

[52] On the identity of these rulers, see Gene Miller, "ΑΡΧΟΝΤΩΝ ΤΟΥ ΑΙΩΝΟΣ ΤΟΥΤΟΥ—A New Look at 1 Corinthians 2:6–8," *Journal of Biblical Literature (JBL)* 91:4 (1972): 522–28; Wesley Carr, "The Rulers of This Age—1 Corinthians II.6–8," *New Testament Studies (NTS)* 23 (1976–77): 20–35; Anthony C. Thiselton, *The First Epistle to the Corinthians: A Commentary on the Greek Text* (Grand Rapids: Eerdmans, 2000), 233–39.

[53] Schmid, *Marcion*, 321: Σοφία (δὲ) λαλοῦμεν ἐν τοῖς τελείοις . . . (σοφίαν δὲ οὐ τοῦ αἰῶνος τούτου οὐδὲ) τῶν ἀρχόντων τοῦ αἰῶνος τούτου τῶν καταργουμένων· (ἀλλὰ) λαλοῦμεν θεοῦ σοφίαν ἐν μυστηρίῳ τὴν ἀποκεκρυμμένην, ἣν προώρισεν ὁ θεὸς πρὸ τῶν αἰώνων εἰς δόξαν ἡμῶν, ἣν οὐδεὶς τῶν ἀρχόντων τοῦ αἰῶνος τούτου ἔγνωκεν· εἰ γὰρ ἔγνωσαν, οὐκ ἂν τὸν κύριον τῆς δόξης ἐσταύρωσαν. In Schmid's reconstruction, words in parentheses supplement firmly attested words and are designed to produce a readable text (*Marcion*, 313).

[54] Robert Ewusie Moses observes: "we are to see them [the god of this age and the rulers of this age] as part of the same phenomenon: opposing powers that lie upon on the opposite side of God and Christ in the cosmic struggle" (*Practices of Power: Revisiting Principalities and Powers in the Pauline Letters* [Minneapolis: Fortress, 2014], 208). "Rulers" (ἄρχοντες) are typically not viewed positively,

second-century readers saw it. The author of the *Ascension of Isaiah*, for instance, related this story:

> The lord [Christ] will indeed descend into the world in the last days ... and
> they [the rulers of this world] will think that he is flesh and a man. And *the
> god of that world* [2 Cor 4:4] will stretch out his hand against the son, and
> they [the evil rulers] will lay their hands upon him [Christ] and hang him
> upon a tree, not knowing who he is.[55]

In this text, the rulers of this world (1 Cor 2:8) are ignorant about the identity of Christ.[56] They are subject to the "the god of this world" (in this text, Beliar) who directs them to crucify Christ. The assumption is that the god and the rulers "of this world" cooperated.

Marcion(ites) were probably familiar with this type of reading even if they identified "the god of this world" with the creator.[57] According to Tertullian, Marcion "argues that the rulers of this age affixed the lord ... to the cross, and this [act] is thrown back in the face of the creator."[58] Tertullian also observed that Marcionites say that the Christ of the true deity was forced onto the cross "by the *forces and powers* of the creator (*a creatoris virtutibus et potestatibus*), as if he [the *creator*] was jealous."[59]

---

but as the enemies of god and Christ (Rom 8:38; Col 2:15). Lieu (*Marcion*, 260) notes: "Although Tertullian passes over in silence his own, or his opponent's, interpretation of 'the rulers of this age who are coming to naught' (2.6), it seems highly probable that Marcion would have found here also a reference to the Creator. This would prepare for the position that Tertullian's subsequent vehement denials project, namely ... that the rulers of this age, being the representatives of the Creator ... crucified 'the Lord of glory', Christ, out of ignorance (*AM* V.6.1–9; cf. III.23.5)."

[55] *Ascension of Isaiah* 9:13–15 (trans. M. A. Knibb in *OTP* 2.170). Compare 10:11–12, where the deity addresses Christ: "none of the angels of that world shall know that you (are) Lord with me of the seven heavens and of their angels. And they shall not know that you (are) with me ... that you may judge and destroy the princes and the angels and the gods of that world" (*OTP* 2.173). Again the "princes" and "gods of that world" are closely aligned—evidence that 2 Cor 4:4 and 1 Cor 2:6–8 were being read together. The interpretation is also reflected in Arnobius, *Against the Nations* 1.53.

[56] The ignorance of the rulers recurs in Sethian texts, for instance, the *Secret Book of John* (II,1) 30.11–21, where Pronoia enters the prison house of the world unrecognized by the powers. Compare the powers who do not see the illuminator but "punish the flesh of the man upon whom the Holy Spirit came" (*Apocalypse of Adam* [NHC V,5]) 77.4–18. For this theme adapted in the fourth century, see Nicholas P. Constas, "The Last Temptation of Satan: Divine Deception in Greek Patristic Interpretations of the Passion Narrative," *Harvard Theological Review* 97:2 (2004): 139–63.

[57] See the citation of 1 Cor 2:8 in Tertullian, *AM* 5.6.1–5. Cf. *AM* 3.6.4: "for unless he had been unrecognized (*ignoratus*) [by the rulers] he [Christ] could surely not have suffered [at their hands]." See also the comment of Lieu in n. 54 above.

[58] Tertullian, *AM* 5.6.5.

[59] Tertullian, *AM* 3.23.5, my emphasis.

Marcion assumed, in short, the connection between the creator and his rulers. There was a link between the actions of the *rulers* of this world and the character of the *god* of this world (the creator). In effect, the creator arranged for his (demonic) powers to crucify Christ.[60]

What world is it that "the god of this world" and his rulers were thought to control? It is the world to which believers must not conform (Rom 12:2); a world whose wisdom they must reject (1 Cor 2:6; 3:18); a world that Paul called "evil" (*ponēros* in Gal 1:4). To be sure, *ponēros* can mean "grievous, painful, toilsome" as well as "useless, good for nothing."[61] Nevertheless, *ponēros* also has a moral sense: "wicked, evil, base"—and it is this moral sense that is accentuated in early Christian texts.[62] The very name for the devil in many of these texts is *ho ponēros*—"the evil one."[63]

Now if Paul spoke of a "present evil world" (Gal 1:4), then the rulers of it are presumably evil—a point confirmed by their actions. Indeed, by crucifying Christ, the rulers performed, in Christian eyes, perhaps the most hideous crime imaginable (1 Cor 2:8).

The actions of both the god and rulers of this world, moreover, relate to spiritual blindness. The rulers crucified the Lord of glory because they did not know secret divine wisdom, a wisdom that would have revealed Christ as lord of glory (2 Cor 2:8). In turn, the "god of this world" blinded unbelievers so that they did not perceive Christ's glory (2 Cor 4:4). Note the parallel: the rulers of this world were blind to Christ's glory; and the "god of this world" inflicted spiritual blindness that hides Christ's glory. In both cases, it is a blindness that conceals Christ's glory.

In the late second century, Irenaeus remarked that unbelievers (evidently including Marcionites) "impute blindness" to the god of this world on the basis of 2 Corinthians 4:4.[64] To understand why they did so requires some reverse engineering. What was it about 2 Corinthians 4:4 that made other early

---

[60] In blaming the creator for Christ's death, Marcion deflected attention from the Jews, whom Tertullian, among others, blamed for killing Christ (*Against Marcion* 2.15.3; cf. 2.28.3). For Marcion and the Jews, see further Lieu, *Image and Reality*, 261–76; Lieu, *Marcion*, 69; Wilson, *Related Strangers*, 207–21; Heikki Räisänen, *Marcion, Muhammad and the Mahatma: Exegetical Perspectives on the Encounter of Cultures and Faiths* (London: SCM, 1997), 73–76; Joseph B. Tyson, "Anti-Judaism in Marcion and His Opponents," *Studies in Christian-Jewish Relations* 1 (2005): 196–208; M. Vinzent, "Marcion the Jew," in *Judaïsme Ancien-Ancient Judaism* 1 (2013): 159–200 at 179–200.

[61] LSJ s.v. I.2, II.1.

[62] LSJ III.1. The first definition of πονηρός in Danker, *Greek-English Lexicon*, is "pert[aining] to being morally or social worthless, wicked, evil, bad, base, worthless, vicious, degenerate" with many examples (851–52).

[63] For instance, Matt 13:19; John 17:15; Eph 6:16.

[64] Irenaeus, *AH* 4.29.1. Moll takes *AH* 4.27–32 to be anti-Marcionite, or at least 4.28–30 (*Arch-Heretic*, 17–21).

Christian interpreters, including Marcion(ites), suppose that the god of this world was himself blind?

At least two considerations may have led to this conclusion. First, in terms of actions, the god of this world was aligned with the lower rulers. These lower rulers were blind to Christ's glorious identity (1 Cor 2:8) and were elsewhere characterized by darkness.[65] Second, the god of this world himself inflicted blindness. If he was aligned with the blind rulers of 1 Corinthians 2:8, he evidently suffered from the same spiritual malady. The spiritual blindness and ignorance that the creator inflicted were proper to him.[66]

The blindness of the creator is well known from Nag Hammadi texts. The author of the *Reality of the Rulers* (NHC II,4) opens his work with the remark: "The leader of the authorities is blind."[67] The warrant for this assertion is the ruler's self-deifying assertion, "I am god and there is no other!" (see Chapter 3). This egotistic boast, however, says nothing directly about the Jewish deity being blind.

The exegetical origin of the blindness is more likely to be an intertextual reading of 1 Corinthians 2:8 (blind world rulers) and 2 Corinthians 4:4 (the god of this world who blinds). The creator's self-deifying assertions were then recalled in a secondary act of narrativizing in order to illustrate the creator's blindness (i.e., ignorance and likely stupidity). Blindness is so fundamental to the portrait of the evil creator that it is inscribed in his very name. Some early Christians called the creator "Samael"—the blind god.[68]

Moral Implications

For Christians, what does it imply about "the god of this world" that he blinds people from Christ's brilliance? We have already seen that hardening hearts and minds is characteristic of the creator (Isa 6:10; 2 Cor 3:14). In his *Antitheses*, Marcion apparently observed: "The god of generation did not restore the sight of Isaac suffering from cataracts, but our lord [Jesus], because

---

[65] Eph 6:12; cf. Col 1:13; *Testimony of Truth* (NHC IX,3) 30.17; 33.1. Accordingly, in the *Second Revelation of James* (NHC V,4), the ignorance of the rulers is transferred to the creator (56.20–57.3).

[66] Marcion's text for 2 Cor 3:14 apparently read ἀλλὰ ἐπωρώθη τὰ νοήματα αἰῶνος, in which αἰών was taken to refer to the creator on the basis of 2 Cor 4:4 ("god, who is this age," θεός τοῦ αἰῶνος τούτου, epexegetic genitive). Marcion could thus have deduced the blindness of the creator more directly from 2 Cor 3:14. See Tertullian, *AM* 5.4.15, 5.11.5 with Schmid, *Marcion*, 118, 259.

[67] *Reality of the Rulers* (NHC II,4) 86.27–28.

[68] *Secret Book of John* (II,1) 11.16–18. Cf. *Reality of the Rulers* (NHC II,4) 87.3; 94.25; *Origin of the World* (NHC II,5) 103.7–18; *Three Forms of First Thought* (NHC XIII,1) 39.27.

he is good, opened the eyes of many blind people" (Luke 7:21).[69] But the contrast ran deeper. The god of this world is not only a god who refrains from healing the blind; he is also a god who actively *inflicts* spiritual blindness on people so that they cannot see Christ's light.

Elsewhere this kind of blinding was seen as morally incriminating. In the *Secret Book of John*, the creator uses fate to blind human beings from seeing the true god (NHC II,1 28.26–29). In the *Apocalypse of Adam*, the creator split the first human into male and female, removing their spiritual insight.[70] We have already seen how in the *Secret Book* the creator inflicted cognitive numbness on Adam in the garden of Eden.[71]

Some early Christians rose to the creator's defense. They believed that people were blinded because of their antecedent unbelief. Yahweh hardened Pharaoh's heart, but Pharaoh hardened his own heart too (Exod 8:32). Thus the creator who inflicted blindness on sinners escaped incrimination.[72]

To be sure, the creator may be just when inflicting blindness on sinners, but his justice was, according to Marcion, rather cruel. After all, is it just for the creator to *keep* people in the dark? What is the point of blinding them after their initial unbelief? Presumably the god of this world would not need to blind unbelievers if there was no chance that they might at some point glimpse Christ's glory and repent. By purposefully blinding them, this god effectively takes away their chance for repentance and hastens their damnation.[73] Thus regardless of whether the god of this world is *originally* responsible for people's unbelief, he is still responsible for them not coming to repentance and salvation in the future.

Evidence for the moral incrimination of the creator based on 2 Corinthians 4:4 comes from the *Adamantius*. The Marcionite Markus remarks: "See that he [Paul] calls the god of this world *evil*, since he does not make enlightenment shine."[74] Any being who blinds people from the enlightenment of Christ cannot be good, *even if* the people blinded previously disbelieved.

---

[69] Adamantius 1.20: ὁ θεὸς τῆς γενέσεως ὑποχυθέντα τὸν Ἰσαὰκ οὐκέτι ἐποίησε διαβλέψαι, ὁ δὲ κύριος ἡμῶν ἀγαθὸς ὤν, πολλῶν τυφλῶν ἤνοιξεν ὀφθαλμούς. Harnack attributed this line to Marcion's *Antitheses* (*Marcion*, 89–92; further sources in his appendix to the German edition, *Marcion*, 266-296).

[70] *Apocalypse of Adam* (NHC V,5) 64.6–65.23; cf. 66.23–25.

[71] *Secret Book of John* (BG) 59.3–4; compare (NHC II,1) 22.26–28.

[72] Irenaeus, *AH* 4.29.

[73] One could say that εἰς τὸ μὴ αὐγάσαι in 2 Cor 4:4 expresses not purpose but result. The intentional action of blinding is clearer in the adaptations of Isaiah 6:10. Cf. John 12:40; Mark 4:12.

[74] *Adamantius* 2.21: ἴδε ὅτι πονηρὸν λέγει τὸν θεὸν τούτου τοῦ αἰῶνος, τὸν μὴ ποιοῦντα καταυγάσαι τὸν φωτισμόν. See further Lieu, *Marcion*, 258–59. Compare Faustus: Paul "adds that [the

Although in the *Adamantius* Markus's interpretation is mocked and opposed, he presses home his point: "Is it characteristic of a good god to blind?"[75] His opponent can only cite analogous cases of extreme but "just" punishment: Christ casting nonbelievers into eternal darkness (Matt 25:41) and Paul handing over a fellow believer to Satan (1 Cor 5:5). These examples of harsh punishment did not, however, exculpate the creator. For Markus, guaranteeing peoples' punishment by blinding them was still problematic.[76]

It was problematic because the people blinded were blinded *from seeing the light of Christ.* If it was a vague physical blinding like that afflicted on the men of Sodom (Gen 19:11), perhaps the punishment could be approved. But the blinding of 2 Corinthians 4:4 is a blinding that specifically results in the inability to know Christ's glory. It is a blinding that, if not healed, results in separation from (the true) god.

Thus from a Marcionite Christian point of view, it was hard to imagine how this sort of blinding could be viewed as good. Actually, Marcionites and their opponents were agreed on this point. To prevent the vision of the light of Christ was enough for them to morally incriminate the character of the blinder in 2 Corinthians 4:4. They disagreed about the blinder's *identity* (the creator versus Satan), but *not* about the wickedness of his character.

Conclusion

To wrap up the argument as a whole: an early Christian group (the Marcionites) understood "the god of this world" in 2 Corinthians 4:4 to refer to the creator. The actions of "the god of this world" (namely, blinding) were viewed as malign and as indicating the creator's wicked character. The evil actions of the creator were deliberately contrasted with the actions of another deity who did the opposite by revealing Christ's brilliance in human hearts (2 Cor 4:6). In terms of actions, this latter being was the true god, while "the god of this world" (2 Cor 4:4) proved to be an immoral imposter.

god of this world] blinds minds so that it is understood he is not the true god (*non esse verus deus*)" (Augustine, *Against Faustus* 21.1).

[75] *Adamantius* 2.21.

[76] Similarly "Mani," after citing 2 Cor 4:4, asks: "Is that god good, who does not want his own people to be saved?" (trans. Mark Vermes and Samuel N. C. Lieu, *Hegemonius, Acta Archelai (The Acts of Archelaus)* [Turnout: Brepols, 2001], 15.7, p. 60, modified).

If Marcion(ites) opposed "the god of this world" to the illuminator deity, they closely aligned "the god of this world" with the "rulers of the world" (1 Cor 2:8). The god and rulers of this world both condemned Christ to the cross and suffered from the same spiritual blindness that they inflicted on others. By keeping people blind (effectively removing their ability to repent), and by incriminating Christ, both the god and rulers of this world demonstrated their wickedness.

Tertullian argued that the so-called evil acts of the creator were acts of just punishment.[77] But the one single act that Christians could not view as just in any sense was the crucifixion of Christ. The rulers who crucified the Christian Savior decisively proved their wicked character.[78] Yet these rulers were only following orders from their lord—the god of this world—who was, for Marcionites, the creator.

In short, Marcionites traced the crime of the crucifixion back to the creator.[79] Blaming the creator for the crucifixion is clearest in the *Adamantius* when a Marcionite speaker claims: "the creator wanted to conspire against him [Christ], and ordained by Law that he be crucified."[80] This interpretive trajectory is the logical endpoint of Marcion's own tendency to concentrate the evil of the crucifying world rulers onto a single villain—namely, the creator himself.

---

[77] E.g., Tertullian, *AM* 2.14.2–4.

[78] Irenaeus observed: "indeed the death of the lord is the damnation of those who affixed him to the cross" (*AH* 4.28.3).

[79] Tertullian, *AM* 5.6.5.

[80] Adamantius 2.9: ὁ δὲ δημιουργός ἠθέλησεν αὐτῷ ἐπιβουλεῦσαι, ὅθεν καὶ ἐνόμισεν αὐτόν σταυροῦν. Cf. Eznik of Kolb, where the good god says to Christ, "Heal . . . so that the lord of creatures [the creator] might see you and be jealous and raise you on a cross"; the creator later admits to the resurrected Christ that "I . . . slaughtered you ignorantly" (*On God*, 358, trans. Blanchard and Young, modified). Marcionites were not alone in this exegesis. According to the "Ophite" report of Irenaeus: "the rulers and the father of Jesus [Yaldabaoth] were indignant [because of Jesus's wonders and announcement of the unknown father] and conspired to kill him" (*AH* 1.30.13). The author of the *Second Revelation of James* (NHC V,4) was so sure the creator killed Christ that he exculpated the Jewish leaders: "it was not you [Jews] who did these things [referring to the events of the crucifixion], but [your] lord [the creator]" (59.8–10. See Armand Veilleux, *La seconde apocalypse de Jacques* [NH V,4] [Quebec: University of Laval, 1986], 177). The creator as crucifier is also assumed by Celsus, who criticized the transcendent father for being "unable to pay back the creator when he has caught the one [Christ] whom he had sent" (ὅν γε ἐξέπεμψεν [πατήρ] . . . τοῦτον ἁλόντα ἐκδικῆσαι μὴ δυνάμενος) (*Cels.* 6.53).

5

Destroyer of the Law I

> Christ wiped out the debt record, the consent to the Law, by his own
> teachings.
>
> —Severian of Gabala[1]

Introduction

According to Ephesians 2:15, Christ "destroyed the Law of commandments
by decrees."[2] This passage, attested in the Apostolikon, provided Marcionite
Christians with perhaps the clearest statement about Christ's destruction of the
creator's Law.[3] Marcionites were not distinct from many other Christian groups
in their (selective) rejection of Mosaic regulations, but they were different in
their view that Christ came to destroy the Law. Christ came to destroy the Law,
in their view, since it was hostile and wicked insofar as it enslaved humanity. The
Law was so destructive, indeed, that Christ had to redeem humanity from its
curse. The wickedness of the Law in terms of both content and effect implied,
for Marcion(ites), the malign nature of the one who gave it, namely, the creator.

Paul and the Law in Marcionite Reception

Marcion's enemies had a penchant for pointing out that for Paul, the Law
was "holy, just, and good" (Rom 7:12).[4] But as they acknowledged in other

---

[1] τὸ χειρόγραφον, τὴν συγκατάθεσιν τὴν πρὸς τόν νόμον, ἐξήλειψε τοῖς ἑαυτοῦ δόγμασιν ὁ
Χριστός, in Staab, *Pauluskommentar*, 323–24. Cf. J. Christian Beker: "Marcion came close to Paul's
intent when he defined the law as the inferior revelation of the Demiurge, which the new revelation of the God of Christ abolishes" (*Paul the Apostle: The Triumph of God in Life and Thought*
[Philadelphia: Fortress, 1997], 186–87).

[2] τὸν νόμον τῶν ἐντολῶν ἐν δόγμασιν καταργήσας. The subject Χριστός is understood from Eph 2:13.

[3] The attestation comes from Tertullian: *si legem praeceptorum sententiis vacuam fecit* ("If he
[Christ] has invalidated the law of commandments in/by decrees") (*AM* 5.17.15). See the text in
Schmid, *Marcion*, 339.

[4] E.g., Tertullian, *AM* 5.14.15; Origen, *First Principles* 2.5.4; Epiphanius, *Panarion* 42, Elenchus 5
and 32; *Adamantius* 2.20. Cf. 1 Tim 1:8: "The Law is good to one who uses it lawfully."

The Evil Creator. M. David Litwa, Oxford University Press. © Oxford University Press 2021.
DOI: 10.1093/oso/9780197566428.003.0007

contexts, Paul associated the Law with divine rage (Rom 4:15), as well as sin (Rom 5:20; 8:2), slavery (Rom 7:25; Gal 4:1–7; 5:1), death (2 Cor 3:6–7; Rom 8:2), imprisonment (Rom 7:6; Gal 3:22–23), and cursing (Gal 3:10).[5]

According to Marcion's version of Galatians 3:10, "As many as are under Law stand under a curse (*hupo kataran*)."[6] The wording indicates that the curse applies to all under the Law, not just to those who fall short of it (for in that case the text would have said: "As many as disobey the Law stand under a curse"). The Law played a role in salvation history, to be sure—as a warden to keep putatively immature Israelites in line (Gal 4:2–3), or as a document of incriminating debt (Col 2:14).[7] As Paul wrote: "I would not have known sin except through Law" (Rom 7:7).[8]

Even though the apostle once considered himself legally "blameless" (Phil 3:6), he later concluded that those who lived by Law did not obtain divine righteousness (Rom 10:4). He even opined that the righteousness obtained from Law was nothing more than "refuse" or "dung" (*skubala*) compared with the righteousness gained by faith in Christ (Phil 3:8–9). Paul resolved that "no one is justified before god by Law" (Gal 3:11). He later put it: "from the works of the Law no flesh will be justified before" god, "since through the Law is the recognition of sin" (Rom 3:20).

---

[5] Here I adapt the language of Michael F. Bird, *Colossians and Philemon: A New Covenant Commentary* (Cambridge: Lutterworth, 2009), 81. On modern views of Paul and the Law, the bibliography is massive. See, e.g., E. P. Sanders, *Paul, the Law, and the Jewish People* (Philadelphia: Fortress, 1983); Hans Hübner, *Law in Paul's Thought: A Contribution to the Development of Pauline Theology*, trans. James C. G. Greig; ed. John Riches (London: T&T Clark, 1984); Jan Lambrecht, "Gesetzverständnis bei Paulus," in *Das Gesetz im Neuen Testament*, ed. Karl Kertelge (Freiberg: Herder, 1986), 88–127; Heikki Räisänen, *Paul and the Law* (Tübingen: Mohr Siebeck, 1983); Paula Fredriksen, *Paul: The Pagans' Apostle* (New Haven: Yale University Press, 2017), 108–30; Karl Olav Sandnes, *Paul Perceived: An Interactionist Perspective on Paul and the Law* (Tübingen: Mohr Siebeck, 2018). C. Marvin Pate argues that the nullification of the Law was already Paul's position, a position he arrived at by reflecting on the curse of the crucified Jesus (*Reverse of the Curse: Paul, Wisdom, and the Law* [Tübingen: Mohr Siebeck, 2000], 212–23). For a similar view, see Räisänen, *Paul and the Law*, 42–40, 56–62.

[6] Schmid, *Marcion*, 316. On the interpretation of this verse, see Christopher D. Stanley, "'Under a Curse': A Fresh Reading of Galatians 3.10–14," *New Testament Studies (NTS)* 36 (1990): 481–511; R. Barry Matlock, "Helping Paul's Argument Work? The Curse of Galatians 3.10–14," in *The Torah in the New Testament: Papers Delivered at the Manchester-Lausanne Seminar of June 2008*, ed. Michael Tait and Peter Oakes (London: T&T Clark, 2009), 154–79.

[7] Although Col 2:14 is unattested in the sources for Marcion's Apostolikon, the next sentence (Col 2:16) is doubly attested (Tertullian, *AM* 5.19.9; Epiphanius, *Panarion* 42.11.7 §1[39]). This gives grounds for inferring the presence of Col 2:14, its (theo)logical basis. Neither Tertullian nor Epiphanius was exhaustive in their quotation of the Apostolikon, especially when it came to Eph and Col. See BeDuhn, *First New Testament*, 317.

[8] See further Räisänen, *Paul and the Law*, 42–202; Räisänen, "Freiheit vom Gesetz im Urchristentum," *Studia Theologica* 46:1 (1992): 55–67.

Around 200 CE, Clement of Alexandria observed that some Christian groups kept shouting Paul's words: "through Law is the knowledge of sin."[9] Clement was referring, at least in part, to Marcionite Christians.[10] These Christians also said (in Clement's summary): "until the Law there was no sin in the world" and "apart from Law sin is dead" (compare Rom 5:13; 7:8).[11] In his *Commentary on Romans*, Origen noted that his opponents "accuse the god of the Law, that the Law is a bad root and a bad tree through which the knowledge of sin comes."[12] This is a distinctly Marcionite argument. In the same work, Origen mentioned Marcion as one who destroys the Law.[13] Tertullian called Marcionites "enemies of the Law" (*adversarii legis*) who ascribe inconstancy to god for the purposes of abrogating the Law.[14]

Ephesians 2:15

Yet it was not hostility to the Law that set Marcionite Christians apart; it was their depiction of *Christ*—not Marcion—as destroyer of the Law. For this idea, they had a biblical basis. The epistle to the Ephesians (known to Marcionites as Laodiceans[15]) read in the Apostolikon:

But now in Christ you who were once far off have come near by his blood. For he is our peace, since he made the two one, broke down the wall of enmity in (his) flesh, and *destroyed the Law* of commandments by teachings, so that, enacting peace, he might make in himself the two into one new human, and reconcile both to god in one body after slaying the enmity in it through the cross. (2:13–16, emphasis added)[16]

---

[9] Clement, *Stromata* 2.7.34.4. Cf. *Acts of Archelaus* 45.6.

[10] See how Tertullian traced the citation of Rom 7:7 to Marcion(ites) in *AM* 5.13.13–14.

[11] Clement, *Stromata* 4.3.9.6.

[12] Origen, *Commentary on Romans* 3.3.10. See further Winrich Löhr, "Die Auslegung des Gesetzes bei Markion, den Gnostikern and den Manichäern," in *Stimuli: Exegese und ihre Hermeneutik in Antike und Christentum: Festschrift für Ernst Dassmann*, ed. Georg Schöllgen and Clemens Scholten (Münster: Aschendorff 1996), 77–95, esp. 77–80.

[13] Origen, *Commentary on Romans* 3.8.2.

[14] Tertullian, *On Idolatry* 5.3.

[15] Tertullian, *AM* 5.11.12 (with Schmid, *Marcion*, 111); 5.17.1; Epiphanius, *Panarion* 42.11.8; 42.12.13. The Latin *Laodiceans* preserved in Codex Fuldensis is a different letter.

[16] Schmid, *Marcion*, 339: νυνὶ δὲ ἐν χριστῷ (Ἰησοῦ) ὑμεῖς οἱ ποτε ὄντες μακρὰν ἐγενήθητε ἐγγὺς ἐν τῷ αἵματι αὐτοῦ. Αὐτὸς γὰρ ἐστιν ἡ εἰρήνη ἡμῶν, ὁ ποιήσας τὰ ἀμφότερα ἕν, λύσας τὸ μεσότοιχον τῆς

The verb translated in the phrase "he destroyed (*katargeō*) the Law" is the same verb Paul used to describe the destruction of the world rulers who crucified Christ (1 Cor 2:6; 2 Thess 2:8), the discharge of the old self from the Law by death (Rom 7:6), and the destruction of death itself (1 Cor 15:26).[17] The tense of the verb indicates that Christ set about his work of destruction at a specific point in time—on the cross (2:16).

The object of destruction is clear: *ho nomos* (Eph 2:15)—*nomos* being Paul's customary word for the Mosaic Law.[18] In context, the Law is thought of as a wall dividing Jews and Gentiles (2:14).[19] When Christ destroyed "the Law of the commandments," he reconciled Jew and Gentile. What kept them at war were the commands of Law. Once this Law was destroyed, peace between Jews and Gentiles was established on the basis of a new way of life.

It has been argued that Paul criticized "(works of) the Law" like circumcision and Sabbath keeping only insofar as these works defined a particular people (the Jews).[20] Nevertheless, Marcion understood "Law" in this letter in the broadest sense of divine "commandments," and he made no apparent attempt to distinguish which commandments were ethical and which we might call ethnic.[21]

ἐχθρὰς ἐν τῇ σαρκί, τὸν νόμον τῶν ἐντολῶν (ἐν) δόγμασιν καταργήσας, ἵνα τοὺς δύο κτίσῃ ἐαυτῷ εἰς ἕνα καινὸν ἄνθρωπον ποιῶν εἰρήνην (καὶ) ἀποκαταλλάξῃ τοὺς ἀμφοτέρους τῷ θεῷ ἐν ἑνὶ σώματι διὰ τοῦ σταυροῦ ἀποκτείνας τὴν ἔχθραν ἐν αὐτῷ.

[17] In Heb 2:14, the one who held the power of death, the devil, is also destroyed (καταργήσῃ).

[18] Pheme Perkins, "The Letter to the Ephesians," in *The New Interpreter's Bible*, ed. Leander E. Keck 12 vols. (Nashville: Abingdon, 2000), Vol. 11, 399. According to Räisänen, "*nomos* in Paul refers to the authoritative tradition of Israel, anchored in the revelation on Sinai, which separates Jews from the rest of mankind" (*Paul and the Law*, 16). Cf. Michael Winger, *By What Law: The Meaning of Νόμος in the Letters of Paul* (Atlanta: Scholars Press, 1992), 197.

[19] The *Letter of Aristeas* (about 150–50 BCE) used a similar metaphor: "the legislator . . . surrounded us [Jews] with . . . iron walls to prevent our mixing with any of the other peoples in any matter" (§139, trans. R. J. H. Shutt in *OTP* 2.22).

[20] James D. G. Dunn, "Works of the Law and the Curse of the Law (Gal 3.10–14)," *NTS* 31:4 (1985): 523–42. Dunn fends off his critics in *Jesus, Paul and the Law: Studies in Mark and Galatians* (Louisville: Westminster/John Knox, 1990), 237–41; "Yet Once More: 'The Works of the Law', a Response," *Journal for the Study of the New Testament (JSNT)* 46 (1992): 99–117. Further interpretive options are reviewed by Markus Barth, *Ephesians: Introduction, Translation, and Commentary on Chapters 1–3* (Garden City: Doubleday, 1974), 287–91. In Col 2:14, Markus Barth and Helmut Blanke understood δόγματα to refer to "OT law, because only this—and not any kind of regulation of a 'religion' designated as deception—can be the legal basis for the divine list of transgressions" (*Colossians: A New Translation with Introduction and Commentary*, trans. Astrid B. Beck [New York: Doubleday, 1994], 370).

[21] Charles H. Talbert: "Jesus' death destroyed the law of commandments in decrees, that is, the Mosaic law covenant (cf. Rom 10:4; Gal 3:23–26), not just the casuistic interpretation of the law or the ceremonial, as opposed to the moral, law" (*Ephesians and Colossians* [Grand Rapids: Baker

The fact that the author of Ephesians cited one of the Ten Commandments (to obey parents, Eph 6:2–3) does not indicate that the Law was considered valid. Early Christians openly rejected the Law while at the same time appropriating all sorts of Jewish precepts into their ethical systems. In the Apostolikon, the command to obey parents (Eph 6:2–3), moreover, was not marked as part of Torah.[22] It simply said "Honor your father and mother" without the phrase, "this is the first command with a promise." Whether or not this was Marcion's deletion, someone else's, or an earlier reading of the letter remains moot.[23]

Decrees or Teachings?

Ephesians 2:15 mentions "the Law of commandments in *dogmata.*"[24] The parallel text in Colossians 2:14 reads: "the document of debt in *dogmata.*" Now *dogmata* could refer to the "decrees" of Jewish Law.[25] If *dogmata* refers to the rulings of the creator in Jewish Law, one could understand them as describing the format of the commands: Christ "destroyed . . . the commandments (which are) in (the form of divine) decrees." When the Marcionite Megethius (in the *Adamantius* dialogue) said that Christ overthrew the decrees (*dogmata*) of the creator, he referred to the decrees of Law.[26] The language possibly derives from Ephesians 2:15 and/or Colossians 2:14—since these are the only places where *dogmata* appear in Pauline writings linked to the Law.

Academic, 2007], 81). See also Perkins, "Ephesians" in *The New Interpreter's Bible*, 11.399–400; John P. Meier, *A Marginal Jew: Rethinking the Historical Jesus*, Vol. 4 (New Haven: Yale University Press, 2009), 43–46; Minna Skhul, *Reading Ephesians: Exploring Social Entrepreneurship in the Text* (London: T&T Clark, 2009), 113–28.

[22] Tertullian, *AM* 5.18.11.

[23] See further Schmid, *Marcion*, 94–95, 113, who notes that there were other motives for removing this clause, since the command to honor parents was not the first (πρώτη) commandment.

[24] Schmid, *Marcion*, 339. It is not clear if Tertullian's *sententiis* represents ἐν δόγμασιν or simply δόγμασιν. Only in P[46] and some manuscripts of the Vulgate is ἐν δόγμασιν omitted, probably by scribal error. C. J. Roetzel accepted the reading of P[46] and drew substantial conclusions from it ("Jewish Christian-Gentile Christian Relations: A Discussion of Ephesians 2.15a," *Zeitschrift für Neutestamentliche Wissenschaft* 74 [1983]: 81–89 at 86).

[25] Cf. the usage of δόγματα in Josephus, *Against Apion* 1.42; *Antiquities* 15.136; 3 Macc 1:3; 4 Maccabees 10:2; Philo, *Allegorical Interpretation* 1.54–55; *Giants* 52.

[26] *Adamantius* 1.4. Similarly, certain "Cainites" according to Epiphanius believed that Christ "wanted to pervert the provisions of the Law" (*Panarion* 38.3.3).

Nevertheless, *dogmata* was also a general term for "teachings." Thus many ancient interpreters understood *dogmata* instrumentally, referring to Christ's instructions. In this reading, Christ destroyed the Law *by* his teachings.[27] This reading is also suggested by the (probably) second-century author of *The Concept of Our Great Power* (NHC VI,4), where Christ's "teaching has abolished the Law of the age."[28] This is hardly a "gnostic" reading. John Chrysostom, bishop of Constantinople (died 407 CE), also proposed it: "What does it mean to say 'He destroyed it [the Law] by teachings? . . . either he calls faith a teaching (*dogma*) . . . or he refers to the precept" of Christ.[29]

On the basis of Ephesians 2:15, then, one can see why Marcionite Christians claimed that Christ destroyed the Law.[30] This point is consistent in their reported views. As Tertullian remarked: "Jesus descended . . . to destroy the Law."[31] According to Epiphanius, Marcion "says that Christ has descended from on high for the salvation of souls and to refute (*epi elegchō*) . . . the Law."[32] Ephrem the Syrian said that the Marcionite Christ "abrogated the former commandments"—meaning those given in Jewish Law.[33] Of course, these opponents of Marcion did not present his teachings as the result of biblical interpretation. Nevertheless, given that Ephesians 2:15 openly stated that Christ "destroyed the Law," Marcionite readers could readily infer that this was one of the purposes for his coming.

Marcionite Evidence

Regrettably, we must admit that we lack direct evidence to show how Marcion(ites) read Ephesians 2:15. We do, however, gain an important glimpse of Marcionite exegesis in Ptolemy's *Letter to Flora*. In the 130s or 140s CE, Ptolemy probably became a student of the Christian teacher

---

[27] So also BeDuhn, *First New Testament*, 253.

[28] *Concept of Our Great Power* (NHC VI,4) 42.5–6: ⲁⲡⲉϥⲗⲟⲅⲟⲥ ⲃⲱⲗ ⲉⲃⲟⲗ ⲙ̄ⲡⲛⲟⲙⲟⲥ ⲙ̄ⲡⲁⲓⲱⲛ. I take "law" here to refer to Jewish Law and "aeon" to refer to "this present evil aeon" (Gal 1:4). For a different interpretation, see Francis E. Williams, *Mental Perception: A Commentary on NHC VI,4. The Concept of Our Great Power* (Leiden: Brill, 2001), 123.

[29] Chrysostom, *Homilies on Ephesians* 5 (PG 62.39.53–58). Cf. Theodoret, *Commentary on Ephesians* in PG 82.524B: "he called gospel teaching *dogmata*."

[30] Irenaeus, *AH* 1.27.2.

[31] Tertullian, *AM* 4.36.11.

[32] Epiphanius, *Panarion* 42.4.2. Epiphanius claimed that Cerdo first took this position, along with many other sects (*Panarion* 41.1.8). Cf. Celsus reported by Origen, *Cels.* 6.53: Christ destroyed the creator's creations (διαφθείρει τὰ τούτου δημιουργήματα).

[33] Ephrem in Mitchell, *Prose Refutations*, lvii.

Valentinus in Rome. There Ptolemy eventually gained disciples of his own. This Ptolemy may be identified with a martyr of the same name who died for confessing Christ about 152.[34] If so, his *Letter to Flora*, evidently a Roman matron, was probably composed around 150 CE. If not, the letter could have been written anytime between 150 and 180 CE, the latter date being when Irenaeus attacked Ptolemy's students, since evidently their master had perished.[35]

In his letter, Ptolemy noted that some Christians vigorously maintain that the Law was given by the devil. The fact that they also conceived of this devil as the creator indicates that these Christians were Marcionites.[36] Now it must immediately be pointed out that Ptolemy misrepresented Marcionite language (Marcionites never directly called the creator "devil").[37] Ptolemy did, however, accurately report that the Marcionite creator was the "opponent" of Christians, the "maker of corruption," and a wicked lawmaker.[38]

Ptolemy portrayed himself as moderating the Marcionite position. Not all the Law is evil, he urged—only the part "entangled with injustice," which Christ "entirely abolished." To illustrate, Ptolemy cited a well-known Marcionite example: the *ius talionis* or law of retaliation (see Chapter 3). This principle was entangled with injustice and abolished by the Savior, who commanded the opposite attitude ("turn the other cheek," Matt 5:38–40).[39]

Ptolemy's direct proof for Christ's destruction of the Law was Ephesians 2:15. The apostle showed that Christ destroyed unjust laws, "when he said that Christ destroyed the Law of commandments by his teachings."[40]

---

[34] For the identity of the two Ptolemies, see Lampe, *From Paul*, 238–40; Dunderberg, *Beyond Gnosticism*, 90–92 with n.97.

[35] Irenaeus, *AH* 1 *pref.* 2.

[36] Ptolemy, *Letter to Flora* 3.2: ὑπὸ τοῦ ἀντικειμένου φθοροποιοῦ διαβόλου τεθεῖσθαι τοῦτον [τὸν νόμον] ἰσχυρίζονται.

[37] Note, however, that "the prince of the power of the air" (Eph 2:2) in patristic exegesis was the devil, but for Marcion it was the creator (Tertullian, *AM* 5.17.7–8). Likewise, Tertullian indicated that Marcion(ites) took the devil in Eph 6:11 to be the creator (Tertullian, *AM* 5.19.12; cf. 5.18.13). See further Moll, *Arch-Heretic*, 48–49, 144–52; Rasimus, "Ptolemaus and the Valentinian Exegesis of John's Prologue," in Rasimus, ed., *Legacy of John*, 145–71, at 147–48.

[38] For different views on how to interpret this passage in Ptolemy, see Roth, "Evil," 346–47; Dunderberg, *Beyond Gnosticism*, 87–90. Dunderberg states that "Marcion did not describe this [creator] god as 'evil' (*kakos*), but only as 'imperfect' or 'wretched' (*ponēros*)" (87). Yet πονηρός also has the sense of "(morally) wicked, base" (Danker, *Greek-English Lexicon*, 851–52).

[39] Ptolemy, *Letter to Flora* 6.2. Compare 5.4, where Ptolemy reveals his own position, that the *ius talionis* is necessary (ἐπάναγκες), and so not entirely evil. Tertullian did not disagree that Christ annulled the *ius talionis* (*On Patience* 6.4–5), although he tried to justify it as a means of deterrence given to a "most calloused" and "unfaithful" people (*AM* 2.18.1).

[40] Ptolemy, *Epistle to Flora* 6.6.

Nevertheless, this passage—though obviously useful to Ptolemy—did not entirely fit his argument. Ephesians 2:15, after all, does not argue for a *partial* nullification of the Law (Ptolemy's position). It says that Christ "destroyed the Law of commandments" *simpliciter*. Thus the verse better fits a Marcionite line of argument, an argument that Ptolemy plausibly adapted from Marcion(ites) just as he did the example of the *ius talionis*. Ptolemy's letter can thus serve as indirect evidence that Marcion(ites) knew Ephesians 2:15 and used it to support their position (that Christ destroyed the Law unconditionally).

Enemy of the Law

Marcion(ites), I propose, inferred from Ephesians 2:15 that Christ was "an enemy of the Law."[41] Tertullian, who reported this point, took the opposite tack. Christ was the Law's "helper." Tertullian agreed that Christ annulled the Law, but only by fulfilling it (Matt 5:17). Instead of mentioning the abolition of the *ius talionis* (Matt 5:38), Tertullian turned to neighboring verses in the gospel called Matthew (a work, it should be noted, not accepted by Marcion as scriptural). The commandment against adultery, for instance, is superseded because Christ made a law against lust (Matt 5:27–28). Likewise, the command against murder became superfluous when Christ condemned slander (Matt 5:21–22).[42] But there is slippage in this argument. Ephesians 2:15 says that Christ *destroyed* the Law, whereas the restrictions that Christ added to the Law in Matthew 5:21–28 did not nullify the creator's laws. Rather, they *reinforced* them and made them stricter—a point emphasized by several early Christians.[43]

Here we can learn something from broader Christian discussions about the Law. In commenting on Colossians 2:16, Tertullian agreed with Marcion that the Law was "pushed aside" (*exclusa*) by Christ.[44] Tertullian made similar

---

[41] Tertullian, *AM* 5.17.15.

[42] Tertullian, *AM* 5.17.15. Cf. *To His Wife* 2: "it was necessary that in former times there be practice which afterwards had to be abrogated . . . For the Law had first to intervene; at a later date, the Word of God was to replace the Law." See further Jorgensen, *Treasure*, 198–99.

[43] Irenaeus, *AH* 4.13.1; Ptolemy, *Letter to Flora* 6.1; Chrysostom, *Homilies on Ephesians* 5 (*PG* 62.39–40); Augustine, *Enemy of the Law* 1.31. This position has many modern reiterations. Cf. Michael Tait: "Matthew's Jesus makes it crystal clear that he has not come to destroy the Law but to fulfil it, which, in the context of the rest of the Sermon, means that none of the Law will be abrogated but rather its demands made radical and interior" ("The End of the Law: The Messianic Torah in the Pseudepigrapha," in *Torah in the New Testament*, 196–207 at 205).

[44] Tertullian, *AM* 5.19.19.

remarks in his opening comments on Romans. Most Christian interpreters, he said, agree that Paul in Romans rebuffs (again, *excludere*) the Law.[45] Tertullian had no dispute with these interpreters, remarking, "We embrace that well-known total destruction (*abolitionem*) of the old Law," citing Luke 16:16, "the Law and the prophets until John," and Romans 10:4, Christ is the "cessation" (*finem*) of the Law.[46] Accordingly, both Tertullian and Marcion actually agreed that Christ destroyed the Law, but for different reasons. For Tertullian, there was nothing morally wrong about the Law. For Marcion, the Law itself was corrupt, enslaving, and not in tune with the character of the true god revealed in Christ.

Bad Law, Bad Lawgiver

"What sort of a tree the Law is," Origen wrote, "is shown by its fruits, that is, by the words of its precepts. For if the Law is found to be good, then undoubtedly he who gave it is believed to be a good god."[47] Origen here employed Marcionite logic, based on Marcion's well-known exegesis of Evangelion 6:43: "a good tree cannot bear bad fruit, nor a bad tree good fruit."[48]

Marcionites, however, made the converse point: if the Law is shown to be *evil*, this indicates that the divine *Lawgiver* is evil as well. To quote Origen again: given that the Law "is a bad tree with a bad root," then Marcionites logically accused "the god of the Law (*deum legis accusant*)."[49] The god of

---

[45] Tertullian, *AM* 5.13.1. See, for instance, *Epistle of Barnabas* 2:6; 9:4; *Diognetus* 4:1; 6:10. The author of the *Holy Book of the Great Invisible Spirit* (probably late second century CE) stated that Jesus "came and crucified what is in the Law" (ⲈⲒ ⲀϤⲤⲦⲀⲨⲢⲞⲨ ⲘⲠⲈⲦϨⲛ̄ ⲠⲚⲞⲘⲞⲤ, NHC III,2 65.18 = IV,2 77.15). Simon of Samaria, according to Epiphanius, claimed that "the Law is not god's, but belongs to the power on the left" (*Panarion* 21.4.5; cf. Pseudo-Clement, *Homilies* 3.2.2). According to Theodore Stylianopoulos, "Justin remains within the older Christian tradition and insists on the radical abolishment of the Law by Christ" (*Justin Martyr and the Mosaic Law* [Missoula: Scholars Press, 1975], 168), citing *Dialogue with Trypho* 11–13. See also Kathleen Gibbons, *The Moral Psychology of Clement of Alexandria: Mosaic Philosophy* (London: Taylor & Francis, 2016), 9–32.

[46] Luke 16:16 in Tertullian, *AM* 5.2.1–2. A. Kroymann in the Corpus Christianorum Series Latina (CCSL) edition prints *legis veteris amolitionem* ("*removal* of the old Law"), as found in codex Montepessulanus 54. Possibly it represents a softening of *abolitionem*, but the meanings are not significantly different. For Rom 10:4 in Tertullian, see his *AM* 5.14.7. Tertullian believed that the creator planned to reject his Law all along, and signaled this in the prophets (*AM* 1.20.5–6). Lieu points out that "it is Tertullian himself who repeatedly identifies slavery with the Law, even supplying it where it is absent from Paul's argument" (*Marcion* 253, 257, citing Tertullian, *AM* 5.4.5–9). Cf. Tertullian, *Exhortation to Chastity* 6; *Monogamy* 7, 13–14.

[47] Origen, *First Principles* 2.5.4.

[48] Origen, *First Principles* 2.5.4; Tertullian, *AM* 4.17.11 (cf. 1.2.1); *Adamantius* 1.28; *Ref.* 10.19.3.

[49] Origen, *Commentary on Romans* 3.6.9.

a hostile and corrupt Law himself must be hostile and corrupt. Therefore Christ came not only to destroy the Law, but also to destroy the Lawgiver.

About 375 CE, Epiphanius observed that "gnostics deny the Law . . . And if they deny the Lord's Law, together with the Law they also carp at the speaker in it."[50] Marcion(ites) (who could be called "gnostic" in Epiphanius's vague way) would have agreed with this line of reasoning. For Marcion(ites), Christ's exposé and destruction of the Law was tied to his exposé and destruction of the creator, since (1) the Law is the Law given by the creator, and thus (2) the Law reveals the creator's character.

The destruction of the Law and the destruction of the creator was a consistent connection made by Marcion's opponents. Marcion taught that Christ not only "abolished . . . the Law" but also "all the works *of his god who made the world*" (Irenaeus).[51] Epiphanius wrote that "The Lord directed his teaching against the Law and *the god* of the Law".[52] Tertullian stated that "Jesus came down from another god *to expose the creator* and to destroy the Law".[53]

It is a tension in Tertullian's argument that Christ destroys the Law but is not a "destroyer of the Law." Tertullian did not want to affirm, with Marcion, that Christ destroyed the creator's work, let alone the creator. Yet for Marcion, the character of the Law was inextricably connected to the character of the creator. Marcionites thus linked Christ's destruction of the Law with his hostility to the creator. But if Christ proved hostile to the creator, then the creator could not be good.

The connection between the hostile Law and the hostile creator partially emerged out of a reading of Paul. Marcionites, according to Origen, often cited Romans 4:15: "The Law brings rage, and where the Law does not exist there is no violation."[54] The violation here is violation of the creator's Law. The rage, then, was taken to be the creator's rage against law-breaking human beings. Paul said that the Law was the power of sin (1 Cor 15:56). By placing

---

[50] Epiphanius, *Panarion* 26.15.1–2.

[51] Irenaeus, *AH* 1.27.2, emphasis added: *et omnia opera eius dei qui mundum fecit.*

[52] Epiphanius, *Panarion* 42.11.16, Elenchus 1: κατὰ τοῦ θεοῦ τοῦ νόμου. In the *Adamantius*, Christ destroyed the "Law *of the creator*" (τὸν νόμον *τοῦ δημιουργοῦ* κατέλυσεν) (*Adamantius* 2.10, emphasis added; cf. 2.15). Lieu underscores the key point: "The character of that Law and the character of the Demiurge are inseparable from each other" (*Marcion*, 356).

[53] Tertullian, *AM* 4.36.11 (*ad detectionem creatoris*), emphasis added.

[54] Origen, *Commentary on Romans* 4.4.3. That Marcion is in view is indicated by Origen, *Commentary on Romans* 5.6.1, where he refers to *Marcion et ceteri heretici*, who, on the basis of Rom 5:20, assert that the Law was given to make sin abound. Marcion and Tertullian agreed that the wrathful god revealed from heaven was the creator (Tertullian, *AM* 5.13.3).

humans under his Law, the creator generated a system in which sin and (eternal) punishment were the inevitable result (think also of the first commandment not to eat from the tree of knowledge, Chapter 3). As the prophet Ezekiel put it: "the soul who sins shall die" (18:20). If death is an evil, then the Law, by Marcionite logic, is evil because it represents the evil character of the one who used it to punish humanity with death.

Colossians 2:14

Ephesians 2:15 affirmed Christ's destruction of the Law to unite Jew and Gentile. But uniting Jew and Gentile was not Marcion's overriding concern. His goals are better represented in the parallel passage of Colossians 2:14, where Christ obliterated the debt record (*cheirograph*) against humanity. Many ancient interpreters took this record to be—or at least to involve—the Law (the list of god-given duties that humans fail to perform).[55] Marcionites likely took it a step further: if Christ destroyed the Law in Ephesians 2:15 and destroyed the debt record in Colossians 2:14, then the Law and the debt record were one and the same.

In Colossians, the debt record is said to be both "against" humans and to be "hostile" to them. If the debt record is the Law itself, as seems likely in Marcionite interpretation, then the Law is hostile to humanity. But if the Law is an enemy to human beings, then it cannot be good. In Romans 7:12, the Law is called good, a goodness qualified by justice. Yet the creator's justice, from a Marcionite point of view, was not in fact good but a mask for cruelty (see Chapters 3–4).[56]

According to Colossians 2:14, Christ paid the debt record that stood against humanity. He paid it not to the devil, but to the one who gave the Law. The devil did not give the Law. Thus humans owed nothing to him. For Marcion(ites), there was only one being to whom the debt of sin was owed: the creator. It was the creator who made people debtors to himself. He

---

[55] E.g., Hilary of Poitiers, *Tractates on the Psalms* 129.9: "who, affixing the debt record of the Law to the cross, destroyed the edict of ancient condemnation (*edictum damnationis veteris delevit*)"; Severian of Gabala: Christ "wiped out (ἐξήλειψε) the debt record, the consent to the Law (τὴν συγκατάθεσιν τὴν πρὸς τόν νόμον), by his own teachings" (Staab, *Pauluskommentar*, 323–24); Theodore of Mopsuestia (350–428 CE): "he calls the Law the debt record, for we were obligated to fulfill all its decrees as laid down by god" (*The Commentaries on the Minor Epistles of Paul*, trans. Rowan A. Greer [Atlanta: SBL Press, 2010], 408–9).

[56] Moll wrote that "[F]or Marcion there was no doubt that the Law was evil" (*Arch-Heretic*, 61).

managed the heavenly ledger and kept tabs on human sin. He was the heavenly lord from whom humanity needed to be redeemed.

Christ's destruction of the Law was thus tied to the Marcionite story of redemption. Christ bought back humans from their status of being "under Law" (Gal 4:5). Being "under Law" was evidently something negative and limiting (otherwise, why be redeemed from under it?). Marcion(ites) took it a step further: if people needed redemption from the Law, then the Law could not be good.

Paul declared that those who lived by the Law were under a curse from which Christ redeemed them (Gal 3:10, 13). Paul euphemistically called it the "curse of the Law," but the Law was not really an agent. The "curse of the Law" was that of the Lawgiver himself. In effect, Christ literally bought humans from the creator who made (and thus owned) them.[57] Marcionite redemption was thus liberation from the creator and his enslaving legal system. When Christians were bought by Christ, they were no longer debtors to the Law and slaves of the creator.

Marcion applied the parable of the strong man to the creator (Evangelion 11:21–22).[58] A strong man (the creator) can protect his property (human beings). But when someone stronger than him arrives (Christ), he overcomes the strong man and takes over his property. In short, Christ came to earth to fight the strong man (the creator). He fought him by undermining his Law and by removing humans from his government.

The redemption occurred at the cross. There, Christ reconciled Jew and Gentile to (the true) god through the cross, and by it (presumably the cross) killed hostility (Eph 2:16). Whose hostility? It could be the hostility between Jew and Gentile, but for Marcion(ites) it was more likely the hostility between humans and the creator (recall the creator's wrath, Rom 1:18; 4:15).

In the parallel passage of Colossians 2:14–15, Christ nailed the damning debt record (for Marcionites: the Law itself) to the cross, thereby parading and triumphing over demonic rulers. When Ephesians and Colossians were read together, a connection was thus formed between destroying the Law

---

[57] Epiphanius, *Panarion* 42.8.1–2: "we were someone else's creation, and he thus bought as at the price of his own life." Ephrem (in Mitchell, *Prose Refutations*, 2.xli) spoke of a "bargain" between Christ and the creator (see Lieu, *Marcion*, 169–73). Eznik of Kolb (*On God* 358) told a more detailed story: the resurrected Christ goes to trial with the creator, and since the creator disobeyed his own Law (by killing Christ), he agrees that Christ can take believing humanity in exchange. Eznik also "quotes" Marcion: "We [believers] are the price of the blood of Jesus" (§386). Christ "purchased humankind" by his crucifixion (§387). Further texts are cited in the German edition of Harnack, *Marcion*, 288; BeDuhn, *First New Testament*, 267. See also Moll, *Arch-Heretic*, 70–71.

[58] Tertullian, *AM* 5.6.7.

(Eph 2:15) and destroying the demonic rulers (Col 2:15). For Marcion, these beings were nothing but minions of the creator. These minions, "the rulers of this world," crucified the Lord of glory under the command of the creator (Chapter 4).

Conclusion

To sum up: Marcion(ites) read Paul's ambiguous portrait of the Law by accentuating its negative functions: it brings rage, death, a curse, and condemnation. The claimed goodness of the Law was a reflection of the creator's justice, which demanded punishment for violations and created a mountain of debt. The Law thereby led to humanity's condemnation, created hostility between humans and the creator (Col 2:14), and enslaved people to the creator himself. Therefore Christ came to destroy it (Eph 2:15). If Christ came to destroy the Law that was pitted against humanity, then the Law itself was part of a system of evil.

Marcion(ites) then deduced the theological implications: if the Law represents the character of the Lawgiver, then a wicked Law comes from a wicked Lawgiver. Christ destroyed the Lawgiver (the creator) not only by his teachings, but also by his death. Christ paid a price to the creator to remove believers from the curse of the Law (Gal 3:13). If Christ performed the ultimate sacrifice to destroy the creator, then the creator was not a good and loving deity, but rather a dark lord, a tyrant. In this way, the creator was shown to be evil.

6

Destroyer of the Law II

> [They will] call him (Christ) "the impious man" and the "[im]pure
> transgressor of the Law."
>
> —*Melchizedek* (NHC IX,1 3.8–9)

Introduction

Marcionites knew from Ephesians 2:15 that Christ destroyed the Law. The
destruction occurred on the cross (2:16). Yet for Marcionites, it did not begin
there. According to them, "Jesus came down from another god to expose the
creator and to destroy the Law (*ad detectionem creatoris, ad destructionem
legis*)."[1] As the purpose of Christ's coming, the destruction of the Law was
also the hallmark of his ministry. It was Christ's continuous conflict with the
Law that indicated his clash with the Law's creator. This clash proved the creator was opposed to Christ. The ultimate opposition was manifested in the
creator's plot to kill Christ by the stipulations of the Law. For Marcionites, the
killing creator could not be good.

Jesus and the Law

According to early Christians, Jesus had several run-ins with the Law. Indeed,
Christ's conflicts with the Law were a theme in the gospels—including
those that became canonical. When speaking to the fictional Jews in John,
Jesus twice referred to the Law as "your Law" (8:17; 10:34; cf. 15:25; 18:31),
insinuating that it was not his own.[2] Early Christians believed that Christ
"taught against the observances of the Law," with regard to foods and Sabbath

---

[1] Tertullian, *AM* 4.36.11.
[2] See further Francis Watson, "Jesus Versus the Lawgiver: Narratives of Apostasy and Conversion,"
in *Telling the Christian Story*, ed. Watson and Parkhouse, 45–62.

The Evil Creator. M. David Litwa, Oxford University Press. © Oxford University Press 2021.
DOI: 10.1093/oso/9780197566428.003.0008

observance especially. "And any observant person," one preacher observed, "will find many other teachings of the same sort."[3]

Marcionite Christians were especially observant in this regard. They noticed that at some points, Christ seemed deliberately to disobey the Law, even rubbing it in the face of Jewish leaders. These leaders regularly pointed out that Jesus failed to obey Mosaic regulations regarding the Sabbath, cleansing before meals, touching impure people, tithing, and so on.[4]

Of course, the historical Jesus was Jewish. But for many early Christians, the Jewish identity of Jesus was not a historical fact in need of recovery. It paled in significance to Jesus's divine identity as son of god and savior. Therefore we cannot assume that merely because Jesus was born Jewish, early Christians understood him to be subject to Jewish Law.[5]

Consider: the Jesus of the canonical gospels is never once portrayed as performing a sacrifice according to Jewish Law. Jewish males were required to appear in festivals at Jerusalem three times a year (Exod 23:14–17; Deut 16:16). The Jesus of the Synoptic gospels never shows independent concern for these holidays. He once desired to eat the Passover meal (Luke 22:15) but in the course of it dramatically changed its meaning.[6] In John, Jesus gave the impression that he would deliberately *not* travel to attend a festival in Jerusalem (7:8). The Jesus of the gospels, finally, was never said to rest on the Sabbath and never encouraged anyone else to do so.[7]

According to canonical Luke, Jesus was presumably circumcised as a child. As an adult, however, he was never heard to recommend circumcision as ordained by Law. He called the proselytes of the Pharisees (who would have

---

[3] Severian of Gabala (in Staab, *Pauluskommentar*, 323). Faustus, bishop of Milevis, invited his readers to undertake this thought experiment: "Imagine that the Jews had also said to him [after hearing that he came to fulfill the Law], 'Why are you acting in such a way that we are able to suspect this? Is it because you mock circumcision, violate the sabbath, reject the sacrifices, and mix different foods together? . . . What more could he have done or what could he have done that was more clearly aimed at the destruction of the Law . . .?" (Augustine, *Against Faustus* 17.2). See further Michael F. Bird, "Jesus as Lawbreaker," in *Who Do My Opponents Say that I Am? An Investigation of the Accusations Against the Historical Jesus*, ed. Scot McKnight and Joseph B. Modica (London: T&T Clark, 2008), 3–26.

[4] H. Basser, *Studies in Exegesis: Christian Critiques of Jewish Law and Rabbinic Responses, 70–300 CE* (Leiden: Brill, 2000), esp. 42, 48, 17–33, 110–15.

[5] Adele Reinhartz argues that "Jesus' discourses employ such a sharp dichotomy between Jesus and believers on the one hand, and the unbelieving Jews on the other, that the term 'Jew' cannot comfortably be used to describe the Jesus we find in this Gospel" ("How 'the Jews' Became Part of the Plot," in *Jesus, Judaism, and Christian Anti-Judaism: Reading the New Testament after the Holocaust*, ed. Paula Fredriksen and Adele Reinhartz [Louisville: Westminster/John Knox, 2002], 103). See further Thomas Kazen, *Jesus and Purity Halakhah: Was Jesus Indifferent to Impurity?* 2nd ed. (Winona Lake: Eisenbrauns, 2010), 2–42.

[6] Roth, *Text*, 433; Klinghardt, *Älteste Evangelium II*, 1019.

[7] Faustus in Augustine, *Against Faustus* 18.2.

been circumcised as adults) children "of hell twice over" (Matt 23:15).[8] Jesus was never said to follow kosher laws. In fact, he proclaimed against Jewish "lawyers" that nothing entering the mouth can defile them (Mark 7:15; Matt 15:11). This latter teaching stands in apparent opposition to lengthy lists of foods prohibited by Jewish Law (Lev 20:25; 11:14–15; Deut 14:13–14).[9]

Finally, in the literary depiction of Jesus's trial, Jesus putatively broke the Law by putting himself on a level with god (consenting, after initial evasion, to be god's son). At least from the Jewish perspective represented in the text, he committed blasphemy and introduced idolatry into Israel by making himself a kind of (subordinate) deity.[10]

The Charge of Destruction

Thus it is hardly surprising when, in Marcion's Evangelion, the Jews accuse Jesus of destroying the Law (23:2).[11] They do so in the indictment before Pilate, which is portrayed as little more than a hurling of accusations. Several charges stand in Luke 23:2. For instance, Jesus perverted the Jewish nation, forbade taxes to Caesar, and called himself a king. In Marcion's Evangelion, the fictional Jews make this additional accusation: "We found this person . . . destroying the Law and Prophets."[12] Epiphanius claimed that Marcion added this clause, though it is well attested in Old Latin witnesses to Luke, indicating that it was a pre-Marcionite reading in the second century.[13]

---

[8] υἱὸν γεέννης διπλότερον ὑμῶν, noted by Faustus in Augustine, *Against Faustus* 18.2.

[9] As pointed out by the Manichean Adimantus in Augustine, *Against Adimantus* 15.1–2. Cf. Augustine, *Answer to Faustus* 16.6. See further Barnabas Lindars, "All Foods Clean: Thoughts on Jesus and the Law," in *Law and Religion: Essays on the Place of the Law in Israel and Early Christianity*, ed. Lindars (Cambridge: James Clarke, 1988), 61–71 at 61; Lindars, *Jesus, Paul and the Law* (London: SPCK, 1990), 37–60; Tom Holmén, *Jesus and Jewish Covenant Thinking* (Leiden: Brill, 2001), 237–51; Sigurd Grindheim, "Jesus and the Food Laws Revisited," *Journal for the Study of the Historical Jesus* 31 (2020): 61–76. For a different view, note Matthew Thiessen, *Jesus and the Forces of Death: The Gospels' Portrayal of Ritual Impurity Within First-century Judaism* (Grand Rapids: Baker Academic, 2020), 187–96.

[10] Mark 14:62–63; Luke 22:70–71; John 19:7; Deut 13:1–16. See further Peter Schäfer, *Jesus in the Talmud* (Princeton: Princeton University Press, 2007), 63–74.

[11] Roth, *Text*, 433 from Epiphanius, *Panarion* 42.11.6, Scholion 69.

[12] Roth, *Text*, 433: τοῦτον εὕρομεν . . . καταλύοντα τὸν νόμον καὶ τοὺς προφήτας. See also Klinghardt, *Älteste Evangelium II*, 1061.

[13] Adolf Jülicher, *Itala: Das Neue Testament in altlateinischer Überlieferung* (Berlin: de Gruyter, 1954), XXIII, 256–57, though note the presence of "our" Law (*solventem legem nostram et prophetas*) in *b e ff² i l q*. See also *The New Testament in Greek: The Gospel according to St. Luke*, Part 2, ed. American and British Committees of the International Greek New Testament Project (Oxford: Clarendon Press, 1987), 204. BeDuhn points out that Jesus destroying the Law in Luke 23:2 was accepted in several editions of the Vulgate and passed without comment in Tertullian (*First New Testament*, 190; cf. Roth, *Text*, 337).

The charge is similar to the indictment of Stephen in Acts 6:14. According to Stephen's opponents: "We have heard him saying that Jesus of Nazareth will destroy this place [the Jewish temple] and alter the customs which Moses handed down to us." These "customs" are evidently synonymous with "the Law" of Moses mentioned in the previous verse.[14] Stephen himself is said to have spoken against the temple and the Law (Acts 6:13), but he spoke in reference to what *Jesus* would do, the very same Jesus who altered Mosaic customs. To be sure, for the author of Acts, Christ was not opposed to Law, but Marcionites would have likely agreed with Stephen's opponents: Jesus quite intentionally undermined both the temple and the Law.

In the so-called *Gospel of the Ebionites* (probably mid–second century CE), Jesus was recorded as saying: "I came to destroy the sacrifices, and if you do not cease from sacrificing, divine rage will not cease from you."[15] Since all manner of sacrifices are mandated by Law, this Jesus annulled a divine ordinance. The author of the Pseudo-Clementine *Recognitions* also argued that Christ, the "true prophet," rejected both Jewish sacrifices and the temple.[16]

The tradition that Christ destroyed the Law is also reflected in the (probably fourth-century) *Gospel of Nicodemus*. In this text, the Jewish leaders accuse Jesus of profaning the Sabbath and wishing "to destroy the Law." Pilate responds: "And what things does he do that he wishes to destroy it?" The Jews explain: "We have a law that we should not heal anyone on the Sabbath. But this man with his evil deeds has healed on the Sabbath the lame, the mutilated, the withered, the blind, the paralytic, the deaf, and the demoniacs."[17] This report is consistent with gospel stories. Jesus did heal such people on

[14] Stephen G. Wilson, *Luke and the Law* (Cambridge: Cambridge University Press, 1983), 1–11; Matthias Klinghardt, *Gesetz und Volk Gottes: Das lukanische Verständnis des Gesetzes nach Herkunft, Funktion und seinem Ort in der Geschichte des Urchristentums* (Tübingen: Mohr Siebeck, 1988), 115–17.

[15] Quoted by Epiphanius, *Panarion* 30.16.5: ἦλθον καταλῦσαι τὰς θυσίας, καὶ ἐὰν μὴ παύσησθε τοῦ θύειν, οὐ παύσεται ἀφ' ὑμῶν ἡ ὀργή. See Bart Ehrman and Zlatko Pleše, *The Apocryphal Gospels: Texts and Translations* (Oxford: Oxford University Press, 2011), 210–11; A. F. J. Klijn, *Jewish-Christian Gospel Traditions* (Leiden: Brill, 1992), 27–43.

[16] Pseudo-Clement, *Recognitions* 37.3; cf. 39.1 ("by the compassion of god he admonished them to stop sacrificing"). These passages go back to *The Ascents of James*, which Robert E. van Voorst dates to the late second century CE, though any date between 135 and 260 CE is possible (*The Ascents of James: History and Theology of a Jewish-Christian Community* [Atlanta: Scholars Press, 1989], 79–80. On anti-sacrificial traditions, see ibid., 166–70, and F. Stanley Jones, *An Ancient Jewish Christian Source on the History of Christianity: Pseudo-Clementine Recognitions 1.27–71* (Atlanta: Scholars Press, 1995), esp. 160. The Clementine *Homilies* (3.51.2) says more directly that Christ appeared to be destroying the Law (φαίνεσθαι αὐτὸν καταλύοντα), but states that what was destroyed did not belong to the Law (ἃ κατέλυεν οὐκ ἦν τοῦ νόμου).

[17] *Gospel of Nicodemus (Acts of Pilate A)* 1.1.

the Sabbath and in some cases seemed to have deliberately chosen that day in order to confront his opponents.

In the *Acts of Philip*, Ananias the high priest declares that Jesus "disregarded both the Law and the temple, and abolished Sabbath observation, the purification rites of Moses as well as New Moon observances, because he said these had not been instituted by god. When we saw that he was destroying the Law in this way, we rebelled and crucified him."[18] It is likely that the widespread Christian view of Christ destroying the Law went back to the reading of proto-Luke 23:2 where that point was explicit.

Even if modern editions of Luke do not print the destruction of the Law in 23:2, the substance of the idea runs through the gospels like a red thread. "There is no one who does not know," remarked one fourth-century bishop, "that the Jews always fiercely attacked the words and deeds of Christ. And since they inferred from them that he was destroying the Law . . . they were necessarily angry."[19]

If Christ "destroying the Law" was original to what became Luke, it was removed from later versions.[20] It was quite possibly removed because it contradicted Matthew 5:17.[21] Epiphanius, for instance, could not accept Christ "destroying the Law" in Luke 23:2 for this very reason.[22] Proto-Luke 23:2 apparently said that Christ came "destroying the Law and Prophets" whereas in Matthew, Christ declared: "Do not suppose that I came to destroy the Law and Prophets" (5:17). The language is virtually identical, simply negated.[23] Even if the author of Matthew did not rebut an ancient version of Luke 23:2, he could have attacked the common (not distinctively Marcionite) Christian understanding that Christ destroyed the Law.

---

[18] Bovon, *The Acts of Philip: A New Translation*, ed. François Bovon and Christopher R. Matthews (Baylor University Press, 2012), 42. See further Hans Josef Klauck, *The Apocryphal Acts of the Apostles: An Introduction*, trans. Brian McNeil (Waco: Baylor University Press, 2008), 232–43.

[19] Augustine, *Against Faustus* 19.1.

[20] On this phenomenon, cf. Bart Ehrman, *The Orthodox Corruption of Scripture: The Effect of Early Christological Controversies on the Text of the New Testament* (New York: Oxford, 1993), entire.

[21] As Roth notes, Matt 5:17 "figures prominently in Tertullian's refutation of Marcion." Roth cites references or allusions to the verse in *AM* 1.23.4; 4.2.2; 4.6.4; 4.9.10; 4.22.11; 4.33.9; 4.36.6; 4.39.17; 4.39.19; and 4.42.6 ("Matthean Texts and Tertullian's Accusations in *Adversus Marcionem*," *Journal of Theological Studies* 59 [2008]: 580–97 at 581, n.2).

[22] Epiphanius, *Panarion* 42.11, Elenchus 69.

[23] For an argument that Matthew was affected by proto-Luke (Marcion's Evangelion), see Matthias Klinghardt, "The Marcionite Gospel and the Synoptic Problem: A New Suggestion," *NovT* 50 (2008): 1–27. Hans Dieter Betz queried: "Has the S[ermon on the] M[ount] picked up such a saying ["I came to destroy the Law"] from actual circulation?" (*A Commentary on the Sermon on the Mount, including the Sermon on the Plain (Matthew 5:3–7:27 and Luke 6:20–49)* [Minneapolis: Fortress1995], 175).

Tertullian claimed that Marcion expunged Matthew 5:17.[24] But since Marcion did not recognize Matthew as scripture, he would have no need to remove the verse.[25] Later Marcionites, however, dealt with it squarely. Markus in the *Adamantius* claimed that Jesus actually said, "I came not to fulfill the Law, but to destroy it."[26] The altered sense of the verse at least accorded with some of Jesus's actions in the gospels and the general Marcionite belief that "Christ came . . . and destroyed the Law of the creator."[27]

Claimed Violations

We now attend to what Marcion(ites) took to be Christ's violations of the Law, limiting ourselves to what is attested in the Evangelion.[28] It is important to note, first of all, what the Evangelion did not contain. It did not feature the Lukan infancy narrative. Thus it did not say anything about John the Baptist's father being a priest, the Law-abiding character of Jesus's parents, or his appearance in the temple as a child.[29] All of these traditions did not exist for Marcionites, or—if they knew them—they considered them corrupt additions to the original gospel.

Other omissions were equally significant. In the Evangelion, Jesus went to the synagogue at Nazareth, but he did not preach a sermon about himself

[24] Tertullian, *AM* 4.7.4; 4.9.15; 4.12.14; 5.14.14. Cf. Augustine, *Against Faustus*, 17–19.

[25] Tertullian referred to Matthew as "that gospel which you [Marcion] have not received" (*non . . . recepisti illud . . . evangelium*) (*AM* 4.34.2). Roth proposed that Tertullian referred to Marcion deleting a passage from the fourfold gospel ("Matthean Texts," 593), though Marcion did not recognize the fourfold gospel either.

[26] *Adamantius* 2.15: οὐκ ἦλθον πληρῶσαι τὸν νόμον ἀλλὰ καταλῦσαι.

[27] *Adamantius* 2.10: ὁ ἐλθὼν χριστὸς . . . τὸν νόμον τοῦ δημιουργοῦ κατέλυσεν. Cf. 2.15. Cf. *Adamantius* 15, where Christ "annuls the Law (τὸν νόμον λύει), destroys the punishment and cancels the judgment."

[28] For modern treatments of the Law in canonical Luke, see Robert Banks, *Jesus and the Law in the Synoptic Tradition* (Cambridge: Cambridge University Press, 1975); Klinghardt, *Gesetz*, 16–17, 314–20; Wilson, *Luke and the Law*; Craig L. Blomberg, "The Law in Luke-Acts," *Journal for the Study of the New Testament (JSNT)* 22 (1984): 53–80; K. Salo, *Luke's Treatment of the Law. A Redaction-Critical Investigation* (Helsinki: Suomalainen Tiedeakatemia, 1991), 43–167; William R. G. Loader, *Jesus' Attitude Towards the Law* (Tübingen: Mohr Siebeck, 1997), 273–38; François Bovon, *Studies in Early Christianity* (Grand Rapids: Baker Academic, 2003), 59–73; Dale C. Allison, *Resurrecting Jesus: The Earliest Christian Tradition and Its Interpreters* (London: T&T Clark, 2005), 149–97. For more general discussions, see Karl Kertelge, ed., *Das Gesetz im Neuen Testament* (Freiberg: Herder, 1986); Ingo Broer, ed., *Jesus und das jüdische Gesetz* (Stuttgart: Kohlhammer, 1992).

[29] According to Roth (*Text*, 412), Luke 1:1–2:52 was not present in Marcion's Evangelion. Luke 3:2–20 is indirectly attested as not present, and 3:21–4:13 was not present. Epiphanius (*Panarion* 42.11.4) noted the absence of these passages. Klinghardt explained their significance in light of his theory of the Evangelion's priority over canonical Luke (" 'Gesetz' bei Markion," 99–128 at 111; *Älteste Evangelium II*, 457–64).

fulfilling Isaianic prophecy (Luke 4:16–30). He refused to heal the people of his hometown (citing not Jewish scripture, but a common proverb). The people responded by throwing him—not just out of the synagogue—but almost off a cliff![30]

In a similar episode, the resurrected Jesus met his disciples on the Emmaus road (Evangelion 24:13–31). But he did not give them a speech about how his sufferings were predicted in the Law. He rebuked them only for not paying sufficient attention to the things he had said to them before his death.[31] This text agrees with Christ's multiple predictions of his death (Evangelion 9:22, 44)—where he himself did not appeal to Hebrew prophecy. It also agrees with the angels' announcement to the women at the tomb: "Remember what *he* spoke to you in Galilee"—Jesus, not the Law (Evangelion 24:6).

Lepers

Let's turn to positive evidence wherein Jesus's actions speak louder than words. In Evangelion 5:12, Christ touched and healed a leper out of compassion. In doing so, Marcion, according to Tertullian, believed that Christ destroyed the Law.[32] The Law forbade people from touching lepers or from having any contact with them at all. According to Leviticus 13:45: "As for the leper . . . let his clothes be rags, his head uncovered, his mouth covered; he will call out 'Unclean!'" This ritual of self-isolation ensured that no one besides a priest came close to a leper. Yet even in this case there was probably no touching. By reaching out to touch the leper, Christ acted in open violation of Jewish Law.[33]

After making contact, Jesus told the leper to appear before the priests as a testimony. According to the Evangelion, the testimony was not for the priests, but for the leper.[34] Priests had the duty of pronouncing lepers clean,

---

[30] For the text, see Roth, *Text*, 412–13; Klinghardt, *Älteste Evangelium II*, 464–65.

[31] Roth, *Text*, 435 (24:25: ὦ ἀνόητοι καὶ βραδεῖς τῇ καρδίᾳ τοῦ πιστεύειν ἐπὶ πᾶσιν οἷς ἐλάληθη πρὸς ὑμᾶς). Epiphanius and *Adamantius* both attest the reading ἐλάλησα πρὸς ὑμᾶς (the things "*I* spoke to you"), a reading printed by Klinghardt, *Älteste Evangelium II* 1131.

[32] Tertullian, *AM* 4.9.4.

[33] Naturally, modern scholars debate this point. See, e.g., John Dominic Crossan, *The Historical Jesus: The Life of a Mediterranean Jewish Peasant* (New York: Harper One, 1991), 263; Kazen, *Jesus and Purity*, 98–127; Thiessen, *Jesus and the Forces of Death*, 43–68.

[34] ἵνα ᾖ εἰς μαρτύριον τοῦτο ὑμῖν attested by Epiphanius, *Panarion* 42.11.6 §1. Who the plural ὑμῖν refers to is disputed, but it presumably includes the leper. Cf. Tertullian, *AM* 4.9.10: *ut sit vobis in testimonium*. See further Roth, *Text*, 413; Klinghardt, *Älteste Evangelium II*, 486.

according to Leviticus 13–14. But Christ proclaimed the leper clean without priestly authority (Evangelion 5:13). Thus the "testimony" was, in effect, that Christ violated the Law.[35] The leper went to the priests, the reader intuits, but to reveal that healing could be pronounced and accomplished without their authority.

Similarly, when Jesus healed the ten lepers (Evangelion 17.11–19), he commanded them to show themselves to the priests. According to Marcion(ites), Christ intended to cast scorn upon the Law, for the lepers were healed apart from the Law's regulations.[36] Tertullian himself conceded that Christ, by healing the ten lepers, "transgressed the solemn rites of the Law."[37]

The Bleeding Woman

According to Harnack, Marcion wrote in his *Antitheses*: "The Law forbids the touching of a woman who has an issue of blood; Christ not only touches them but heals them."[38] In the report of Tertullian, it was first the bleeding woman who disobeyed the creator's Law by touching Jesus in a clandestine way (Evangelion 8:42–48). The fact that Jesus readily healed her only reinforced his (later explicit) approval of her action and breach of the creator's Law.

In this case, even if Jesus did not himself reach out his hand, he still involuntarily broke the Law, for "anyone who touches her [a woman with a flow of blood] will be unclean" (Lev 15:19). Yet Jesus was not defiled. He did not return to his home and remain unclean until evening. His purity and healing power showed that he was not under the Law's authority.[39] Jesus approved the woman's faith, a faith that he shared and that, according to Marcion, held the Law in contempt.[40]

---

[35] See further Tertullian, *AM* 4.9.11–1.

[36] Roth, *Text*, 427–28; Klinghardt, *Älteste Evangelium II*, 895.

[37] Tertullian, *AM* 4.35.4: *praevenientem sollemnia legis etiam in curatione decem leprorsorum.*

[38] Harnack, *Marcion*, 62.

[39] Naturally, modern scholarly opinion differs on this point. See, e.g., Marla Selvidge, "Mark 5:25–34 and Leviticus 15:19–20: A Reaction to Restrictive Purity Regulations," *Journal of Biblical Literature (JBL)* 103 (1984): 619–23; Amy-Jill Levine, "Discharging Responsibility: Matthean Jesus, Biblical Law, and Hemorrhaging Woman," in *Treasures New and Old: Contributions to Matthean Studies*, ed. David Bauer and Mark Allan Powell (Atlanta: Scholars Press), 379–97; Kazen, *Jesus and Purity*, 127–64; Cecilia Wassen, "Jesus and the Hemorrhaging Woman in Mark 5:25–34: Insights from Purity Laws from Qumran," in *Scripture in Transition: Essays on Septuagint, Hebrew Bible, and Dead Sea Scrolls in Honour of Raija Sollamo*, ed. Anssi Voitila and Jutta Jokiranta (Leiden: Brill, 2008), 641–60; Thiessen, *Jesus and the Forces of Death*, 69–96.

[40] Tertullian, *AM* 4.20.9–10: *Sed hanc vis mulieris fidem constituere, qua contempserat legem.*

Dead Gravediggers

In the Evangelion 9:60, Christ invited a man to become his disciple. Though the man was willing, he asked first to bury his father. Such was the sacred obligation of the Jews, modeled by the patriarchs (Gen 25:9), and widely considered to be part of the fifth Commandment to honor parents (Exod 20:12).[41] Nevertheless, Christ told the man to follow him despite his father's demise, commenting simply: "Let the dead bury their own dead."[42]

In response to the Marcionite use of this passage, Tertullian stated that Jesus (and apparently others) were free from the obligation to bury parents by virtue of laws applying to high priests and Nazirites.[43] The fact that neither in Luke nor in the Evangelion is Jesus a priest or Nazirite undermines this objection. One scholar has argued that Jesus took a Nazirite vow at the Last Supper.[44] But these vows, even if we accept them, came too late in the story. When Jesus addressed his would-be disciple in Evangelion 9, he not only failed to mention his Nazirite status, but also affronted those people who bury their parents by calling them (metaphorically or spiritually) "dead." Here there is more than a suspicion that Jesus demanded a discipleship that superseded Mosaic regulations.[45]

Marcion(ites) would have agreed with several later interpreters that Jesus annulled the commandment to honor parents by his order to neglect a father's burial.[46] This point is specifically mentioned by Adimantus, Manichean Christian writer of the *Disputations* (late third century CE).[47]

---

[41] Martin Hengel, *The Charismatic Leader and His Followers*, trans. James Greig (New York: Crossroad, 1981), 8. On the requirement to bury, see Tobit 4:3; 6:14; 14:11–12; Jub 23:7; 36:2, 18–19; *m. Berakhot* 3:1a. Holmén notes, "In the Old Testament, being denied burial is pictured as the ultimate punishment and horror" (*Jesus and Jewish Covenant*, 188, citing Deut 28:26; Jer 7:33; 8:1–2; Ezek 6:5; 29:5). See further Thiessen, *Jesus and the Forces of Death*, 97–122.

[42] We know from Clement of Alexandria that Marcionites appealed to this passage (*Stromata* 3.4.25.3).

[43] Tertullian, *AM* 4.23.10–11 (appealing to Lev 21:1; Num 6:6–7).

[44] Markus Bockmuehl, *Jewish Law in Gentile Churches: Halakah and the Beginning of Christian Public Ethics* (Edinburgh: T&T Clark, 2000), 23–48. Bockmuehl writes that "Jesus himself appears to have uttered a Nazirite vow on the eve of his execution" but admits that "This evidence is too weak to support a direct Nazirite setting for Matt 8.22 par." (47). For a critique of Bockmuehl, see Crispin H. T. Fletcher-Louis, "'Leave the Dead to Bury Their Own Dead': Q 9.60 and the Redefinition of the People of God," *JSNT* 26 (2003): 39–68 at 42–48.

[45] See further Allison, *Resurrecting Jesus*, 169–71.

[46] Hengel, *Charismatic*, 13, n.31, 14. Hengel also quoted A. Schlatter: "such sayings [as Luke 9:60] could easily suggest to the disciples the thought that Jesus was abolishing the Law" (14).

[47] Augustine identified Adimantus as Addas, one of Mani's disciples (*Retractions* 1.22.1; *Enemy of the Law* 2.12.41–42). See further Giulea Sfameni Gasparro, "Addas-Adimantus unus ex discipulis Manichaei: For the History of Manichaeism in the West," in *Studia Manichaica IV: Internationaler Kongress zum Manichäismus Berlin 14–18 Juli 1997*, ed. Ronald E. Emmerick et al. (Berlin: Akademie,

Adimantus is important because, since Harnack, scholars have (with good reason) judged that his *Disputations* was a revised version of Marcion's *Antitheses*.[48] Adimantus wrote that the command in Exodus, "Honor your father and mother" (20:12), is contrary to Jesus's command to "let the dead bury the dead."[49] In the latter verse, according to one modern interpreter, Christ "consciously require[d] disobedience of a commandment understood by all Jews to have been given by God."[50]

Related to Evangelion 9:60 is Jesus's saying, "If someone does not leave one's own father and mother and brothers and wife and children . . . such a person is not worthy to be my disciple" (Evangelion 14:26).[51] In this case, we are not dealing with a one-time, situation-based command to follow Christ at a certain place and time. It is presented as a universal rule. Loyalty to Christ supersedes loyalty to family. The fifth commandment demands that one honor one's father and mother. Abandoning father and mother (not to mention wife and children) is presumably not a way to honor them. Here it seemed to Marcion(ites) that Christ annulled the Law—indeed, one of its central pillars.

The Law Until John

In Evangelion 16:16, Jesus, after criticizing the greed of the Pharisees, said that "The Law and the Prophets were until John; from then the kingdom of god is being proclaimed as good news."[52] Here Jesus delimited two eras: the

---

2000); 546–59; Jacob Albert van den Berg, *Biblical Argument in Manichean Missionary Practice: The Case of Adimantus and Augustine* (Leiden: Brill, 2010), 11–48.

[48] Here I adopt the language of BeDuhn, *Frontiers*, 139. BeDuhn cites the German edition of Harnack, *Marcion*, 97, 219, 292, 349–50. See further W. H. C. Frend, "The Gnostic-Manichaean Tradition in Roman North Africa," *Journal of Ecclesiastical History* 4 (1953): 13–26 at 20; van den Berg, *Biblical Argument*, 24–25, 157–58, 218–20 (Adimantus was a former Marcionite). Augustine, *Enemy of the Law* 1.20.43.

[49] Augustine, *Against Adimantus* 6.

[50] E. P. Sanders, *Jesus and Judaism* (London: SCM, 1985), 254. Cf. Holmén, *Jesus*, 198–99.

[51] Attested in Tertullian, *AM* 4.19.12; Epiphanius, *Panarion* 42.11.17; Elenchus 70. Roth (*Text*, 78, n.74) says that it is not clear that Epiphanius drew from Marcion's Evangelion. Cf. Klinghardt, *Älteste Evangelium II*, 843.

[52] Roth (*Text*, 426): ὁ νόμος καὶ οἱ προφῆται ἕως Ἰωάννου (ἐξ or ἀφ') οὗ ἡ βασιλεία τοῦ θεοῦ εὐαγγελίζεται (Klinghardt prints ἀπαγγελίζεται, *Älteste Evangelium II*, 868). Matthew's version of the saying presented a different meaning. Instead of "the Law and the prophets [were] until John," Matthew used a different verb: "for all the prophets and the Law was prophesied until John" (Matt 11:13).

time when the Law was valid, and the time when it became invalid—the ministry of John the Baptist serving as the pivot.

Early patristic writers supported this view. Irenaeus wrote that "Since the Law originated with Moses, it then ceased with John. Christ had come to fulfill it: and so the Law and the Prophets were with them until John."[53] Tertullian also agreed with Marcion that the Law was destroyed (*destrui*) since John's time. There was a moment, then, when "Judaism" ceased, according to Tertullian, and "Christianity" began.[54] The new period of Christianity is characterized by the "cessation of the Law" (*sedatio legis*), its "sunset," or even "destruction" (*occasu*).[55] Other Christians of his time—not just Marcionites—understood Luke 16:16 to mean that "the legal and prophetical antiquities have been abolished."[56]

Yet the following verse in Luke (16:17) seems to contradict the preceding: "It is easier for heaven and earth to pass away than for a single jot of the Law to fall." Significantly, however, Marcion's Evangelion had an alternative and seemingly more logical reading: "It is easier for the heaven and the earth to pass away than for a single jot of *my words* to fall."[57] Tertullian accepted this latter reading without qualm.[58] The reading is consistent with Jesus's statement in Luke 21:33 (attested in the Evangelion): "heaven and earth will pass away, but *my words* will not." In short, Jesus heralded the end of the Law while proclaiming the eternity of his own teachings. Without mincing words, he opposed the temporary Mosaic Law to his own eternal revelation.[59]

[53] Irenaeus, *AH* 4.4.2 (*quoniam igitur a Moyse lex inchoavit, consequenter in Johannem desivit, ad impletionem eius advenerat Christus: et proper hoc lex et prophetae apud eos usque ad Johannem*).

[54] Tertullian, *AM* 5.3.8.

[55] Tertullian, *AM* 4.33.8. According to the *OLD* (*Oxford Latin Dictionary*) (p. 1232), *occasus* can mean "downfall, decline, destruction, ruin." Cf. Tertullian's citation of Luke 16:16 in *AM* 5.8.5.

[56] Tertullian, *On Fasting* 2.2: *abolitis legalibus et propheticis vetustatibus*; cf. 11.6. Tertullian thought that the "burdens" of the Law lasted until John, but the "remedies" (*remedia*) remained (*On Modesty* 6.2–3). Cf. *Acts of Archelaus* 45.7: Mani "would say that 'the law and prophets were until John,' . . . for by the fact his head was cut off it was made manifest that all his predecessors and superiors had been cut off."

[57] Following Roth, *Text*, 426: εὐκοπώτερον . . . τὸν οὐρανὸν καὶ τὴν γῆν παρελθεῖν ἢ τῶν λόγων μου μίαν κεραίαν παρελθεῖν. Cf. Klinghardt: ταχύτερον ἢ μία κεραία τῶν λόγων τοῦ κυρίου (*Älteste Evangelium II*, 868).

[58] Tertullian, *AM* 4.33.9.

[59] For modern interpretations of Luke 16:16, see Hans Conzelmann, *The Theology of St Luke*, trans. Geoffrey Buswell (New York: Harper & Brothers, 1960), 12–17, 20–27, 101, 112; W. G. Kummel, "Das Gesetz und die Propheten gehen bis Johannes'—Lukas 16,16 im Zusammenhang der heilgeschichtlichen Theologie der Lukasschriften," in *Verborum Veritas: Festschrift für Gustav Stählin zum 70. Geburtstag*, ed. Otto Böcher and Klaus Haacker (Wuppertal: Rolf Brockhaus, 1972), 89–102; Wilson, *Luke and the Law*, 43–51; Allison, *Resurrecting Jesus*, 173.

Sabbath Violations

Perhaps the crowning violation of Jesus was his reputed failure to keep the Sabbath. According to Raymond E. Brown, "That Jesus violated the rules of the scribes for the observance of the Sabbath is one of the most certain of historical facts about his ministry."[60] It was part of Marcion's *Antitheses*, at any rate, that "the creator of the world ordained the Sabbath, but Christ banishes it."[61] In the late fourth century CE, bishop Faustus of Milevis presented the theological background for Sabbath keeping:

> Moses above all teaches that one should abstain from all work on the Sabbath, and he claims that the reason for this observance is that, when god made the world and everything in it, he devoted six days to work, but stopped on the seventh, which is the Sabbath. Consequently he blessed it, that is, made it holy, as the haven of his tranquility, and issued a law that anyone who violated it should be put to death. (Exod 20:8–11; 31:13–15)[62]

The bishop knew that Sabbath law was not just part of the Ten Commandments, spoken by the Jewish deity (Exod 20:8–11); it was the law of creation, built into the cosmos by the creator himself. Sabbath law was, as it were, the script of nature, and it was performed as a precedent by the creator (Gen 2:3).[63] To violate the Sabbath, therefore, had direct implications for one's attitude toward the creator.

The Evangelion attested three of Jesus's Sabbath violations, two of which are shared with the gospels called Mark and Matthew. The shared episodes are plucking grain (Evangelion 6:1–5//Mark 2:23–28//Matt 12:1–8), and the man with a shriveled hand (Evangelion 6:6–11//Mark 3:1–6//Matt 12:9–14). The Evangelion had another violation story: the crippled woman in the synagogue (13:10–17). It may also have included the story of the man healed from dropsy (Luke 14:1–6), though it is unattested.

We begin with the grain rubbing episode. In Evangelion 6:1–2, Jesus's disciples pick and rub heads of grain on the Sabbath. Some of the Pharisees inform them that this act is unlawful, since it is a form of harvesting, an act that

---

[60] Brown, *Gospel According to John*, 2 vols. (Garden City: Doubleday, 1966), 1:210. Cf. Yong-Eui Yang, *Jesus and the Sabbath in Matthew's Gospel* (Sheffield: Sheffield Academic, 1997). For a different view, see Thiessen, *Jesus and the Forces of Death*, 149–78.

[61] Harnack, *Marcion*, 62.

[62] Augustine, *Against Faustus* 16.6.

[63] For the connection of Sabbath and creation, see Aristobulus, frag. 5 (*OTP* 2.841–42).

was not permitted on the Sabbath.[64] The Pharisees were not just nitpickers. Both Irenaeus and Tertullian agreed that the act of harvesting performed in these verses was unlawful.[65] There was, moreover, no life-threatening need for the disciples to pluck the grain since, despite their hunger, they were in no danger of starvation.

Yet Jesus stoked the rhetorical fire. He justified his disciples based on the example of David, who took—one might say stole—prohibited bread from the creator's tent shrine (1 Sam 21:1–6). (For Marcionites, Christ's appeal to this story did not indicate that he accepted Jewish scripture as divine truth. Christ used it, like Marcion, as an illustration, authoritative for his enemies and thus useful in debate.)

Yet Jesus did not stop there. To ground his allowance of Sabbath violation, he presumed to call himself "Lord of the Sabbath."[66] Tertullian confessed that this claim put Christ in apparent conflict with the Law.[67] Christ as Lord of the Sabbath was also "destroyer of the Sabbath" (*sabbati destructor*).[68] Epiphanius concluded from the harvesting episode that "the Sabbath was abolished."[69] Eznik of Kolb concluded that Christ, "like a lord of the Law, put a stop to the Law."[70] Several modern interpreters follow this line of interpretation. S. G. Wilson, for instance, wrote that, "As lord of the sabbath he [Christ] stands above the law."[71]

Christ proclaiming himself lord of the Sabbath not only made him lord of the Law, but also lord over creation. He was lord *over* creation, not *of* it, since Christ evidently did not agree with the script of creation established by the creator. The Sabbath was written into nature and kept by the creator, but Christ annulled it. He defended the violation of the Sabbath on his own personal status as superior to the creator's ordinance.

---

[64] Exod 34:21: "on the seventh day you shall rest . . . in harvest you shall rest." Cf. Philo: "it is not permitted [on the Sabbath] to cut any shoot or branch, or even a leaf, or to pluck any fruit whatsoever" (*Life of Moses* 2.22).

[65] Irenaeus, *AH* 4.8.3; Tertullian, *AM* 4.12.5.

[66] Tertullian, *AM* 4.12.11; Irenaeus's claim that David was a priest is inaccurate (*AH* 4.8.3).

[67] Tertullian, *AM* 4.12.1: the question concerning Sabbath violation, "could have no substance if Christ had not proclaimed himself lord of the Sabbath."

[68] Tertullian, *Spectacles* 30.

[69] Epiphanius, *Panarion* 30.32.3.

[70] Eznik, *On God*, 392 (trans. Blanchard and Young).

[71] Wilson, *Luke and the Law*, 33, citing Bank, *Law*, 121–22. Later Wilson adds: "the sabbath institution as such is subordinated to its lord, the Son of Man. Taken to its logical conclusion this Christological claim mounts a fundamental challenge to the sabbath and ultimately to the law itself" (39). For a counterpoint, see Joseph A. Fitzmyer, *Luke the Theologian: Aspects of His Teaching* (New York: Paulist Press, 1989), 183–85.

Jesus did not only defend the Sabbath violation of others; he also transgressed it himself. He performed two Sabbath healings in synagogues before the astounded eyes of Jewish leaders. The first was a man with a shriveled hand (6:6–11); the second was a crippled woman (13:10–16). Both individuals did not need to be healed on the Sabbath since their conditions were not lethal. In spite of this, Jesus publicly healed them in Jewish religious spaces. In each case, Jesus ignited a conflict, first by asking provokingly whether one can do good on the Sabbath (6:9), and secondly by calling his opponents hypocrites because on that day they untie farm animals (13:15).[72]

The creator, at least as portrayed in Jewish scripture, was hostile to any Sabbath breaker. Setting a precedent, Yahweh condemned a man to death for collecting sticks on a Saturday morning (Num 15:32–34). Adimantus, possibly dependent on Marcion's *Antitheses*, believed that this story of execution contradicted the spirit and action of Jesus, who healed the man with a shriveled hand.[73]

To be sure, there is no explicit law against healing on the Sabbath—only against work.[74] But the Sabbath disputes hinged on the idea that Jesus's healings were a form of labor. The synagogue leader in Evangelion 13:14 declared, "There are six days in which one must *work*; come on these days to be *healed* and not on the Sabbath day" (emphasis added).

The Jesus of the gospels never disagreed that his healings were a form of work.[75] He even agreed with the charge of illegality in the grain rubbing episode. The disciples did something "unlawful" on the Sabbath and were justified because David also did something "unlawful" (Luke 6:2, 4). The repetition of "unlawful," and the fact that it is precisely the element of illegality that binds the two (otherwise different) incidents together, indicates that Jesus made no attempt to evade the charge that he worked on the Sabbath and that he approved of such transgression when others performed it.[76]

---

[72] Roth, *Text*, 414, 425; Klinghardt, *Älteste Evangelium II*, 519, 813. See further Allison, *Resurrecting Jesus*, 173. According to Lutz Doering, *Schabbat: Sabbathalacha und -praxis im antiken Judentum und Urchristentum* (Tübingen: Mohr Siebeck, 1999), 446: "healing on the Sabbath in the eyes of his opponents represented a *breaking of Sabbath Law*" (*Heilen am Sabbat in den Augen seiner Gegenspieler einen Sabbatbruch darstellt*, emphasis his).

[73] Augustine, *Against Adimantus* 22; cf. *Acts of Archelaus* 44.9–10 (which also mentions the disciples plucking grain on the Sabbath).

[74] A point made by Irenaeus, *AH* 4.8.2.

[75] In John, Jesus implicitly treats healing as a form of work. He publicly heals a paralytic on the Sabbath. When he is accused of Sabbath violation, he declares: "I am working and my father is working" (John 5:17). Here Jesus's "father" is evidently different than the Jewish god since Yahweh observed the Sabbath (Gen 2:2; Jub 2:18; *Gen. Rabb.* 7.5; 11.5, 9).

[76] Wilson, *Luke and the Law*, 33; Holmén, *Jesus*, 101–2; David B. Gowler, *Host, Guest, Enemy and Friend: Portraits of the Pharisees in Luke and Acts* (New York: Peter Lang, 1991), 207–8; Allison,

For Marcion(ites), this was not merely an issue of interpreting the Law differently. The Evangelion nowhere made the distinction between Law and human tradition as is found in Mark 7:1–2; 10:2–3. The Jesus of the Evangelion (the only Jesus Marcionites held as authoritative) knew exactly what would be offensive to Jewish Law observers and performed it based on his own personal authority.[77]

Christ Against the Law(giver)

Heresiologists underscored the (solely Matthean) tradition that Christ came to fulfill the Law (Matt 5:17), but as R. Hakola has commented, "It is not likely that any Jew would have understood how one can fulfil the purpose of the law by acting deliberately against one of its principal commandments"—here referring to sabbath keeping.[78] In context, Hakola quoted the famous scholar of ancient Judaism, E. P. Sanders: "obedience to the Torah is the condition for retaining the covenant promises; intentional and unrepenting disobedience implies rejection of the law, rejection of the covenant for which it is the condition, and rejection of the God who gave the law."[79]

Here Sanders—no Marcionite to be sure—put his finger on something Marcion and his followers saw in the second century. Repeated repudiation of the Law implied rejection of the god who gave it. But Jesus would only have rejected the Lawgiver if this Lawgiver was not good. Thus if Jesus rejected the Law, then, so Marcion(ites), he did not confirm the goodness of the god who gave the Law.

As we saw in the last chapter, Marcionite Christians made an even stronger point: undermining the Law meant undermining the Law giver. If Jesus was hostile to the Law of the creator, then he was hostile to the creator. For the one who gave teaching contrary to the Law is, as Tertullian voiced the Marcionite

---

Resurrecting Jesus, 167. The Mishnah equates practicing medicine with work (*m. Sabb.* 14:3–4). See further Robert Doldenberg, "The Jewish Sabbath in the Roman World," *ANRW* II.19.1, ed. Wolfgang Haase (Berlin: de Gruyter, 1979), 414–47 at 430–34.

[77] See further Allison, *Resurrecting Jesus,* 168.

[78] Hakola, *Identity,* 129–30.

[79] Quoted in Hakola, *Identity,* 130. Holmén concluded that Jesus "did not take part in the activity integral to the covenant thinking of his time which aimed at learning how to keep the covenant" (*Jesus,* 333). For similar opinions, see Berndt Schaller, *Jesus und der Sabbat: Franz-Delitzsch-Vorlesung 1992* (Münster: Delitzsch Judaic Institute, 1994), 126–27.

inference, "contrary to the creator."[80] If Christ was the destroyer of the Law, he was "destroyer of the creator."[81]

The inference may seem extreme today, but its basis was taken to be Jewish and Christian scripture. The Law is the Law of the creator. Attacks on the Law, therefore, are not simple transgressions, but acts of sacrilege against the creator. The author of Acts, for instance, makes a connection between blaspheming the Law and blaspheming god. Jewish opponents accuse Stephen of saying blasphemous words "against Moses [i.e., the Law], and against god" (Acts 6:11).[82] To say words against the creator's Law was in effect to speak against the Judean "god."

The Law Killed Christ

What decisively showed the wickedness of the Lawgiver was that Jesus died under his regulations. Historically, it seems, Jesus was put to death for sedition against Rome. According to the Evangelion, however, he was arrested and executed for destroying the Law (23:2). The culmination of Christ's Law-destroying activity was his blasphemy against the creator.[83]

In Jesus's trial, the high priest asked him if he considered himself to be god's son. Jesus was initially evasive: "If I tell you, you won't believe" (Evangelion 22:67). Nonetheless, he went on to state that he, in his capacity as the heavenly redeemer, would rule from a throne at god's right hand (22:69). The high priest needed no additional testimony. He rent his robe and declared Jesus a blasphemer (v.71).

Jesus, as every Christian knew, was god's child. Yet Jesus as god's child could not—so Marcion—be the child of the creator, for he consistently, and seemingly intentionally, transgressed the creator's laws. Internal to the text, Jesus's actions were interpreted to be an insult to the creator and his Law. The fictional Jews in Jesus's trial believed that he could not be the son of their god. Marcion(ites) inferred that he was the son of another, true deity. In either

---

[80] Tertullian, *AM* 4.7.8: *adversus legem . . . et hoc nomine adversus creatorem.*

[81] Tertullian, *AM* 4.8.7: *destructor creatoris.*

[82] For "Moses" as a reference to Jewish Law, see Klinghardt, *Gesetz*, 121–23.

[83] See further Tobias Nicklas, "'Du bist nur ein Mensch und machst dich selbst zu Gott' (Johannes 10,33): Das Motiv der Gotteslästerung bei Johannes vor dem Hintergrund der Synoptiker," in *Studies in the Gospel of John and its Christology: Festschrift Gilbert van Belle*, ed. Joseph Verheyden et al. (Leuven: Peeters, 2014), 239–56; Darrell L. Bock, "Jesus as Blasphemer," in *Who Do My Opponents*, 76–94.

reading, Christ committed blasphemy against the creator by admitting that he was, as it were, a deity himself.

Tertullian was willing to admit that Jesus destroyed "Judaism," thereby provoking the Jews to kill him by their law (*suo iure*).[84] A later church father wrote that according to Marcion, Jesus "was found worthy of death many times over by those laws" since he was curtailing and obstructing Jewish Law.[85] The Law commanded that "Every Jew who breaks the Law" be killed—in particular Sabbath breakers. Thus by the Law, Jesus was "worthy of death."[86] But if the Law of the creator could kill the innocent Christ, could the Law be good? And if it was not good, how could its creator be good?

The Creator Killed Christ

Instead of blaming the Jews for killing Christ, Marcion(ites) ultimately accused the creator. In the words of Megethius, "The creator, having seen the good [Christ] dissolving his Law, conspired against him." Yet the creator not only conspired, he ordained by law—namely his own Law—that Christ be crucified.[87]

The Lawgiver had a motive for killing Christ, for Christ undermined the creator by dissolving his Law. This destruction of the Law is the charge that the Jews brought to Pilate (Evangelion 23:2)—but Pilate himself cared not a fig for Jewish Law. The one chiefly offended by Jesus's blasphemy was not the Roman establishment, but the lord of this world, the creator. The Jewish plot to kill Christ was only a reflection, so Marcion, of the creator's machinations against the child of the true deity.

In brief: for Marcion(ites), Christ was attacked and killed by the one most threatened by him. This was neither the Romans nor the Jews, but the Jewish lord. The creator was threatened by Christ because Christ was destroying his Law. As a result, the creator attempted to destroy Christ by a "lawful" execution. Jesus died as a violator of the Law and received the punishment mandated for blasphemers.

---

[84] Tertullian, *AM* 3.7.10.

[85] Eznik, *On God*, 387 (trans. Blanchard and Young).

[86] Eznik, *On God*, 389 (trans. Blanchard and Young).

[87] *Adamantius* 2.9. Tertullian also assumed that the creator, in the Marcionite conception, fixed Christ to the cross (*in cruce eum figere*, *AM* 5.6.7). Manicheans asked: "If he [Adonai, the Jewish deity] is the Lord of all, why did he crucify his own son?" (Hans-Joachim Klimkeit, *Gnosis on the Silk Road: Gnostic Texts from Central Asia* [New York: HarperSanFrancisco, 1993], 127).

Christ died according to the Law because he broke it. But the judgment Christ experienced exposed the Law's falsity—along with the falsity and cruelty of the one who gave it. Christ was innocent, as every Christian confessed. Therefore his crucifixion in accordance with the Law showed once and for all that the Law was corrupt, as was the one who gave it.

Conclusion

From a Jewish perspective, Christianity could be depicted as a kind of mass idolatry because it involved the worship of a human being, a being distinct from the creator known from Jewish scripture. Marcionites who worshiped Jesus hardly considered themselves to be idolaters. But they took seriously the Jewish viewpoint that Christ's claim to be divine undermined a core teaching of the Law and ignited the jealousy of the creator. The fictional Jews were fulfilling the regulations of Torah when they pushed for the execution of a Law breaker. They were doing the will of their deity, at least as they perceived it.

Jesus worked to destroy the Law, and the Law ended up by destroying him. But the Law was only the instrument of the Lawgiver. One had only to assume that the Law represented the will of the Lawgiver (a basic Jewish and Christian assumption). If, according to the Law, Jesus had to die, then Jesus's death was the will of the Lawgiver. So it was ultimately the creator, according to Marcionites, who fixed Christ to the cross.[88] Christ's death at the hands of the creator proved decisively that the creator could not be the father of Jesus Christ, and furthermore, that the creator who opposed Christ—scheming to crucify him—was not good and in fact nothing short of evil.

---

[88] Tertullian's discussion assumed this point: *nec in cruce eum figere* ("he [the creator] did not fix him to the cross . . . ") (*AM* 5.6.7). Cf. *AM* 3.23.7, where the creator is said to be going to kill Christ (*interempturus*).

7

The Curse of the Creator

Jesus conformed to the terms of the creator's law in order to "purchase" mankind from sin and death, so Christ becomes the victim of the creator's curse.

—J. Christiaan Beker[1]

Introduction

Our final chapter focuses on the Marcionite reception of Galatians 3:13—itself an interpretation of Deuteronomy 21:23 ("every person hung on a tree is cursed by god"). The latter verse was widely taken to mean that the Judean deity cursed the victims of crucifixion. This interpretation gave grounds for perceived Jewish charges against Jesus. In the early second century CE, Marcion adapted these charges in the service of his anti-creator reading. His interpretive trajectory was opposed by patristic writers who attempted to undercut, by various strategies, the creator's curse against Christ. Manichean Christians continued the Marcionite line of interpretation and to a certain extent allow us to look back, as through a mirror, onto their Marcionite predecessors.

The Pauline Context

We begin by translating Galatians 3:10–13 from Marcion's Apostolikon. Since sizable chunks of Galatians 3 were absent from this version of the letter, verse 13 was brought into further relief:[2]

---

[1] J. Christiaan Beker, "Christologies and Anthropologies of Paul, Luke-Acts and Marcion," in *From Jesus to John: Essays on Jesus and New Testament Christology in Honour of Marinus de Jonge*, ed. Martinus C. de Boer (Sheffield: Sheffield Academic Press, 1993), 174–82 at 180.

[2] According to Schmid (*Marcion*, 316), Gal 3:6–9, 14a, 15–18, and 19 were absent.

The Evil Creator. M. David Litwa, Oxford University Press. © Oxford University Press 2021.
DOI: 10.1093/oso/9780197566428.003.0009

For as many as are under Law are under a curse, since the righteous person will live from faith. The one who does them shall live by them. Christ purchased us from the curse of the Law by becoming a curse on our behalf: "Accursed is everyone hung upon a tree." (Deut 21:23)[3]

Paul's source text (Deut 21:23) records that every person hanging on a tree is cursed by god (*hupo theou*).[4] The perfect tense of the verb "to curse" (*kekatēramenos*) expresses the completeness and continuance of the curse. Paul replaced this word with the adjective *epikataratos*, "accursed"—perhaps taken from Deuteronomy 27:26.

Paul omitted the words "by god." Possibly this change was unintentional, since Deuteronomy 27:26 left the agent of cursing unmentioned. It is conceivable, however, that Paul already wanted to avoid the thought that the Jewish deity cursed his own son on the cross.[5] Whatever the case may have been, Paul's omission of "by god" is important because a reader unfamiliar with Deuteronomy 21:23 would not conclude from Galatians 3:13 that Christ was cursed by the creator. Only someone independently familiar with Deuteronomy 21:23 could arrive at this conclusion.

Those independently familiar with this verse were the traditional caretakers of Jewish scripture, the Jews. Around the turn of the fifth century CE, Jerome complained that "the Jews, to disgrace us [Christians], customarily raise the objection that our Lord and Savior became a curse at the hands of god (*sub dei*)."[6] This was not a debate that started in Jerome's time. The same charge was made around 160 CE by the Jewish interlocuter in Justin's *Dialogue with Trypho*.[7]

---

[3] Schmid, *Marcion*, 316: ὅσοι γὰρ ὑπὸ νόμον (εἰσίν), ὑπὸ κατάραν εἰσίν ὅτι ὁ δίκαιος ἐκ πίστεως ζήσεται, (ἀλλὰ) ὁ ποιήσας αὐτὰ ζήσεται ἐν αὐτοῖς. Χριστὸς . . . γενόμενος ὑπὲρ ἡμῶν κατάρα (ὅτι γέγραπται) ἐπὶ κατάρατος πᾶς ὁ κρεμάμενος ἐπὶ ξύλου. Cf. BeDuhn, *First New Testament*, 231, 264–65.

[4] Some MSS read "by *the* god" (τοῦ θεοῦ) with definite article or "by the lord" (κυρίου)—κύριος being the standard substitution for Yahweh (John William Wevers, ed., *Genesis* [Göttingen: Vandenhoeck & Ruprecht, 1974], 249).

[5] So Gert Jeremias, *Der Lehrer der Gerechtigkeit* (Göttingen: Vandenhoeck & Ruprecht, 1963), 133–34; F. F. Bruce, *The Epistle to the Galatians: A Commentary on the Greek Text* (Grand Rapids: Eerdmans, 1982),165; Pate, *Reverse*, 215. Note also Stanley, "Under a Curse," 505, n.64. In the post-LXX Greek translations of the Hebrew text of Deut 21:23, god is also disassociated from the curse. See the versions quoted by Jerome, *Commentary on Galatians 2* on 3:13b.

[6] Jerome, *Commentary on Galatians 2* on 3:13b–14.

[7] Justin, *Dialogue with Trypho* 32.1: "Your so-called Messiah became dishonored and robbed of glory to such an extent that he fell headlong under the most extreme curse in god's Law (τῇ ἐσχάτῃ κατάρᾳ τῇ ἐν τῷ νόμῳ τοῦ θεοῦ)—for he was crucified."

In fact, some scholars believe that Paul himself, when he first opposed Christians, opposed them for worshiping a crucified—and thus cursed—Messiah.[8] These developments suggest that the creator's curse against Christ was originally—at least perceived to be—a first-century Jewish charge supported by Deuteronomy 21:23.[9] The *Didascalia* (an early third-century Christian document probably originating in Syria) even claims that Deuteronomy 21:23 was added to scripture in a deliberate attempt to blind the Jews by making them believe that their deity cursed Jesus on the cross.[10]

Cursing

What, in second-century Christianity, did it mean to curse? In its most basic sense, to curse meant to wish evil or harm on another person or thing.[11] When the agent of a curse was a deity, the harm inflicted was often permanent. In this case, "to curse" meant "to damn."[12] For the creator in particular,

---

[8] P. Feine, *Das gesetzesfreie Evangelium des Paulus* (Leipzig: J. C. Hinrichs, 1899), 18. See further A. J. Hultgren, "Paul's Pre-Christian Persecutions of the Church: Their Purpose, Locale, and Nature," *Journal of Biblical Literature (JBL)* 95 (1976): 97–111 at 102–4; Seyoon Kim, *The Origin of Paul's Gospel* (Tübingen: Mohr Siebeck, 1981), 46–48; Räisänen, *Paul and the Law*, 249; Mark A. Seifrid, *Justification by Faith: The Origin and Development of a Central Pauline Theme* (Leiden: Brill, 1992), 164–65; Pate, *Reverse*, 150–52.

[9] See Jeremias, *Lehrer*, 134–35; Barnabas Lindars, *New Testament Apologetic: The Doctrinal Significance of the Old Testament Quotations* (London: SCM Press, 1973), 232–37; Heinz-Wolfgang Kuhn, "The Impact of Selected Qumran Texts on the Understanding of Pauline Theology," in *The Bible and the Dead Sea Scrolls Volume Three: The Scrolls and Christian Origins*, ed. James H. Charlesworth (Waco: Baylor University Press, 2006), 153–86 at 173–74; Florentino García Martínez, "Galatians 3:10–14 in the Light of Qumran," in *The Dead Sea Scrolls and Pauline Literature*, ed. Jean-Sébastian Rey (Leiden: Brill, 2014), 51–67 at 56–60; David W. Chapman, *Ancient Jewish and Christian Perceptions of Crucifixion* (Tübingen: Mohr Siebeck, 2008), 241–52. For a different view, see Kelli S. O'Brien, "The Curse of the Law (Galatians 3.13): Crucifixion, Persecution, and Deuteronomy 21.22–23," *Journal for the Study of the New Testament (JSNT)* 29 (2006): 55–76.

[10] R. Hugh Connolly, *Didascalia apostolorum: The Syriac Version Translated and Accompanied by the Verona Latin Fragments* (Oxford: Clarendon, 1969), 222, 230, 233 (comments on lx–lxi). It is significant that in the *Acts of Pilate* 16:7, Deut 21:23 is put in the mouth of the Jewish teachers (J. K. Elliott, *The Apocryphal New Testament* [Oxford: Clarendon, 1993], 184). Herod the Jew is also the one who quotes Deut 21:23 in *Gospel of Peter* 2:5 (ibid., 154).

[11] For cursing in antiquity, see Werner Riess, *Performing Interpersonal Violence: Court, Curse, and Comedy in Fourth-century BCE Athens* (Berlin: de Gruyter, 2012); Dan Levene, *Jewish-Aramaic Curse Texts from Late Antique Mesopotamia* (Leiden: Brill, 2004); Daniela Urbanová and Natalia Gachallová, *Latin Curse Tablets of the Roman Empire* (Innsbruck: Innsbruck University Press, 2018).

[12] Matt 25:41 (κατηραμένοι, spoken of the damned on the Day of Judgment); Job 3:5 (καταραθείη, Job curses—wishing to annihilate—the day of his birth); 4 Kings 9:34 (κατηραμένην, of the dead Jezebel eaten by dogs); Num 22:6 (ἄρασαι, Balak's intended curse of annihilation against Israel). Cf. Origen, *Homily 17 on Numbers*: "the one who curses Christ . . . is damned by an everlasting curse" (PG 12.711d, *qui maledicit Christo . . . perpetua maledictione damnatus est*); Augustine, *Ennarations on Psalms* 108.20: "a curse, by which I mean eternal punishment" (*maledictionem, hoc est poenam aeternam*).

speech results in action (as we learn from the "Let there be" refrain in Genesis 1). Thus when the creator pronounced his curse over the serpent, the ground, and Cain in Jewish scripture (Gen 3:14–19; 4:11–12), it took immediate effect—the snake ate dust, the ground bore thorns and thistles, and Cain trembled upon the earth.

In Galatians 3:13, Paul spoke of the "curse of the Law." Yet the Law was given by the Jewish deity, as Paul knew.[13] Paul's comments about the Torah thus raise the question, "if the Law itself brings a curse, what does this say about the Lawgiver?"[14] To adapt the question of the *Testimony of Truth*: "What kind of god is this?"[15] He curses people in and after a harsh method of execution. He commands that their bodies be taken down before sunset. Yet he does so not out of mercy, but because his land would otherwise be defiled (Deut 21:23).[16]

Perhaps, as Paul described, Christ assumed the curse for Christians as an act of interchange.[17] Yet the positive result of assuming the curse did not exculpate the one who inflicted it. The divine character, in other words, is not justified by its salvific result. The curse stands, and Paul never denied its reality. In fact, he accentuated it: Christ *became* (*genomenos*) a curse at the hands of god. The creator's act of cursing Jesus—whatever its results—communicated something about his character.

God Does Not Curse

As underscored in the Introduction to Part II, a popular philosophical principle of Marcion's time was that god could only be and thus do good. A god who inflicted harm—especially the harm of cursing—could not be good and therefore could not be god.

---

[13] Rom 7:22; 8:7; 1 Cor 9:9, 21; Gal 3:21.

[14] Richard N. Longenecker comments: "of course, 'the curse of the law' is another way of saying 'cursed by God' " (*Galatians*, Word Biblical Commentary 41 [Columbia: Word, 1990], 122). Similarly, Seifrid: "Paul's citation of Deut 21:23 . . . carries the implication that God himself—not merely the Law— pronounced the curse on the crucified" (*Justification*, 168).

[15] *Testimony of Truth* (NHC IX,3) 47.15.

[16] 11QTemple 64.10–11 is the only Jewish text to interpret Deut 21:22–23 to mean that the crucified person is also cursed: "those hanged on the tree are cursed of god (מקוללי אלוהים) and men." The meaning of this phrase, according to James L. Kugel, is: "it is [only] the accursed by God who is to be hanged" (*Traditions of the Bible*, 873). See further Martin Hengel, *Crucifixion in the Ancient World and the Folly of the Message of the Cross* (Philadelphia: Fortress, 1989), 84–85.

[17] For interchange, see Morna Hooker, *From Adam to Christ: Essays on Paul* (Cambridge: Cambridge University Press, 1990).

Understandably, then, the Jewish philosopher Philo (about 20 BCE–45 CE) soft-pedaled divine cursing. The scriptural passages in which the creator inflicted a curse Philo either avoided or transformed by allegorical interpretation.[18] Yet what would a Gentile Christian do with these same passages—a Christian who held Philo's philosophical presuppositions while shunning his allegorical impulse? There are many possibilities, of course, but one logical chain of inference has already been presented: If the creator cursed Jesus on the cross (Gal 3:13), then he could not be good. If the creator was not good, then he could not be god.

Marcion

Such, I think, was the conclusion made by Marcion and his followers. Admittedly, we do not know exactly how Marcion arrived at this conclusion. But Galatians 3:13—or more broadly the notion that the Jewish deity cursed Jesus—seemed to have played a significant role.

Galatians 3:13 was probably one of the texts showcased in Marcion's *Antitheses*.[19] If so, Marcion would likely have contrasted it with Christ, who was accustomed to bless— possibly with an extra appeal to the command in Romans 12:14, "Bless and do not curse." Tertullian acknowledged that in the Sermon on the Mount, Jesus forbade people from speaking curses against their neighbors (Matt 5:22). Even if a Christian had cause to curse—such as extreme injury—the act was utterly prohibited.[20]

Tertullian reported Marcion's view that Christ "received in himself the creator's curse by being hung from a tree."[21] Here it is specifically the *creator's* curse.[22] The words are Tertullian's, but in this case they accurately convey a Marcionite emphasis. The curse of the crucified was inflicted *by the creator*,

---

[18] For instance, Philo quotes Deut 21:23 in *Posterity of Cain* 26 (including the ὑπὸ θεοῦ phrase) but interpreted it to mean that the life of the evildoer "hangs" on the body (cf. § 61; *On Dreams* 2.213). Philo expositiod Deut 21:23 in *Special Laws* 3.151–52 but did not mention the curse. The only place to my knowledge where he acknowledged that god cursed is in his account of Cain (*Rewards and Punishments* 72, ἀρὰν ἐπηράσατο τῷ ἀδελφοκτόνῳ). See further Chapman, *Crucifixion*, 133–35, 186–88.

[19] Harnack, *Marcion*, 61–62. See the sources cited in the German edition, 288, 307.

[20] Tertullian, *On the Shows* 16: *deus etiam cum causa maledicere non sinit* ("god does not permit cursing even with just cause").

[21] Tertullian, *AM* 1.11.8. Tertullian preferred the language of *crucis maledicto* ("the curse of the cross") (*AM* 4.21.11).

[22] Cf. Tertullian, *AM* 5.3.10: *a creatore iam tunc in lege maledictus* ("in the Law Christ is now cursed by the creator").

for it is his Law that announced the curse (Deut 21:23), and—as already seen in Chapter 4 and 6—the creator plotted to put Christ on the cross.

For Marcion, a god who curses is *atrox*, a Latin word that can mean "savage," "harsh," "cruel," "fierce," "dreadful," "shocking," "heinous," "ruthless," "inflexible," or "unrelenting."[23] Jerome said that Marcion, based on Galatians 3:13, called the creator "a bloodthirsty, cruel judge."[24] A god who is savage and cruel could be just in name only. An unjust and savage deity could not be the god of Jesus Christ.[25] The fact that Jesus was cursed by the creator indicated to Marcion that the Law was opposed to Jesus, and that Jesus belonged to a higher deity incapable of cursing.[26] From this data, we can retrace the Marcionite logic. Galatians 3:13 indicated: (1) that the Jewish creator was savage in character, therefore (2) not good, and accordingly (3) not (the true) god.

These points were distinct from prior Jewish criticisms of Jesus based on Deuteronomy 21:23 for two reasons. First, the Marcionite criticisms were based on a reading of Galatians 3:13 and not independently on Deuteronomy 21:23. Second, they sought to discredit not the cursed Christ of the Christians, but the *author* of the curse—the creator imagined by some Christians (wrongly, according to Marcionites) to be Jesus's divine father.

The Marcionite debate concerning Galatians 3:13, in other words, was an intra-Christian one about the nature and character of deity.[27] The Marcionites who inferred an evil creator from Galatians 3:13 had a persuasive goal: to convince their fellow Christians that the true deity was not and could not be the creator who cursed Christ on the cross.

Justin Martyr

Writing in the wake of Marcion, Justin Martyr (died around 165 CE) denied that the crucified Jesus was cursed. He presented Trypho, a Jew in a fictional

---

[23] Tertullian, *AM* 5.3.9–10. See *OLD*, s.v. *atrox*.

[24] Jerome, *Commentary on Galatians* 2 at 3:13a (*sanguinarium, crudelem . . . iudicem*). Jerome's witness is important because it selectively reproduces Origen's commentary on Galatians. Harnack (*Der kirchengeschichtliche Ertrag der exegetischen Arbeiten des Origenes*, 2 vols. [Leipzig: Hinrichs, 1918–1919], 149) identified this very passage as deriving from Origen.

[25] Philosophically speaking, gods only bless whereas demons curse (Origen, *Homilies on Numbers* 13.4.6).

[26] Tertullian, *AM* 5.3.9–10, cf. 3.18.1.

[27] Lieu, *Marcion*, 356.

debate, as saying that Jesus "fell headlong under the most extreme curse in the Law of god—for he was crucified."[28] Justin waited nearly fifty chapters of his *Dialogue with Trypho* to answer this objection; when he did so, however, he offered a full defense.[29]

First, Justin avoided restating Paul's view that Christ "became" a curse.[30] Only in passing did Justin speak of Jesus "receiving" a curse.[31] In the main, Justin dealt with the curse by undercutting it: the curse was only "seeming," and Jesus was only "supposedly cursed."[32]

In making these points, Justin was keen to defend the creator's innocence. As in Plato's *Republic*, the true god is blameless of wrongdoing.[33] The creator willed Christ to receive the curses meant for all people.[34] He prophesied Jesus's death in symbols.[35] These prior signs indicated that Christ was not actually cursed.[36] Justin concluded: "the passage spoken in the Law, 'Cursed is every person hanging upon a tree,' does not indicate that god cursed this crucified one."[37]

Justin's quote, however, was selective. Deuteronomy 21:23 says that the crucified is "cursed by god,"[38] and Justin's mention of "god's curse" shows that he was well aware of this reading.[39] The fact that the Christian Messiah was cursed "by god" was certainly not lost upon Trypho, the fictional Judean who

---

[28] Justin, *Dialogue with Trypho* 32.1 (τῇ ἐσχάτῃ κατάρᾳ τῇ ἐν τῷ νόμῳ τοῦ θεοῦ περιπεσεῖν). Trypho was not concerned to distinguish the true deity from the creator. Yet anti-Marcionite polemic plays a role later in the dialogue (89.2; 90.1), and Justin argued against Marcionites in 35.2–6. See further Andrew Hayes, *Justin Against Marcion: Defining the Christian Philosophy* (Minneapolis: Fortress, 2017), esp. 156–62; Matthijs den Dulk, *Between Jews and Heretics: Refiguring Justin Martyr's Dialogue with Trypho* (London: Routledge, 2018); Sebastian Moll, "Justin and the Pontic Wolf," in *Justin Martyr and His Worlds*, ed. Sara Parvis and Paul Foster (Minneapolis: Fortress, 2007), 145–51.

[29] Justin, *Dialogue with Trypho* 89–96. On this section, see Craig D. Allert, *Revelation, Truth, Canon, and Interpretation: Studies in Justin Martyr's Dialogue with Trypho* (Leiden: Brill, 2002), 232, 236–38.

[30] Rodney Werline, "The Transformation of Pauline Arguments in Justin Martyr's *Dialogue with Trypho*," *Harvard Theological Review* 92:1 (1999): 79–93 at 91.

[31] Justin, *Dialogue with Trypho* 95.2 (ἀναδέξασθαι). See further Chapman, *Crucifixion*, 247–48.

[32] Justin, *Dialogue with Trypho* 90.3 (τὴν δοκοῦσαν κατάραν); 95.2 (ὡς κεκατηραμένου).

[33] Justin, *Dialogue with Trypho* 94.5.

[34] Justin, *Dialogue with Trypho* 95.2.

[35] Justin, *Dialogue with Trypho* 90–95.

[36] Justin, *Dialogue with Trypho* 94.5.

[37] Justin, *Dialogue with Trypho* 96.1: οὐχ ὡς τοῦ θεοῦ καταρωμένου τούτου τοῦ ἐσταυρωμένου. It did not even indicate, according to Justin, that Christ was cursed by the Law (111.2: Χριστὸς οὐ κατηράθη ὑπὸ τοῦ νόμου).

[38] See Joost Smit Sibinga, *The Old Testament Text of Justin Martyr* (Leiden: Brill, 1963), 96–99.

[39] Justin, *Dialogue with Trypho* 96.1. Elsewhere (91.4), Justin was content to add that the serpent was cursed "by god" (ὑπὸ τοῦ θεοῦ) even when these words are lacking in Gen 3:14.

used the passage to say that Christ was god's enemy and accursed,[40] nor was it lost upon Marcionite Christians who saw implied in it a negative portrayal of the creator.[41]

Tertullian

About fifty years after Justin, Tertullian denied that Christ was cursed, offering two reasons. First, Jesus did not die for his own sins, and second, he died to fulfill prophecies (largely restating Justin's arguments).[42] Yet Marcion knew that even a sinless Christ can be cursed, for in Deuteronomy 21:23—as quoted by Tertullian—"*everyone* hung on a tree is cursed by god." Moreover, a curse still applies even if predicted. Indeed, the fact that Jesus was sinless and that the Jewish deity *planned* to curse Jesus ahead of time seems only to worsen the problem.

Elsewhere Tertullian accepted the reality of the curse against Christ but avoided connecting it with the creator. Following Paul's emphasis, he insisted that it applied "to the son from the Law."[43] In his treatise *On Patience*, Tertullian remarked: "When you are cursed, rejoice, The lord himself was cursed in the Law."[44] "In saying that Christ is crucified," Tertullian elsewhere urged, "we do not curse him, but refer to the curse of the Law."[45] In short, it is the Law, not the creator, who is blamed for the curse—even though the creator is the (unacknowledged) author of the Law.

---

[40] Justin, *Dialogue with Trypho* 93.4. See further Chapman, *Crucifixion*, 248–51.

[41] See further Willem Cornelis van Unnik, "Der Fluch der Gekreuzigten: Deuteronomium 21,23 in der Deutung Justinus des Märtyrers," in *Theologia Crucis, Signum Crucis: Festschrift für Erich Dinkler zum 70*, ed. C. Andresen and G. Klein (Tübingen: Mohr Siebeck, 1979), 483–99.

[42] Tertullian, *Against the Jews* 10.3–4 (written between 198 and 208 CE). For the authenticity of this work, see Claudio Moreschini and Enrico Norelli, *Early Christian Greek and Latin Literature: A Literary History*, trans. Matthew J. O'Connell, 2 vols. (Peabody: Hendrickson, 2005), 1.339; Geoffrey D. Dunn, *Tertullian's Adversus Iudaeos: A Rhetorical Analysis* (Washington, DC: Catholic University of America Press, 2003), 5–30.

[43] Tertullian, *Against Praxeas* 29.3.

[44] Tertullian, *On Patience* 8.3. In context, Tertullian argued for the joyful acceptance of persecution.

[45] Tertullian stated that it is blasphemy if the father god is said to be cursed, but not blasphemy in the case of the son: "Just as concerning a being who is said to have a capacity for something, this is said without blasphemy, so with regard to one who does not have the capacity, to say it is blasphemy" (*sicut autem de quo quid capit dici sine blasphemia dicitur, ita quod non capit, blasphemia est si dicatur, Against Praxeas* 29.3–4).

Ambrosiaster

A Roman clergyman now called "Ambrosiaster," writing between 366 and 384 CE, openly denied that Christ "became accursed." To argue this point, he had to make a subtle distinction. Christ, he said, was *made* "a curse" (*maledictum*), but he was not accursed (*maledictus*). Christ was *made* a curse because he bore the creator's curse on the cross. Since he was innocent, however, he did not become accursed.[46]

This kind of distinction, though innovative, is lacking in the text of Galatians. Paul says that Christ became a curse and immediately quotes the text in which the crucified victim is said to be "accursed." To become a curse and to be accursed are equivalent expressions. Arguably, "to become a curse," even says *more* than calling Jesus "accursed." If Christ was accursed, we could distinguish the curse and Christ, but if Christ *became* a curse, there is no apparent distinction.

Epiphanius

Ambrosiaster did not tell us whose interpretation he tried to overcome. Epiphanius (about 375 CE) made his arguments explicitly against Marcion(ites). He vitriolically denied the reality of god's curse. "The fool"—referring to Marcion—"is wholly unaware that Christ has not become a curse either—god forbid!"[47] Like Justin, Epiphanius appealed to interchange theology and fulfilled prophecy to mitigate the force of the curse.[48] In this way, he discounted the notion that cursing reflected poorly on the creator.

Jerome

Taking a different tack, Jerome contended that it is only because of one's *crime* that one is cursed, not because one is crucified. Nevertheless, the text

---

[46] Ambrosiaster, *Commentary on Galatians* 3.13.
[47] Epiphanius, *Panarion* 42.8.3; cf. 66.79.10.
[48] Epiphanius, *Panarion* 42.12, Elenchus 2.

he dealt with said: "cursed by god is *everyone* who hangs on a tree" (Deut 21.23)—*everyone*, whether innocent or guilty. Jerome was so bothered by the creator's curse that he claimed (in line with the *Didascalia*) that interpolators added "cursed *by god*" to Deuteronomy 21:23 in both Christian and Jewish versions of the text. He added that, "in no place is it written [in scripture] that anyone is cursed by god and wherever a curse is made, the name of god is not added."[49]

But when Jerome quoted the curse against Cain ("You are accursed," Gen 4:11), he failed to mention that it is the creator who speaks.[50] In the other curse texts Jerome mentioned, the creator brings the curses as well. When Noah cursed his grandson Canaan (Gen 9:25), for instance, the creator fulfilled that curse by later commanding and overseeing the annihilation of the Canaanites (Deut 20:17; Josh 10:28, 30, 32, 35, 37, 39; 11:11, 14).

But it was not just the creator's enemies that he cursed, but his own people. In the fifty-four verses of Deuteronomy 28:15–68 there are eighty-two curses that threaten the Israelites. To quote just a sample:

> It will happen if you do not obey the voice of the lord your god to keep and perform all his commandments . . . there will come upon you all these curses—and they will overtake you. You will be accursed in the city, accursed in the country, accursed will be your storehouses and reserves, accursed the offspring of your womb and the products of your land, the herds of your cattle and the flocks of your sheep. Accursed you will be in your leaving and accursed in your coming. The lord will send you poverty, wasting hunger, and the withering of everything you attempt, whatever you do, until you are annihilated . . . (Deut 28:15–20)

When one goes looking, in fact, there are many examples of the creator cursing, and Jerome's discussion helps to bring these out.[51]

---

[49] Jerome, *Commentary on Galatians* 2 at 3.13: *nullo loco scriptum a deo quemquam esse maledictum et ubicumque maledictio ponitur nunquam dei nomen adiunctum.*

[50] This point was not lost on Adimantus in Augustine, *Against Adimantus* 3.4.

[51] Origen wrote that the creator threatens and speaks abusively (ἀπειλεῖ . . . ὁ θεὸς καὶ λοιδορεῖ) in the Law and the Prophets, and that "abundant curses" (ἀραὶ πλεῖσται) are recorded in Leviticus (26:14–46) and Deuteronomy (*Cels.* 2.76). Ephrem also commented that god said "concerning the unjust, 'You are cursed' " (*Prose Refutations* in Mitchell, 2.xxv, modified).

The Cursing God

Indeed, it is useful to study these curses more fully to understand the Marcionite critique. In Genesis 3, Adam and Eve disobey the creator by eating from the tree of knowledge. The creator responds with a double curse:

> To the woman he said: "I will greatly increase your sufferings and your groans; with suffering you will bear children; you will resort to your husband and he will dominate you." To Adam he said: "Because you listened to your wife and ate from the tree, . . . accursed is the soil when you work it; with sufferings you will eat it all the days of your life; thorns and thistles it will produce for you and you will eat field grass. By the sweat of your face you will eat bread until you resort back to the soil from which you were taken." (Gen 3:16–20)

Despite the harshness of these punishments (physical suffering, male domination, lifelong labor, and so on), only the snake and the soil are expressly said to be cursed, as some interpreters pointed out. Philo, for instance, argued that Adam could not be cursed because he represents mind or intelligence, the precipitate of the creator's breath.[52] Irenaeus denied that the creator cursed Adam, in part because a curse implied damnation.[53]

Adamantius, the early catholic exponent in the dialogue named after him, argued that the creator did not curse the first human—only the ground. His Marcionite opponent countered that the creator did curse Adam, for Adam was taken from the ground. This curse, moreover, implied the creator's condemnation: "he bestowed on [Adam] a curse—how could this not be condemnation?"[54] Origen of Alexandria agreed that the creator's curse against "the earth in your works" was directed "to Adam."[55] He also spoke generally of "the curse of Adam" and the "curses pronounced against Eve."[56]

In certain Nag Hammadi retellings of the Paradise story, the creator's curse against the first humans is accentuated. In the shorter version of the

---

[52] Philo, *Questions on Genesis* 1.50.

[53] Irenaeus, *AH* 3.23.3. For Irenaeus, indeed, the idea that Adam was not saved was heresy (1.28.1).

[54] *Adamantius* 2.7: κατάραν αὐτῷ ἔδωκε, πῶς οὖν οὐ κατεδίκασεν;

[55] Origen, *Homilies on Numbers* 15.3.1.

[56] Origen, *Cels.* 4.40. Augustine rejected the idea that Adam was subject to god's curse (*Enemy of the Law* 1.24).

Secret Book of John, the chief creator sees Adam and Eve separate from him after eating the fruit and curses them.[57] An expanded set of curses appears in *On the Origin of the World*, where blind rulers first curse the instructing serpent, then Eve and her children, and finally Adam, the earth, and the fruit because of him: "Everything they created they cursed. There is no blessing from them. Good cannot be born from evil."[58]

The last line may go back to Marcion's explanation of Jesus's parable that a bad tree does not bear good fruit (Evangelion 6:43).[59] If so, both the Christian and philosophical backgrounds of the criticism are evident. The true god, who is good and can only do good, cannot curse. Accordingly, the god who *does* curse cannot be good and thus forgoes his claim to be god.

In some cases, the "god" who curses is himself an accursed god. Origen claimed that, since the creator cursed the knowledge-giving snake, "Ophite" Christians directed their curses against the creator.[60] Origen's opponent Celsus (writing about 178 CE) scored rhetorical points by highlighting this "accursed god" of the Christians.[61] The creator and his minions are also said to be cursed in the *Reality of the Rulers* (NHC II,4): they "have no blessing," to give, "for they are under a curse." In the same text, the main heroine, Norea, calls the rulers "accursed."[62]

Based on these texts, we gather that for some ancient Christians, there was a connection between a *cursing* creator and an *accursed* creator. A tree is known by its fruit, and a cursing god is himself accursed. Although Marcionites did not, on present evidence, argue this specific point, they would have plausibly agreed that a cursing creator is himself cursed—in particular one who cursed the sinless Christ.

---

[57] *Secret Book of John* (BG 8502,2) 61.7–10. Yaldabaoth immediately makes Adam master of Eve, has his angels chase them from Paradise, and clothes them in thick darkness.

[58] *Origin of the World* (NHC II,5) 120.3–11. The cursing of Adam and Eve is also explicit in the "Ophite" report of Irenaeus, *AH* 1.30.8: "so that the spirit [of Adam] from the principality . . . might not share in the [creator's] curse."

[59] See the re-established text in Roth, *Text* 415; Klinghardt, *Älteste Evangelium II* 555. See also ibid., 4.4.20; 7.4.7; 8.8. Cf. Origen, *First Principles* 2.5.4 ("that famous question of theirs"); 3.1.18; *Commentary on John* 13.73; *Ref.* 10.19.2; Pseudo-Tertullian, *AAH* 6.2; Filastrius, *Diverse Heresies* 45; Augustine, *Enemy of the Law* 1.47. For the Manichean reception, see J. Kevin Coyle, "Good Tree, Bad Tree: The Matthean/Lukan Paradigm in Manichaeism and Its Opponents," in *The Reception and Interpretation of the Bible in Late Antiquity: Proceedings of the Montreal Colloquium in Honour of Charles Kannengiesser*, ed. Lorenzo DiTommaso and Lucian Turcescu (Leiden: Brill, 2008), 122–44.

[60] Origen, *Cels.* 6.28.

[61] Origen, *Cels.* 6.27–28.

[62] *Reality of the Rulers* (NHC II,4) 91.6–7, 92.23.

Manichean Reception

There is one final way to reconstruct what would appear plausible in Marcionite interpretation, and that is through its Manichean reception. Following Marcionites, Manicheans—who claimed to be the true followers of Christ—were avid interpreters of Galatians 3:13. One such interpreter we have already met—Adimantus, writer of the *Disputations*. Adimantus is particularly important because his *Disputations* may have been a revised expansion of Marcion's *Antitheses* (see Chapter 6).

Following the format of the *Antitheses*, Adimantus highlighted the following tension: whereas the Jewish deity cursed crucified people (Deut 21:23), Jesus invited his disciples to take up their cross and follow him (Matt 19:21; cf. 16:24). The conflict highlighted here was between the character of Christ—who invited people to die sacrificially on the cross—and the character of the creator, who cursed the righteous sufferers of crucifixion.[63]

Centuries after the cessation of crucifixion, it is easy to read Christ's command, "take up your cross" in figurative fashion, but as early Christian literature indicates, several of Jesus's disciples (for instance, Peter and Andrew) embraced literal crucifixion for their commitment to Christ.[64] Manicheans believed that their founder Mani was also crucified, making him, by extension, a victim of the creator's curse.[65] The fact that the Jewish deity cursed the righteous victims of crucifixion manifested his wicked character.

Against Adimantus, the North African church father Augustine (died 430 CE) took a figurative reading of Matthew 19:21. The person who takes up the cross, he said, is not literally crucified like Christ. Rather, only one's "old self" is crucified (using the language of Rom 6:6). Augustine identified the old self with the "old life" inherited from Adam.

In his response to Adimantus, Augustine avoided the idea that god actually cursed Christ. "It was not the lord. . . but death itself that merited the curse which our lord annulled in the act of assuming it." The language indicates that Augustine, like Justin before him, was more comfortable with

---

[63] Augustine, *Against Adimantus* 21: *maledictus omnis, qui in ligno pependerit . . . quod ex evangelio Adimantus obponendum putavit, ubi dominus ait: si vis perfectus esse . . . tolle crucem tuam* (Corpus scriptorum ecclesiasticorum latinorum [CSEL] 25.1:179–80); translated as *Disputation* 21 in van den Berg, *Biblical Argument*, 116.

[64] *Acts of Andrew* 54–55; *Martyrdom of Peter* 36–40 translated by Elliott, *Apocryphal*, 262, 424–26.

[65] Asmussen, *Manichaean Literature*, 54.

Christ *assuming* a curse than with actually *becoming* a curse, as is written in Galatians 3:13. Augustine's wording was careful: he admitted that Christ assumed "the most shameful kind of death known to human beings," but he did not concede that Christ was cursed.[66]

Augustine returned to Galatians 3:13 in his *Answer to Felix*. Felix, a "learned man" in the Manichean church, came to spread his faith in Augustine's city (Hippo Regius) toward the end of 404 CE.[67] Felix's scriptures were confiscated according to a law that sentenced Manicheans to be burned along with their writings. Felix offered to discuss the contents of the books with Augustine in order to prove their harmlessness. If he failed in his endeavor, Felix agreed to be burned.[68]

In the second day of the debate, Felix argued that the power which is against the true god—the evil power that crucified Christ—cannot belong to god. Augustine countered that this power, which catholics called Satan, derived from god. Manicheans thought this position blasphemous, because it traced evil back to god. It made Satan himself "a power of god"; and if he was a power of god, then he was effectively god's employee. If god's employee holds power over humans by divine permission, this reflected poorly on god, or what the catholics took to be god.

The true view, according to Felix, is that humans are in bondage to a hostile power, one who does *not* belong to god. The hostile power proves its evil nature by cursing everyone hung on a cross (Gal 3:13). This power was not the devil —though he too was evil— but the creator. The creator, Felix concluded, was not the true (that is, good) god.[69]

There is one final piece of evidence. This comes from Faustus of Milevis, whom we have met in Chapter 6. Faustus was a Manichean bishop of North Africa who wrote a critical and exegetical work, the *Capitula*, between 386 and 390 CE. Faustus had met Augustine around 382 when the latter was a young and inquisitive Manichean.[70] Four years later, Augustine converted to early catholicism, and some thirteen years after that (between 398 and 400), Augustine wrote a reply to Faustus that preserved most of Faustus's *Capitula* through quotations.

---

[66] Augustine, *Against Adimantus*, 21.
[67] Augustine, *Retractions* 2.8 (35).
[68] Augustine, *Against Felix* 1.12. See further Richard Lim, *Public Disputation, Power, and Social Order in Late Antiquity* (Berkeley: University of California Press, 1995), 99–102.
[69] Augustine, *Against Felix* 2.10.
[70] Augustine, *Confessions* 5.6.10–5.7.11.

In the *Capitula*, Faustus proffered his interpretation of Galatians 3:13. Although the bishop focused his attack on Moses, the creator's prophet, his comments still apply to the creator. According to Faustus, Manicheans curse Moses because Moses "knowingly and willingly cursed" the crucified Christ. Indeed, Moses in Deuteronomy 21:23 cursed "all righteous people and martyrs, as many as left this life by a like suffering . . . Moses does not say that they are cursed before the world—that is humans only—but cursed *by god*."[71] Early catholics, claimed Faustus, did not want to admit god's curse, because this curse would also include Jesus.[72]

In his reply, Augustine at first seemed only prepared to allow—as he did with Adimantus—that god cursed death: "Is it any wonder that god curses what he hates?" Yet since only death was cursed, god hated not Christ, but death. But then Augustine changed tactic. He conceded to Faustus that "absolutely every person" crucified is cursed, including the son of god. This is what Manicheans do not want, Augustine claimed, "For you are displeased that he is cursed for us, because you are displeased that he died for us."[73]

This is an interesting attempt to turn the tables. Augustine argued that, since Manicheans did not accept that Christ was actually hurt on the cross, they did not accept his death, and therefore they could not accept that he was cursed. But Faustus did accept that he was cursed, and that by "god". The problem, then, was with the god worshiped by early catholics, as Faustus urged: "a divine spirit would not curse Christ."[74]

In a subsequent critique of Faustus, Augustine brought in the Jews. If Faustus really believed, said Augustine, that Jesus was cursed by the creator, then logically Faustus would have been the first to attack Christ if they were contemporaries. In this regard, Faustus would have no quarrel with the Jews "who, in persecuting Christ with heart and soul, acted in obedience to their own god."[75]

The fact that Augustine could refer to the god of the Jews (*dei sui*, as if this being was different from his god), and acknowledge—if only for the sake of argument—that the Jews obeyed their god in crucifying Christ, returns us to the heart of the Manichean—and earlier Marcionite—critique. At least one

---

[71] Augustine, *Against Faustus* 14.1.
[72] Augustine, *Against Faustus* 32.5.
[73] Augustine, *Against Faustus* 14.6.
[74] Augustine, *Against Faustus* 16.5.
[75] Augustine, *Against Faustus* 32.5.

reason why the idea of an evil creator arose is because some Christians realized that the creator *was the driving cause* of Christ's crucifixion, and that he added his imprimatur by cursing Christ on the cross.

Indeed, Felix made this point explicitly: "See what the apostle said (Rom 8:7; 2 Cor 4:4; 12:7–8); see what the evangelist said (Matt 25:34, 41). Mani said that he who wages war against god is external to god. Christ was crucified as well as all the apostles *for the sake of god's command*."[76] If the creator commanded Christ's crucifixion, Christ could not belong to the creator. By attacking Christ, the creator "wages war against [the true] god" and so proves that he is evil, foreign to Christ, and to what is truly divine.

Again, these Manichean sources are not direct witnesses to Marcionite interpretations of Galatians 3:13. Still, I would argue that they give us a sense for what would have been a plausible Marcionite reading of this verse. Marcion probably engaged with Galatians 3:13 in his *Antitheses*. Adimantus probably rewrote—or at least borrowed—from the *Antitheses*. We know that Faustus read Adimantus's work, and likely the same can be said for Felix. All three Manichean leaders agreed with Marcion that Christ "received in himself the creator's curse by being hung from a tree."[77] They all concluded that a "god" who curses the crucified Christ—not to mention all other victims of crucifixion—was not good and thus not (the true) god.

Conclusion

Patristic authors employed various strategies to confront the creator's curse against Christ (Gal 3:13). Yet virtually all agreed that this curse must somehow be avoided or denied, despite Paul's language that Christ "became" a curse. Early catholic writers like Epiphanius, Jerome, and Augustine must have had strong motives for overriding what was for them biblical language. One of these motives, I believe, was to protect the goodness of the creator against Marcionite—and later, Manichean—attacks.

Marcionites and their interpretive heirs viewed the creator's curse against Christ as incriminating the creator's character. Whatever good resulted from the curse was not planned by the creator and could not exculpate his cursing character. A being who cursed the sinless savior could not under any

---

[76] Augustine, *Against Felix* 2.2 (end), italics added.
[77] As reported by Tertullian, *AM* 1.11.8.

circumstances be considered good. But the creator who cursed Christ not only lacked goodness; he also proved himself to be malign. In short, the creator's curse against the sinless Christ manifested once and for all the creator's hostility toward Christ and served to hoist up, as it were, his wicked character for all to behold.

Conclusion

The Evil Creator at Large

> We should assuredly be quite different if the Christian era had been
> inaugurated by the execration of the Creator, for the permission
> to abuse Him would not have failed to lighten our burden, and to
> render the last two millennia that much less oppressive.
>
> —M. Cioran[1]

In 1995, Jack Miles published a book called *God: A Biography*. In this volume, he performed a character analysis on the deity of the Hebrew Bible. He pointed out significant character development in this figure and was not afraid to hide his destructive side. "God is no saint," he remarked. "There is much to object to in him, and many attempts have been made to improve him. Much that the Bible says about him is rarely preached from the pulpit because, examined too closely, it becomes a scandal."[2]

In the fifth century BCE, the playwright Aeschylus—or an imitator—performed another kind of character analysis. He focused on Zeus, who chained Prometheus, benefactor of humanity, to the face of a cliff. In the Roman era, this punishment was understood to be a form of crucifixion.[3] (One might liken it to offshore detention and torture.) Parading before Prometheus, the various characters in the play do not hesitate to berate Zeus as a tyrant.[4]

Marcionite Christians performed a similar kind of character analysis on the creator—not out of literary interest, but from theological concern. Based

---

[1] M. Cioran, *The New Gods*, ed. Richard Howard (Chicago: University of Chicago Press, 2013), 8.
[2] Jack Miles, *God: A Biography* (London: Simon & Schuster), 6.
[3] Hengel, *Crucifixion*, 11–12. For Prometheus crucified, see Lucian, *Sacrifices* 6; *Zeus Catechized* 8; Tertullian, *AM* 1.1.3–4.
[4] [Aeschylus], *Prometheus Bound* 222, 310, 736, 761, 942, 957.

The Evil Creator. M. David Litwa, Oxford University Press. © Oxford University Press 2021.
DOI: 10.1093/oso/9780197566428.003.0010

on biblical stories, they pointed out flaws in his character (that he was blood-thirsty, jealous, arrogant, irascible, and so on).[5] They exposed questionable actions like preventing knowledge, sending a flood, and killing children. From these biblical stories, as channeled through their theological assumptions and hermeneutical frameworks, they concluded that the creator was wicked.

Today it seems strange that some early Christians would read biblical documents without the felt need, in Milton's phrase, "to justify the ways of God to men."[6] Yet this assumes that all early Christians presupposed that the Judean deity was the universal god of pure goodness, and that so-called gnostic and Marcionite Christians were responsible for a subsequent "split" in the deity.[7]

But what if this isn't true? After all, Gentile Christians of the early second century may never have been acculturated to Jewish theological traditions.[8] Even if they became familiar with Jewish scripture, they may never have viewed the Judean deity as either universal or good. They lived in a culture in which widespread social antagonism toward perceived Jewish peculiarities was already fused with theological criticism.[9] Celsus (about 178 CE) observed that some Christians "will concede that their god is the same as that of the Jews, while others will maintain that he is a different one, to whom the latter is in opposition."[10] Celsus is usually thought to be referring to Marcionite Christians, but it is possible that he had several groups of Christians in mind.[11] After all, according to Celsus, all it took was an interpretation of Plato to derive the idea of "a God above the heavens . . . higher than the heaven in which the Jews believe."[12]

Note also, on this score, Marcion's contemporary Basilides, a Gentile Christian theologian from Alexandria.[13] He lived through both Jewish

---

[5] Documented by Lieu, *Marcion*, 337–49, 357–66. Cf. Augustine, *Enemy of the Law* 1.30.

[6] John Milton, *Paradise Lost*, 1.26. For theodicy-oriented readings of scripture, see Williams, "Demonizing," 90–91.

[7] For the split theory, see Birger A. Pearson, "Gnosticism as a Religion," in *Was There a Gnostic Religion?* ed. Antti Marjanen (Helsinki: Finnish Exegetical Society, 2005), 81–101 at 83. DeConick speaks of a "bifurcation" of the Jewish god into a good father and a malicious lawgiver performed by a transitional gnostic Christian—the author of the fourth gospel ("Why" at 178; *Gnostic New Age*, 146–47). Irenaeus already accused the Marcionites of "slicing the godhead in two" (*dividens deum in duo*, AH 3.25.3). Cf. Origen's "they divide the godhead" (διακόπτουσι τὴν θεότητα, *On Prayer* 29.12).

[8] Cf. Arnobius, a Gentile Christian from North Africa: "Jewish fables . . . do not concern us and have nothing at all in common with us"; those that are shared require the allegorical interpretation of exegetical experts (*Against the Nations* 3.12).

[9] Helpfully summarized in Schäfer, *Judeophobia*, 34–196.

[10] Origen, *Against Celsus* 5.61.

[11] Horacio E. Lona, *Die "Wahre Lehre" des Kelsos* (Freiburg: Herder, 2005), 310.

[12] Origen, *Against Celsus* 6.19.

[13] For Basilides, see esp. Winrich Alfried Löhr, *Basilides und seine Schule: Eine Studie zur Theologie-und Kirchengeschichte des zweiten Jahrhunderts* (Tübingen: Mohr Siebeck, 1996); Löhr, "Christliche

uprisings (the revolt under Trajan, 115–117 CE, and the Bar Kochba war, 132–135 CE). Perhaps in response to these uprisings, Basilides developed his own theory as to why the Jews rose up and why the other nations joined forces to suppress them. The god of the Jews, he thought, was actually a powerful angel in charge of Judea who sought to expand his power and subdue the nations. This angelic "god" repeatedly incited his own people to revolt, an act that inspired the backlash of other peoples (led by *their* angelic lords).[14] In deriving this theory, Basilides never "split" the Jewish god away from a transcendent father deity. He never actually assumed that these two different entities were one. The Judean deity was always a subordinate ruler, whose local rule in Judea actually had a biblical foundation (Deut 32:8–9).

Both Basilides and Epiphanius's "Phibionites" lived in Egypt along with several other Christian groups (Carpocratians, Valentinians, among others) over the course of two centuries (from at least 115–350 CE). Egypt was the land where—centuries before Basilides and Marcion—hostile intellectuals had propagated the view of Yahweh as a form of Seth-Typhon. This understanding of Yahweh gained cultural currency by the late first century. In this environment, it seems that many Gentiles who became Christians in the context of the Jewish revolts began by considering the local god of Judea to be "other," dangerous, and bellicose—especially when compared with the god revealed in Jesus Christ.[15]

In opposing this "split" theory of deity, I seek to undermine the assumed originality of a particular constructed tradition: that all early Christians, Jew or Gentile, adopted Yahweh as their deity and worshiped him as "the lord." In my view, this understanding gained much of its traction in hindsight when historical reconstructions, such as those we find in the book of Acts, began to leaven the Christian imagination in the late second century. The author of Acts depicted earliest Christianity as chiefly spread by Jewish missionaries

'Gnostiker' in Alexandria im zweiten Jahrhundert," in *Alexandria*, ed. Tobias Georges, Felix Albrecht, and Reinhard Feldmeier (Tübingen: Mohr Siebeck, 2013), 413–33.

[14] Basilides, as reported by Irenaeus, *AH* 1.24.4.

[15] Hostility toward Judaism and the Jewish deity may have increased across the empire after the Jewish uprisings of 66–71, 115–17, and 132–35 CE. See further Martin Goodman, "Trajan and the Origin of Roman Hostility to the Jews," *Past & Present* 182 (2004): 3–29; John M. G. Barclay, "The Politics of Contempt. Judeans and Egyptians in Josephus' *Against Apion*," in *Pauline Churches and Diaspora Jews* (Tübingen: Mohr Siebeck, 2011), 277–300; Bar-Kochva, *Image*, 206–52; Daniele Tripaldi, "From Philo to Areimanios: Jewish Traditions and Intellectual Profiles in First-Third Century Alexandria in the Light of the *Apocryphon of John*," in *Jews and Christians in Antiquity*, ed. Lanfranchi and Verheyden, 101–20.

who first targeted Jews. He is significantly silent, however, about the spread of Christianity in places like Egypt, North Africa, Pontus, Edessa—among other places.[16] Truth be told, we still do not know how Christianity was spread in these areas and whether the converts had any significant inculturation in Jewish customs and theology. Thus we cannot assume that they all adopted the Judean deity as their supreme lord, as opposed to the deity revealed in gospel proclamations (whether oral or written).

I would propose that at least some Christians, including intellectuals like Basilides (from Alexandria) and Marcion (from Pontus), did not have any significant commitment to Jewish theology prior to their faith in Christ. These Christians, that is, never adopted the Judean creator as their deity and did not feel any need to do so. In this development, I think, Marcion and Basilides are only representatives. They represent, that is, segments of Christians who never worshiped the creator as the true and universal god. Their form of Christianity thus already had a different framework for understanding the creator, who—as in Platonic theology—was not identical to the supreme deity.

Gradually, Gentile Christians became familiar with stories in the Septuagint, stories that were also reflected in historical texts, spells, amulets, and oral lore in antiquity. Their interpretation of stories in which Yahweh floods the earth, plagues Egypt, destroys Amalek, and so on, eventually convinced some of them to view the Jewish creator as actually evil and tyrannical in character.

But they did not limit themselves to Jewish scriptures. In fact, the most critical evidence for the creator's wickedness came from a central story in what are distinctly Christian scriptures. I refer to the story of the crucifixion, a story in which the "rulers" of this world, in obedience to "the god of this world" (the creator) plotted behind the scenes to nail Christ to the cross (1 Cor 2:8; 2 Cor 4:4). The Judean deity's plot might have been forgiven if it occurred under a different dispensation for pedagogical purposes against someone who truly deserved it. Instead, the creator plotted against, killed, and cursed the Christian savior, whom Christians identified with the spotless lamb (1 Cor 5:7) of the (true) god. Since crucifying the innocent Christ was, in the Christian imagination, demonstrably evil, Marcionite—among other—Christians concluded that the creator himself was evil. My overall argument agrees with Simone Pétrement's older observation that the notion

---

[16] See the classic study of Bauer, *Orthodoxy and Heresy* (entire).

of the evil creator was primarily "brought about within and by Christianity, the crucifixion of Christ, the Pauline theology of the cross."[17] Yet we need to make this formulation sharper: it was the creator who *put* Christ on the cross and therefore decisively proved, beyond any lurking doubt, the corruption of his character.

Whatever one thinks of this thesis, my argument has shown at the very least that Marcionites—among several other early Christian groups—had exegetical reasons for believing that the creator was evil. I do not deny that there were other—potentially many other—reasons for ancient Christians to conclude that the creator of this world was hostile to both Christ and to themselves. Yet the key inspiration, as developed in this book, were particular readings of Christian scripture (both "Old" and "New" Testaments).

To be sure, Marcionite (among other) Christians did not read their Bibles in a vacuum. They already carried with them (1) a predetermined oppositional stance toward rabbinic-style Judaism motivated (at the very least) by the need to assert their Christian identity, and (2) popular philosophical assumptions of the day that informed them about what traits were and were not appropriate for a deity.

Merely by virtue of being Christian, Marcionites (among other Christians) were opposed to a religious ideology that centered on the temple and obedience to the Torah. Their opposition to this ideology was born out of their need to craft their own Christian identity, which—while trying to avoid the disgrace of the Jewish tax and the stigma of perceived treason (between 115 and 135 CE)—was constantly trying to siphon off symbolic capital from Jewish scripture and tradition.[18]

This growing Christian animus against what they took to be recalcitrant Jews was, I surmise, in some cases re-expressed as an animus against the Jewish god. This animus might have motivated them to find and accentuate passages wherein the biblical creator failed to measure up to what was considered to be divine (omnibenevolent) status. The creator's statements, actions, and character proved that he was not only *not* good, but also positively evil—jealous, hostile, and angry—in particular at Christ and those Christians endowed with deeper insight about the nature of the divine.

---

[17] Simone Pétrement, *A Separate God: The Christian Origins of Gnosticism*, trans. Carol Harrison (San Francisco: Harper & Row, 1990), 10.

[18] For nuanced discussion, see Judith M. Lieu, "Self-definition vis-à-vis the Jewish Matrix," in *Cambridge History of Christianity*, Vol. 1, ed. Margaret M. Mitchell (Cambridge: Cambridge University Press, 2006), 214–29; Lieu, *Image and Reality* (entire).

Terminology

As my argument now draws to a close, I want to offer a practical suggestion regarding terminology that might in some way help us to surmount the current impasse about the use of "Gnosis" or "gnostic" as a global term. I propose that we call the idea (or ideology) of an evil creator, present in several early Christian groups, "negative demiurgy." The related phrase "biblical demiurgy," as proposed by Michael A. Williams in 1996, was generally not accepted by scholars.[19] I myself understand it to be overly vague—since effectively it could apply to all theories of the biblical creator, whether he is viewed as good, evil, or as something in between. "*Negative* demiurgy" is more precise and thus more useful as an analytical tool and comparative category. In the second century CE, it would describe the views of Marcionite and Sethian Christians, for instance—neither of whom we need call "gnostic" in a global sense.

Negative demiurgy, I think, should not be understood as the central idea of a separate religion or religious phenomenon. Instead, I take it as a particular view possible in several discrete traditions, though mostly within what I would prefer to call summodeistic faiths (including early Judaism and Christianity).[20] It is, to be sure, a minority position in the Abrahamic traditions. Yet it should not be left unstudied, not only since it is important for early Christian history and the history of biblical interpretation, but also because it is alive and well in modern times.

The Evil Creator Today

A key inspiration for negative demiurgy in contemporary discourse is—once again—Christian scripture.[21] This time, however, the most vocal critics of the biblical creator are not alternative Christian theologians but humanists and freethinkers still endeavoring to detach politics, science, and education

---

[19] William, *Rethinking*, 218. See, e.g., the critique of Burns, *Did God Care*, 184–86.

[20] For summodeism, see Litwa, *We Are Being Transformed*, 229–57.

[21] On the continued influence of the Bible, see Mark A. Noll, "The Bible Then and Now," in *The Bible in American Life*, ed. Philip Goff, Arthur Farnsley, and Peter Thuesen (Oxford: Oxford University Press, 2017), 331–44; Corwin E. Smidt, "The Continuing Distinctive Role of the Bible in American Lives," ibid., 203–24.

from the structures of religious ideology.[22] In so doing, they continue the project of the Enlightenment, which proved so influential for the founding of Western democracies.

In 1979, Ruth Hurmence Green, in the throes of her battle against cancer, published *The Born Again Skeptic's Guide to the Bible.* By her own report, she had been a skeptic the previous fifty years of her life, but an in-depth examination of scripture in her sunset years made her an outright atheist.[23] It was in the Bible that she observed the "unspeakable cruelty of the Christian God, manifested in his sentencing of a man who picked up sticks on the Sabbath to be stoned to death." Such cruelty reached its height when god "destroyed all the inhabitants of the earth [with a flood] except for one family of his own choosing."[24] God preordained human sin but blamed humankind" in Eden.[25] He sent she-bears to "devour 42 children . . . [who were] playfully teasing Elisha."[26] "God also," she observed, "makes use of evil spirits. He sends one upon Saul."[27] Furthermore, god ordered the Amalekites to be slaughtered by the edge of the sword—every man, woman and child.[28]

Green's criticisms were not limited to the Hebrew Bible. What most horrified her was the story of the "capture, torture, and crucifixion of Jesus." She was both astounded and disgusted that human beings were blamed for such a tragedy, since it is none other than god who needed to cause "all this ghastly panorama in order to fulfill the prophecies."[29] She inquired: "If the concept of a father who plots to have his own son put to death is presented to children as beautiful and as worthy of society's admiration, what types of human behavior can be presented to them as *reprehensible*?"[30] Green—a churchgoing Methodist most of her life—then made a peculiarly Marcionite conclusion—though ultimately more daring than Marcion—"The God of the Bible is a demon."[31]

---

[22] An exception here is Archbishop Jonathan Blake, *The Old Devil Called God Again: The Scourge of Religion* (Winchester: John Hunt, 2014), 30–38. In the book, Blake argues that "the biblical God is immoral, cruel, and abusive" (8).

[23] Ruth Hurmence Green, *The Born-again Skeptic's Guide to the Bible with the Book of Ruth* (Madison: Freedom from Religion Foundation, 1979), vii.

[24] Green, *Guide,* 21.

[25] Green, *Guide,* 23–24.

[26] Green, *Guide,* 27.

[27] Green, *Guide,* 30.

[28] Green, *Guide,* 103, 129.

[29] Green, *Guide,* 97.

[30] Green, *Guide,* viii, emphasis hers.

[31] Green, *Guide,* 30.

In 2001, American atheist Richard Carrier e-published an intellectual biography explaining how he had become an atheist. As it turns out, simply
reading the Bible, by his own report, proved to be the decisive factor. Someone
had encouraged him to read "the good book" cover to cover. Accordingly,
Carrier picked up the New International Version (an American Evangelical
translation) and began to search the scriptures. Between the covers, Carrier
discovered, to his surprise,

> a terrible, sinful God . . . a jealous, violent, short-tempered, vengeful
> being whose behavior is nonsensical and overly meddlesome and
> unenlightening. . . .
>
> Though called a wise father, there is not a single example in the Old
> Testament of God sitting down and kindly teaching anyone, and when
> asked by Job, the best of men, to explain why He went out of His way to
> hurt a good man by every possible means, including killing his loved ones,
> this "wise father" spews arrogant rhetorical questions, ultimately implying
> nothing more than "might makes right" as his only excuse. I revulsed in
> horror at this demonic monster . . .[32]

When Carrier closed his Bible after finishing the final page, he (by his
own testimony) declared aloud, though alone in his bedroom: "Yep, I'm an
atheist." In this case, "atheist" meant not only that he did not believe in the
biblical god but also that he indignantly opposed the character of its putative
deity. In Carrier's own mind, at least, the act of Bible reading played a consti-
tutive role in helping him toward his negative demiurgical conclusions.

These experiences are hardly unique. An article of an anonymous
American author was published on News24 (a South African online news
outlet) on October 25, 2012. It is entitled, "What if God was the Evil One?" In
it we find statements such as these:

> Throughout the bible there are numerous accounts of god dishing out di-
> vine punishment by way of genocide, plagues, ethnic cleansing, and the like.
> If the bible were the word of god, then god supports infanticide, slavery,
> torture, genocide and all manner of death, destruction, and suffering. Just
> take the crucifixion as an example—the foundation of the Christian reli-
> gion. This is nothing less than a human sacrifice, and purportedly to allow

---

[32] https://infidels.org/library/modern/testimonials/carrier.html. Visited on September 25, 2019.

sinners to go free of punishment for their sins. What father would have his own son, a "good man" by all accounts, brutally tortured and murdered so that "bad" people could be let off their crimes? If the answer is that god loves us all and wants us to be forgiven, why did he not just do that? Why insist on a bloodthirsty crucifixion?[33]

The implied conclusion is that the god who enforces Christ's crucifixion is in fact malign. This line of thought has analogies in Marcionite Christian theology. Unlike ancient Marcionites, however, this anonymous author does not assume that there is a beneficent deity higher than the creator. Like Carrier and Green, s/he assumes and responds to a traditional Christian theology that seems to have muscled out other interpretive options. According to this theology, there is one god, the creator who does battle with a completely separate but subordinate lord of evil (Satan). Yet this was only one option, as it turns out, in early Christian theology.

Still more criticisms of the creator appear on a website called the "Evil Bible.com." This site first appeared in 2003 and is apparently the work of atheist Chris Thiefe.[34] On the home page, we encounter this remark:

The so called God of the Bible makes Osama Bin Laden look like a Boy Scout. This God, according to the Bible, is directly responsible for many mass-murders, rapes, pillage, plunder, slavery, child abuse and killing . . .

Here Marcionite-like criticisms crop up once more. The difference, again, is that atheists like Thiefe do not envision the creator as a subordinate ruler. Instead, they renounce their belief in what they consider to be the only version of god on the market (the all-powerful, all-good creator).

In 2009, David Plotz, a writer of Jewish heritage, published a work called *The Good Book: The Bizarre, Hilarious, Disturbing, Marvelous, and Inspiring Things I Learned When I Read Every Single Word of the Bible*.[35] At the end of this work, Plotz concluded: "After reading about the genocides, the plagues, the murders, the mass enslavements, the ruthless vengeance for minor sins (or no sin at all), and all that smiting—every bit of it directly performed,

[33] https://www.news24.com/MyNews24/What-if-God-was-actually-the-evil-one-20121025. Visited on September 21, 2019.
[34] We learn this from an article on Rational Wiki, https://rationalwiki.org/wiki/Evil_Bible.com (accessed September 23, 2019).
[35] Plotz, *The Good Book: The Bizarre, Hilarious, Disturbing, Marvelous, and Inspiring Things I Learned When I Read Every Single Word of the Bible* (New York: Harper Perennial, 2010).

authorized, or approved by God—I can only conclude that the God of the Hebrew Bible, if He existed, was awful, cruel, and capricious. He gives us moments of beauty—sublime beauty and grace!—but taken as a whole, He is no God I want to obey, and no God I can love. Why would anyone want to be ruled by a God who's so unmerciful, unjust, unforgiving, and unloving?"[36]

When later asked if he still believed in god, Plotz paused for a moment and mused, "I guess not." He later reflected, "Even if somehow it was true that the God of the Hebrew Bible existed, who would want to believe in him? Why would I want any 'relationship' with such a jealous, erratic, brutal, unmerciful, unloving, unkind God?"[37]

Particularly helpful for discovering an evil god in scripture is Steve Wells's *The Skeptic's Annotated Bible*. This work highlights in the margins of the (admittedly outdated) King James Version all of the putatively questionable passages of Christian scripture, with mini-icons indicating categories of perceived "absurdity" (2,178 instances), "injustice" (1,541 instances), "cruelty and violence" (1,316 instances), and "intolerance" (701 instances).[38] Wells's two appendices identify 471 perceived contradictions in scripture, and 135 cases wherein god kills people, beginning with Noah's flood and ending with Jesus's crucifixion.[39]

In his introduction, Wells notes that to make the Bible "a truly good book . . . would require massive surgery . . . for nearly all passages in the Bible are objectionable in one way or another. But with a little luck and much careful editing, perhaps a small pamphlet could be produced from the Bible—one that could honestly be called good."[40] Wells seems unaware that "purifying" the canon of scripture was one of Marcion's most (in)famous accomplishments. Wells's statement that "the believer is simply stuck with the Bible" indicates an unawareness of diverse canons today and the plethora of Christian literature that pointed out problematic passages (such as the *Antitheses*) in antiquity.[41]

On the American Humanists Association website, Joseph C. Sommer explains why secular Humanists reject the Bible. It is because, he says,

---

[36] Plotz, *Good Book*, 302–3.
[37] Plotz, *Good Book*, "Afterward," 8–9.
[38] Steve Wells, *Skeptic's Bible* (Moscow, ID: SAB, 2013), xi–xii.
[39] Wells, *Skeptic's Bible*, 1597–632. See further Steve Wells, *Drunk with Blood: God's Killings in the Bible* (Moscow, ID: SAB, 2010).
[40] Wells, *Skeptic's Bible*, ix–x.
[41] Wells, *Skeptic's Bible*, x.

It approves of outrageous cruelty and injustice. In civilized legal systems, a fundamental principle is that the suffering of the innocent is the essence of injustice. Yet the Bible teaches that God repeatedly violated this moral precept by harming innocent people.

Sommer offers examples of the creator's cruelty:

> He damned the whole human race and cursed the entire creation because of the acts of two people ([Adam and Eve] Genesis 3:16–23; Romans 5:18); he drowned pregnant women and innocent children and animals at the time of the Flood (Genesis 7:20–23); he tormented the Egyptians and their animals with hail and disease because Pharaoh refused to let the Israelites leave Egypt (Exodus 9:8–11, 25); and he killed Egyptian babies at the time of the Passover (Exodus 12:29–30). After the Exodus he ordered the Israelites to exterminate the men, women, and children of seven nations and steal their land (Deuteronomy 7:1–2) . . . He sent wild animals such as bears (II Kings 2:23–24).[42]

Just as Marcion implicitly compared the creator with unstated philosophical assumptions about the goodness of god, Sommer sees the creator as violating a baseline morality embodied in "modern legal systems." He appeals, in other words, to a concrete instance of shared morality to show how the biblical creator falls short. This is basically a Marcionite procedure, though Sommer, like all the other writers mentioned here, has evidently never heard of Marcion or radical diversity in early Christianity. Nor is he interested in contrasting the mentality of Christ with the character of the creator. The Bible, in the view of Sommers and most other atheistic critics, seems monolithic and univocal, which—as the history of biblical interpretation shows—is not at all accurate.

A similar univocal reading of scripture is manifest in Dan Barker's 2016 book *God: The Most Unpleasant Character in All Fiction*. In this work, Barker unpacks Richard Dawkins's (in)famous statement that the "Old Testament" god is "jealous and proud of it; a petty, unjust, unforgiving control-freak; a vindictive, bloodthirsty ethnic cleanser; a misogynistic, homophobic, racist, infanticidal, genocidal, filicidal, pestilential, megalomaniacal

---

[42] Visited on September 21, 2019.

sadomasochistic, capriciously malevolent bully."[43] To this (already rather full) list, Barker adds negative attributes of his own: god is "a pyromaniacal, angry, merciless, curse-hurling, vaccicidal [cow killing!], aborticidal, cannibalistic slavemonger."[44]

Ninety percent of Barker's book is comprised of proof-texting biblical passages stripped of their contexts, and with the most gory, violent, and lurid bits printed in boldface. His last chapter turns to Jesus with some interesting theological conclusions. "According to the New Testament," he says, "Jesus *was* the God of the Old Testament."[45] Barker concludes that Jesus "was identical with the God of the Old Testament" based on passages in John where Jesus appears to claim unity or identity with his father (John 10:30; 14:9).[46] Though hardly nuanced in his Christology, Barker assumes orthodox Christian theology in identifying Jesus's father with the creator. Captivated by American Evangelical frameworks—or, rather, his need to undermine them—Barker seems unaware of any other interpretive options.

To my mind, it is regrettable that these modern critics of the biblical god do not know enough of the history of biblical interpretation to realize the host of interpretive options available to them. They end up endlessly having to reinvent the wheel, even though much of what they have been saying was already said nineteen centuries ago in a more thoroughgoing and nuanced way. Presumably if these critics knew more about the history of biblical interpretation, they could better understand the issues at stake and craft better arguments. At the very least, they would not assume the sole legitimacy of a particular tradition (that Jesus's father is the creator) that was constructed in dialogue with other interpretive options presented by Marcion and other early Christian thinkers in antiquity.

Marcion did not reject the existence of the creator; instead, he redescribed him as a tyrannical being whose influence and power were both dangerous and deadly. This particular viewpoint may seem bizarre today, but it at least takes seriously the need for an honest character analysis of the biblical creator. It also witnesses to a certain resilience in Christian theology. Even if the Flood-sending, plague-bearing, Christ-cursing creator proves to be an evil being, Christians can still worship the true god. Their first act of worship is

---

[43] Richard Dawkins, *The God Delusion* (London: Bantam, 2006), 31. See also Dawkins, *Outgrowing God: A Beginner's Guide* (New York: Random House, 2019), 72–92.

[44] Barker, *God: The Most Unpleasant Character in All Fiction* (n.p.: Sterling, 2016), 291.

[45] Barker, *God*, 289.

[46] Barker, *God*, 289.

actually coming to know what true deity is. God is only good, so the basic principle is: if a god is not good, he's not god.

Whatever its truth value, Marcionite, Phibionite, and Sethian Christian teaching (etc.) reminds us that, in the struggle to generate an ethical and informed culture, the Bible need not be utterly rejected, but reframed. It is reframed simply by viewing it not as the word of the (potentially evil) creator but as the historical expression of thoughts about a very particular deity at discrete times and in different locales of the Mediterranean basin. The Bible is also reframed by viewing it as a secret code sent by the true god in allegories and parables—unfortunately misunderstood and adulterated by human beings.

By their precipitous rejection of the biblical creator, the so-called new atheists reverse the conclusions but maintain the hard-line mentality featured among so-called orthodox Christian writers (past and present). These writers actively endeavored to uproot any interpretation that could be used to support the idea of an evil creator. But they were and continue to be unsuccessful. This dangerous and disturbing idea keeps cropping up even without the Marcionite trademark, among people with strikingly different social contexts, cultures, and interpretive horizons.

Why does the idea of an evil creator constantly reinvent itself? It keeps resurfacing, I surmise, because the very scriptures still upheld as the word of god are susceptible to an alternative, yet still sensible, construction (despite shifting cultural presuppositions). According to this construction, the biblical creator does not simply lack goodness; he is a kind of tyrant who proved his evil nature in numerous acts of violence, jealousy, and self-glorification. His wicked character is clinched by his secret but successful plot to kill Jesus, who was at minimum an innocent man and at maximum the savior and child of the true deity. To be sure, my language here is deliberately provocative to drive home a point easily missed by readers who start from within the tradition of a divine, sinless creator. That tradition hardly represents all the data of scripture. As long as people continue to read scripture, they will persist in discovering data that undermines what have become (outdated, insufficient) traditional readings.

If this book does anything in the lives of modern readers, I hope that it will further enhance our collective ability to read the Bible through the eyes of the "other," and that it will inspire new thoughts and categories allowing us to read this monument of literature in more nuanced, honest, and ethical ways. We must never allow negativity about the character of the biblical creator to translate into hostility toward those who worship the creator by their own lights and according to their own traditions. At the same time, we should continue to think seriously about developing positive images of god, for we are what we imagine. If deity is tyrannical, bloodthirsty, egoistic, jealous, and evil, then there is and always will be an excuse for us to be so. Thankfully, the sword cuts both ways: in portraying deity as good, loving, kind, and merciful, we uphold a flourishing exemplar for the divine image, which is, or is at least imagined to be, ourselves.

Bibliography

Primary Sources

Adler, Ada. *Suidae Lexicon*. 5 vols. Leipzig: Teubner, 1928–38.

[Aeschylus.] *Prometheus Bound*. Edited by Alan H. Sommerstein. LCL 145. Cambridge, MA: Harvard University Press, 2008.

Alcinous. *Enseignement des doctrines de Platon*. Edited by John Whittaker. Paris: Belles Lettres, 1990.

Ambrosiaster. *Commentarius in epistulas paulinas Pars tertia*. Edited by Henricus Iosephus Vogels. Vienna: Tempsky, 1969.

The American and British Committees of the International Greek New Testament Project, eds. *The New Testament in Greek: The Gospel according to St. Luke*, Part 2. Oxford: Clarendon Press, 1987.

Apostolic Fathers. Edited by Bart D. Ehrman. 2 vols. Cambridge MA: Harvard University Press, 2003.

Apuleius. *Opuscules philosophiques*. Edited by Jean Beaujeu. Paris: Belles Lettres, 2018.

Ascensio Isaiae. Edited by Enrico Norelli. 2 vols. Turnhout: Brepols, 1995.

Augustine. *Contra adversarium legis et prophetarum*. Edited by K.-D. Daur. Turnholt: Brepols, 1997.

Augustine. *Contra Faustum, Contra Felicem*. CSEL 25/1–2. Vienna: Tempsky, 1891.

Augustine. *Enarrationes in Psalmos CI–CL*. CCSL 40. Edited by D. Eligius Dekkers and Iohannes Fraipont. Turnholt: Brepols, 1956.

Bakhuyzen, W. H. van de Sande, ed. *Der Dialog des Adamantius ΠΕΡΙ ΤΗΣ ΕΙΣ ΘΕΟΝ ΟΡΘΗΣ ΠΙΣΤΕΩΣ*. Leipzig: Hinrichs, 1901.

Beeson, Charles Henry. *Hegemonius. Acta Archelai*. Leipzig: Hinrichs, 1906.

Betz, Hans Dieter, ed., *The Greek Magical Papyri in Translation Including the Demotic Spells*, 2nd ed. Chicago: University of Chicago Press, 1992.

Black, M., ed. *Apocalypsis Henochi Graece*. Leiden: Brill, 1970.

Charlesworth, James, ed. *The Old Testament Pseudepigrapha*. 2 vols. New York: Doubleday, 1985.

Coptic Gnostic Library, A Complete Edition of the Nag Hammadi Codices. Edited by James M. Robinson. 5 vols. Leiden: Brill, 2000.

Cyril of Jerusalem. *Catechetical Lectures*. Translated by John Henry Parker. London: Rivington, 1845.

Cyril of Jerusalem. *Opera quae supersunt omnia*. Edited by W. K. Reischl and J. Rupp. 2 vols. Hildesheim: Olms, 1967.

Dio Cassius. Translated by Earnest Cary and Herbert Baldwin Foster. 9 vols. LCL. London: Heinemann, 1914–1927.

Elliott, J. K. *The Apocryphal New Testament*. Oxford: Clarendon, 1993.

Epiphanius. *Ancoratus* and *Panarion*. Edited by Karl Holl, Marc Bergermann, Christian-Friedrich Collatz, and Jürgen Dummer. 2nd ed. 4 vols. Berlin: Akademie, 1980–2013.

Evans, Ernst, ed. *Tertullian: Adversus Marcionem*, 2 vols. Oxford: Clarendon, 1972.

Gardner, Iain, ed., *The Kephalaia of the Teacher: The Edited Coptic Manichaean Texts in Translation with Commentary*. Leiden: Brill, 1995.

Hanhart, Robert, ed. *Tobit*. Göttingen: Vandenhoeck & Ruprecht, 1983.

Harris, J. Rendel, and J. Armitage Robinson, eds. *The Apology of Aristides on Behalf of the Christians*. Cambridge: Cambridge University Press, 1891.

Heine, Ronald E. *The Commentary of Origen on the Gospel of Matthew*. 2 vols. Oxford: Oxford University Press, 2018.

Irenaeus. *Contre les hérésies*. 10 vols. Edited by Adelin Rousseau and Louis Doutreleau. SC. Paris: Cerf, 1974.

Jerome. *Opera Pars I Opera Exegetica 6 Commentarii in epistulam Pauli Apostoli ad Galatas*. Edited by Giacomo Raspanti. CCSL 77a. Turnhout: Brepols, 2006.

Josephus. Translated by H. St. J. Thackeray et al. 10 vols. LCL. Cambridge, MA: Harvard University Press, 1926–1965.

Jülicher, Adolf. *Itala: Das Neue Testament in altlateinischer Überlieferung*. Berlin: de Gruyter, 1954.

Justin Martyr. *Dialogus cum Tryphone*. Edited by Miroslav Marcovich. Berlin: de Gruyter, 1997.

Le Bas, Philippe, and William Henry Waddington. *Inscriptions grecques et Latin de la Syrie*. Vol. 3. Rome: L'Erma, 1968.

Minucius Felix. *Octavius*. Edited by H. A. Holden. Cambridge: Cambridge University Press, 1853.

Mitchell, C. W., trans. *S. Ephraim's Prose Refutations: Mani, Marcion and Bardaisan*. 2 vols. Piscataway: Gorgias Press, 2008.

Numenius. *Fragments*. Edited by Édouard des Places. Paris: Belles Lettres, 2003.

Origen. *Commentaire sur l'Épître aux Romains. Tome II, livres III–V*. Edited by Caroline P. Hammond Bammel. SC 539. Paris: Cerf, 2010.

Origen. *Contra Celsum libri VIII*. Edited by M. Marcovich. Leiden: Brill, 2001.

Origen. *Matthäuserklärung*. Edited by Erich Klostermann and Ernst Benz. 3 vols. Leipzig: Hinrichs, 1935.

Origen. *Origenes Werke 2*. Edited by P. Koetschau. Griechischen Chritlichen Schriftsteller 3. Leipzig: Hinrichs, 1899.

Petronius. Translated by Michael Heseltine. LCL 15. Cambridge, MA: Harvard University Press, 1969.

Philo. *Opera*. Edited by Leopold Cohn and Paul Wendland. 7 vols. Berlin: de Gruyter, 1962–1963.

Plato. *Opera*. Edited by E. A. Duke, W. F. Hicken, W. S. M. Nicoll, D. B. Robinson, and J. C. G. Strachan. 5 vols. Oxford Classical Texts. Oxford: Clarendon, 1995.

Plotinus. *Opera*. Edited by Paul Henry and Hans-Rudolf Schwyzer. 3 vols. Oxford: Clarendon, 1951–1973.

Plutarch. *De Iside et Osiride*. Edited by J. Gwynn Griffiths. Cardiff: University of Wales Press, 1970.

Preisendanz, K., and A. Henrichs, eds. *Papyri Graecae magicae*. 3 vols. 2nd ed. Stuttgart: Teubner, 2001.

Pseudo-Clement. *Die Pseudoklementinen. Homilien; Rekognitionen in Rufins Übersetzung*. Edited by Bernhard Rehm and Georg Strecker. Berlin: Akademie, 1992–1994.

Ptolemy. *Lettre a Flora*. Edited by Gilles Quispel. 2nd ed. SC 24. Paris: Cerf, 1966.

Scheck, trans. Thomas P. *Ancient Christian Texts: Commentaries on the Twelve Prophets. Vol. 1: Jerome.* Downers Grove: IVP Academic, 2016.

Schmidt, Carl, ed. and Violet MacDermot, trans. *Pistis Sophia.* Leiden: Brill, 1979.

Schmidt, Carl, ed., and Violet MacDermot, trans. *The Books of Jeu and the Untitled Text of the Bruce Codex.* Leiden: Brill, 1978.

Sextus Empiricus. *Opera 1: ΠΥΡΡΩΝΕΙΩΝ ΥΠΟΤΥΠΩΣΕΩΝ.* Edited by Hermann Mutschmann, and I. Mau. Leipzig: Teubner, 1958.

Staab, K. *Pauluskommentar aus der griechischen Kirche aus Katenenhandschriften gesammelt.* Münster: Aschendorff, 1933.

Tcherikover, Victor A., and Fuks, Alexander. *Corpus Papyrorum Judaicarum*, 3 vols. Cambridge, MA: Harvard University Press, 1957–1964.

Tertullian. *Adversus Iudaeos mit Einleitung und kritischem Kommentar.* Edited by Hermann Tränkle. Wiesbaden: Franz Steiner, 1964.

Tertullian. *Contre Marcion.* Edited by René Braun and Claudio Moreschini. 5 vols. SC. Paris: Cerf, 1990–2004.

Tertullian. *De Idololatria: Critical Text, Translation and Commentary.* Edited by J. H. Waszink and J. C. M. van Winden. Leiden: Brill, 1987.

Tertullian. *Opera.* Edited by A. Kroymann and E. Evans. 2 vols. CCSL 2/1–2. Turnholt: Brepols, 1954.

Theodore of Mopsuestia. *The Commentaries on the Minor Epistles of Paul.* Translated by Rowan A. Greer. Atlanta: SBL Press, 2010.

Theodoret. *Correspondence II–III.* Edited by Yvan Azéma. 2 vols. SC 98, 111. Paris: Cerf, 1964–65.

Theophilus. *Ad Autolycum.* Edited by Robert M. Grant. Oxford: Clarendon, 1970.

Tromp, J., ed. *The Life of Adam and Eve in Greek: A Critical Edition.* Leiden: Brill, 2005.

Von Arnim, Hans, ed. *Stoicorum veterum fragmenta.* 4 vols. Leipzig: Teubner, 1903.

Westerink, L. G., trans. *Anonymous Prolegomena to Platonic Philosophy.* Wiltshire: Prometheus, 2011.

Wevers, John William, ed. *Exodus.* Göttingen: Vandenhoeck & Ruprecht, 1991.

Wevers, John William, ed. *Genesis.* Göttingen: Vandenhoeck & Ruprecht, 1974.

Ziegler, Joseph, ed. *Isaias*, 3rd ed. Göttingen: Vandenhoeck & Ruprecht, 1983.

Ziegler, Joseph, and Olivier Munnich, ed. *Susanna, Daniel, Bel et Draco. Editio secunda versionis iuxta LXX interpretes textum plane novum constituit.* Göttingen: Vandenhoeck & Ruprecht, 1999.

Secondary Sources

Aland, Barbara. "Marcion: Versuch einer neuen Interpretation," *Zeitschrift für Theologie und Kirche* 70 (1973): 420–47.

Allen, J. "Ezekiel the Tragedian and the Despoliation of Egypt," *Journal for the Study of the Pseudepigrapha* 17:1 (2007): 3–19.

Allert, Craig D. *Revelation, Truth, Canon, and Interpretation: Studies in Justin Martyr's Dialogue with Trypho.* Leiden: Brill, 2002.

Allison, Dale C. *Resurrecting Jesus: The Earliest Christian Tradition and Its Interpreters.* London: T&T Clark, 2005.

Alt, Karin. *Weltflucht und Weltbejahung: Zur Frage des Dualismus bei Plutarch, Numenius, Plotin.* Stuttgart: Franz Steiner, 1993.

Ando, Clifford. *The Matter of the Gods: Religion and the Roman Empire.* Berkeley: University of California Press, 2008.

Annas, Julia. *Platonic Ethics, Old and New.* Ithaca: Cornell University Press, 1999.

Armstrong, Arthur H. "Dualism: Platonic, Gnostic, and Christian." Pages 33–54 in *Neoplatonism and Gnosticism*, ed. Richard T. Wallis and Jay Bregman. Albany: SUNY Press, 1992.

Arnold, Clinton. *Powers of Darkness.* Downers Grove: InterVarsity, 1992.

Armstrong, J. M. "After the Ascent: Plato on Becoming Like God." *Oxford Studies in Ancient Philosophy* 26 (2004): 171–83.

Assmann, Jan. *Moses the Egyptian: The Memory of Egypt in Western Monotheism.* Cambridge, MA: Harvard University Press, 1997.

Assmann, Jan. *Of God and Gods: Egypt, Israel, and the Rise of Monotheism.* Madison: University of Wisconsin Press, 2008.

Asmussen, Jes P. *Manichean Literature: Representative Texts Chiefly from Middle Persian and Parthian Writings.* Delmar: Scholars' Facsimiles, 1975.

Auffarth, Christoph. "Herrscherkult und Christuskult." Pages 283–318 in *Die Praxis der Herrscherverehrung in Rom und seinen Provinzen*, ed. Hubert Cancik & Konrad Hitzl. Tübingen: Mohr Siebeck, 2003.

Aziza, Claude. "Recherches sur l'Onokoites' des écrits apologétiques de Tertullien." Pages 283–90 in *Hommage à Pierre Fargues (Philologie, Littératures et histoire anciennes).* Edited by Jean Granarolo, et al. Paris: Belles Lettres, 1974.

Aziza, C. "L'utilisation polémique du récit de l'Exode chez les écrivains alexandrins (IV siècle av. J.-C.-1 siècle ap. J.C." Pages 41–65 in *Aufstieg und Niedergang der römischen Welt (ANRW).* Edited by Wolfgang Haase. Vol. I.20.1. Berlin: de Gruyter, 1987.

Bagnall, Roger S. *Egypt in Late Antiquity.* Princeton: Princeton University Press, 1993.

Banks, Robert. *Jesus and the Law in the Synoptic Tradition.* Cambridge: Cambridge University Press, 1975.

Barc, Bernard. "Samaèl-Saklas-Yaldabaôth: Recherche sur le genèse d'un mythe gnostique." Pages 132–50 in *Colloque international sur les Textes de Nag Hammadi: Québec 22–25 août 1978.* Leuven: Peeters, 1981.

Barclay, John M. G. *Against Apion: Translation and Commentary.* Leiden: Brill, 2007.

Barclay, John M. G. "Hostility to Jews as a Cultural Construct: Egyptian, Hellenistic, and Early Christian Paradigms." Pages 365–86 in *Josephus und das Neue Testament: Wechselseitige Wahrnehmungen*, ed. Christfried Böttrich and Jens Herzer. Tübingen: Mohr Siebeck, 2007.

Barclay, John M. G. *Jews in the Mediterranean Diaspora: From Alexander to Trajan (323 BCE–117 CE).* Edinburgh: T&T Clark, 1996.

Barclay, John M. G. "The Politics of Contempt. Judeans and Egyptians in Josephus' *Against Apion.*" Pages 277–300 in *Pauline Churches and Diaspora Jews.* Tübingen: Mohr Siebeck, 2011.

Barker, Dan. *God: The Most Unpleasant Character in All Fiction.* N.p.: Sterling, 2016.

Bar-Kochva, Bezalel. *The Image of the Jews in Greek Literature.* Berkeley: University of California Press, 2010.

Barnes, Timothy David. *Tertullian: A Historical and Literary Study.* Oxford: Clarendon, 1971.

Barth, Markus. *Ephesians: Introduction, Translation, and Commentary on Chapters 1–3.* Garden City: Doubleday, 1974.

Barth, Markus, and Blanke, Helmut. *Colossians: A New Translation with Introduction and Commentary*, trans. Astrid B. Beck. New York: Doubleday, 1994.

Bauer, Walter. *Orthodoxy and Heresy in Earliest Christianity*. Philadelphia: Fortress, 1971.

Basser, H. *Studies in Exegesis: Christian Critiques of Jewish Law and Rabbinic Responses, 70–300 CE*. Leiden: Brill, 2000.

BeDuhn, Jason D. *The First New Testament: Marcion's Scriptural Canon*. Salem, OR: Polebridge, 2013.

BeDuhn, Jason D., and Paul Mirecki, eds. *Frontiers of Faith: The Christian Encounter with Manichaeism in the Acts of Archelaus*. Leiden: Brill, 2007.

Behr, John. *Irenaeus of Lyon: Identifying Christianity*. Oxford: Oxford University Press, 2013.

Beker, J. Christiaan. "Christologies and Anthropologies of Paul, Luke-Acts and Marcion." Pages 174–82 in *From Jesus to John: Essays on Jesus and New Testament Christology in Honour of Marinus de Jonge*, ed. Martinus C. de Boer. Sheffield: Sheffield Academic Press, 1993.

Beker, J. Christian. *Paul the Apostle: The Triumph of God in Life and Thought*. Philadelphia: Fortress, 1997.

Benko, Stephen. "The Libertine Sect of the Phibionites According to Epiphanius, *VC (Vigiliae Christianae)* 21:2 (1967): 103–19.

Ben Zeev, Miriam Pucci. *Diaspora Judaism in Turmoil 116–117 CE: Ancient Sources and Modern Insights*. Leuven: Peeters, 2005.

Berendts, A. *Studien über Zacharias-Apokryphen und Zacharias-Legenden*. Leipzig: Deichert'sche, 1895.

Bergmann, Michael, Michal J. Murray, and Michael C. Rea. *Divine Evil? The Moral Character of the God of Abraham*. Oxford: Oxford University Press, 2011.

Berzon, Todd. *Classifying Christians: Ethnography, Heresiology, and the Limits of Knowledge in Late Antiquity*. Berkeley: University of California Press, 2016.

Betz, Hans Dieter. *A Commentary on the Sermon on the Mount, Including the Sermon on the Plain (Matthew 5:3–7:27 and Luke 6:20–49)*. Minneapolis: Fortress, 1995.

Belayche, Nicole. "Deus deum . . . summorum maximus (Apuleius): Ritual Expressions of Distinction in the Divine World in the Imperial Period." Pages 141–66 in *One God: Pagan Monotheism in The Roman Empire*, ed. Stephen Mitchell and Peter van Nuffelen. Cambridge: Cambridge University Press, 2010.

Bianchi, Ugo. "Marcion théologien biblique ou docteur gnostique?" *VC* 21 (1967): 141–49.

Bilde, Per. "2 Cor. 4,4: The View of Satan and the Created World in Paul." Pages 29–41 in *Apocryphon Severini*, ed. Per Bilde, Helge Kjaer Nielson, and Jorgen Podemann Sørensen. Aarhus: Aarhus University Press, 1993.

Bird, Michael F. *Colossians and Philemon: A New Covenant Commentary*. Cambridge: Lutterworth, 2009.

Bird, Michael F. "Jesus as Lawbreaker." Pages 3–26 in *Who Do My Opponents Say that I Am? An Investigation of the Accusations Against the Historical Jesus*, ed. Scot McKnight and Joseph B. Modica. London: T&T Clark, 2008.

Blackman, Edwin Cyril. *Marcion and His Influence* London: SPCK, 1948.

Blake, Archbishop Jonathan. *The Old Devil Called God Again: The Scourge of Religion*. Winchester: John Hunt, 2014.

Blanchard, Monica J., and Darling Young. *A Treatise on God Written in Armenian by Eznik of Kolb (floruit c.430–c.450): An English Translation, with Introduction and Notes*. Leuven: Peeters, 1998.

Blomberg, Craig L. "The Law in Luke-Acts," *Journal for the Study of the New Testament (JSNT)* 22 (1984): 53–80.

Bock, Darrell L. "Jesus as Blasphemer." Pages 76–94 in *Who Do My Opponents*, ed. Scot McKnight and Joseph B. Modica.

Bockmuehl, Markus. *Jewish Law in Gentile Churches: Halakah and the Beginning of Christian Public Ethics*. Edinburgh: T&T Clark, 2000.

Bohak, Gideon. *Ancient Jewish Magic: A History*. Cambridge: Cambridge University Press, 2008.

Borgeaud, Philippe. "The Death of the Great Pan: Problems of Interpretation," *History of Religions* 22:3 (1983): 254–83.

Borgeaud, Philippe. "Quelques remarques sur Typhon, Seth, Moïse et son âne, dans la perspective d'un dialogue reactive transcultural." Pages 173–85 in *Interprétations de Moïse: Égypte, Judée, Grèce et Rome*, ed. Borgeaud et al. Leiden: Brill, 2009.

Bovon, François. *Studies in Early Christianity*. Grand Rapids: Baker Academic, 2003.

Bovon, François, and Christopher R. Matthews, eds. *The Acts of Philip: A New Translation*. Baylor University Press, 2012.

Boys-Stones, George. *Platonist Philosophy 80 BC to AD 250: An Introduction and Collection of Sources in Translation*. Cambridge: Cambridge University Press, 2018.

Boys-Stones, George. "Providence and Religion in Middle Platonism." Pages 317–38 in *Theologies of Ancient Greek Religions*, ed. Esther Eidinow et al. Cambridge: Cambridge University Press, 2019.

Brakke, David. *Demons and the Making of the Monk: Spiritual Combat in Early Christianity*. Cambridge, MA: Harvard University Press, 2009.

Brakke, David. *The Gnostics: Myth, Ritual, and Diversity in Early Christianity*. Cambridge, MA: Harvard University Press, 2010.

Braun, René. *Deus Christianorum: Recherches sur le vocabulaire doctrinal de Tertullian*. Paris: Études Augustiniennes, 1977.

Broer, Ingo, ed. *Jesus und das jüdische Gesetz*. Stuttgart: Kohlhammer, 1992.

Brown, Derek. *The God of This Age: Satan in the Churches and Letters of the Apostle Paul*. Tübingen: Mohr Siebeck, 2015.

Brown, Raymond E. *Gospel According to John*, 2 vols. Garden City: Doubleday, 1966.

Brox, Norbert. "Non huius aevi deus (Zu Tertullian adv. Marc. V 11,10," *Zeitschrift für die neutestamentliche Wissenschaft (ZNW)* 59 (1968): 259–61.

Bruce, F. F. *The Epistle to the Galatians: A Commentary on the Greek Text*. Grand Rapids: Eerdmans, 1982.

Burns, Dylan. *Did God Care? Providence, Dualism and Will in Later Greek and Early Christian Philosophy*. Leiden: Brill, 2020.

Busch, Austin. "Characterizing Gnostic Scriptural Interpretation," *Zeitschrift für Antikes Christentum (ZAC)* 21:2 (2017): 243–71.

Busch, Austin. "Gnostic Biblical and Second Sophistic Homeric Interpretation," *ZAC* 22:2 (2018): 195–217.

Cahana-Blum, Jonathan. *Wrestling with Archons: Gnosticism as a Critical Theory of Culture*. London: Lexington, 2018.

Cappelletto, Pietro. *I Frammenti di Mnasea: Introduzione testo e commento*. Milan: LED, 2003.

Carr, Wesley. *Angels and Principalities: The Background, Meaning and Development of the Pauline Phrase hai archai kai hai exousiai*. Cambridge: Cambridge University Press, 1981.

Carr, Wesley. "The Rulers of This Age—1 Corinthians II.6–8," *New Testament Studies (NTS)* 23 (1976–77): 20–35.

Carroll, M., R. Daniel, and J. Blair Wilgus. *Wrestling with the Violence of God: Soundings in the Old Testament*. Winona Lake: Eisenbrauns, 2015.

Ceruti, M. V. "'Pagan Monotheism?' Towards a Historical Typology." Pages 15–32 in *Monotheism Between Pagans and Christians in Late Antiquity*, ed. Stephen Mitchell and Peter van Nuffelen. Leuven: Peeters, 2010.

Chapman. David W. *Ancient Jewish and Christian Perceptions of Crucifixion*. Tübingen: Mohr Siebeck, 2008.

Chiapparini, Giuliano. "Irenaeus and the Gnostic Valentinus: Orthodoxy and Heresy in the Church of Rome Around the Middle of the Second Century," *ZAC* 18:1 (2013): 95–119.

Cioran, M. *The New Gods*, ed. Richard Howard. Chicago: University of Chicago Press, 2013.

Connolly, R. Hugh. *Didascalia apostolorum: The Syriac Version Translated and Accompanied by the Verona Latin Fragments*. Oxford: Clarendon, 1969.

Constas, Nicholas P. "The Last Temptation of Satan: Divine Deception in Greek Patristic Interpretations of the Passion Narrative," *Harvard Theological Review* 97:2 (2004): 139–63.

Conti, Marco, ed. *Ancient Christian Commentary on Scripture V: 1–2 Kings, 1–2 Chronicles, Ezra, Nehemiah, Esther*. Downers Grove: InterVarsity, 2008.

Conzelmann, Hans. *The Theology of St Luke*, trans. Geoffrey Buswell. New York: Harper & Brothers, 1960.

Cook, Granger. *The Interpretation of the Old Testament in Greco-Roman Paganism*. Tübingen: Mohr Siebeck, 2004.

Coyle, J. Kevin. "Good Tree, Bad Tree: The Matthean/Lukan Paradigm in Manichaeism and Its Opponents." Pages 122–44 in *The Reception and Interpretation of the Bible in Late Antiquity: Proceedings of the Montreal Colloquium in Honour of Charles Kannengiesser*, ed. Lorenzo DiTommaso and Lucian Turcescu. Leiden: Brill, 2008.

Crossan, John Dominic. *The Historical Jesus: The Life of a Mediterranean Jewish Peasant*. New York: Harper One, 1991.

Crum, W. E. *A Coptic Dictionary*. Oxford: Clarendon, 1939.

Dahl, Nils Alstrup. "Der Erstgeborene Satans und der Vater des Teufels (Polyk. 7.1 und Joh 8.44)." Pages 69–84 in *Apophoreta: Festschrift für Ernst Haenchen zu seinem 70. Geburtstag*, ed. Walther Eltester and Franz H. Kettler. Berlin: de Gruyter, 1965.

Dahl, Nils Alstrup. "Arrogant Archon." Pages 689–712 in *Rediscovery of Gnosticism*, Vol. 2, ed. Bentley Layton.

Danker, Frederick William. *A Greek-English Lexicon of the New Testament and Other Early Christian Literature*, 3rd ed. Chicago: University of Chicago Press, 2000.

Davies, Andrew. *Double Standards in Isaiah: Re-Evaluating Prophetic Ethics and Divine Justice*. Leiden: Brill, 2000.

Davies, Eryl W. *The Immoral Bible: Approaches to Biblical Ethics*. London: Bloomsbury, 2010.

Dawkins, Richard. *The God Delusion*. London: Bantam, 2006.

Dawkins, Richard. *Outgrowing God: A Beginner's Guide*. New York: Random House, 2019.

Deakle, David W. "Harnack and Cerdo: A Reexamination of the Patristic Evidence for Marcion's Mentor." Pages 177–90 in *Markion und seine kirchengeschichtliche Wirkung*, ed. Gerhard May and Katharina Greschat. Berlin: de Gruyter, 2002.

de Angelis, Franco, and Benjamin Garstad. "Euhemerus in Context," *Classical Antiquity* 25:2 (2006): 211–42.

De Boer, Martinus C. "Expulsion from the Synagogue: J. L. Martyn's *History and Theology in the Fourth Gospel* Revisited," *NTS* 66 (2020): 367–91.

DeConick, April D. "From the Bowels of Hell to Draco: The Mysteries of the Peratics." Pages 3–38 in *Mystery and Secrecy in the Nag Hammadi Collection and Other Ancient Literature: Studies for Einar Thomassen at Sixty*, ed. Christian H. Bull, Liv Ingeborg Lied, and John Turner. Leiden: Brill, 2012.

DeConick, April D. *The Gnostic New Age: How a Countercultural Spirituality Revolutionized Religion from Antiquity to Today*. New York: Columbia University Press, 2016.

DeConick, April D. "Why Are the Heavens Closed? The Johannine Revelation of the Father in the Catholic-Gnostic Debate." Pages 147–79 in *John's Gospel and Intimations of Apocalyptic*, ed. Catrin H. Williams and Christopher Rowland. London: Bloomsbury, 2013.

de la Torre, Miguel A., and Albert Hernández, *The Quest for the Historical Satan*. Philadelphia: Fortress, 2011.

den Dulk, Matthijs. *Between Jews and Heretics: Refiguring Justin Martyr's Dialogue with Trypho*. London: Routledge, 2018.

Denzey, Nicola. "Stalking Those Elusive Ophites." Pages 89–122 in *Essays in Honour of Frederik Wisse: Scholar, Churchman, Mentor*, ed. Warren Kappeler. Montreal: ARC, 2005.

de Strycker, Émile. *La forme la plus ancienne du Protevangile de Jacques*. Brussels: Bollandist Society, 1961.

Dillery, John. *Clio's Other Sons: Berossus and Manetho*. Ann Arbor: University of Michigan Press, 2018.

Dinkler, Erich. *Signum Crucis: Aufsätze zum Neuen Testament und zur christlichen Archäologie*. Tübingen: Mohr Siebeck, 1967.

Doering, Lutz. *Schabbat: Sabbathalacha und -praxis im antiken Judentum und Urchristentum*. Tübingen: Mohr Siebeck, 1999.

Dohmen, Christoph. "Eifersüchtiger ist sein Name (Ex 34,14). Urprung und Bedeutung der alttestamentlichen Rede von Gottes Eifersucht," *Theologisches Zeitschrift* 46:4 (1990): 289–304.

Doldenberg, Robert. "The Jewish Sabbath in the Roman World." Pages 414–47 in *ANRW* II.19.1. ed., Wolfgang Haase. Berlin: de Gruyter, 1979.

Dreyer, Oskar. *Untersuchungen zum Begriff des Gottgeziemenden in der Antike mit besonderer Berücksichtigung Philons von Alexandrien*. Hildesheim: Georg Olms, 1970.

Drijvers, Hans J. W. "Marcion's Reading of Gal 4:8. Philosophical Background and Influence on Manichaeism." Pages 339–48 in *A Green Leaf. Papers in Honour of Jes. P. Amussen*. Leiden: Brill, 1988.

Droge, Arthur J. "The Apologetic Dimensions of the *Ecclesiastical History*." Pages 492–509 in *Eusebius, Christianity, and Judaism*, ed. Harold W. Attridge and Gohei Hata. Leiden: Brill, 1992.

Drozdek, Adam. "Plato and the Demiurge." Pages 151–68 in *Greek Philosophers as Theologians: The Divine* Arche. Hampshire: Ashgate, 2007.

Dubois, Jean-Daniel. "Hypothèse sur l'origine de l'apocryphe *Genna Marias*," *Augustinianum* 23 (1983): 263–70.

Dubois, Jean-Daniel. "La mort de Zacharie: mémoire juive et mémoire chrétienne," *Revue des Études Augustiniennes* 40 (1994): 23–38.

Dunderberg, Ismo. *Beyond Gnosticism: Myth, Lifestyle and Society in the School of Valentinus.* New York: Columbia University Press, 2008.

Dunderberg, Ismo, "Gnostic Interpretations of Genesis." Pages 383–96 in *The Oxford Handbook of the Reception History of the Bible,* ed. Michael Lieb, Emma Mason, and Jonathan Roberts. Oxford: Oxford University Press, 2011.

Dunn, Geoffrey D. *Tertullian's Adversus Iudaeos: A Rhetorical Analysis.* Washington, DC: Catholic University of America Press, 2003.

Dunn, James D. G. "Works of the Law and the Curse of the Law (Gal 3.10–14)," *NTS* 31:4 (1985): 523–42.

Dunn, James D. G. "Yet Once More: 'The Works of the Law,' a Response," *Journal for the Study of the New Testament (JSNT)* 46 (1992): 99–117.

Dunn, James D. G. *Jesus, Paul and the Law: Studies in Mark and Galatians.* Louisville: Westminster/John Knox, 1992.

Eck, Werner. "The Bar Kokhba Revolt: The Roman Point of View," *Journal of Roman Studies* 89 (1999): 76–89.

Edsall, Benjamin A. *The Reception of Paul and Early Christian Initiation: History and Hermeneutics.* Cambridge: Cambridge University Press, 2019.

Ehrman, Bart. *Lost Christianities: The Battles for Scripture and the Faiths We Never Knew.* Oxford: Oxford University Press, 2003.

Ehrman, Bart. *The Orthodox Corruption of Scripture: The Effect of Early Christological Controversies on the Text of the New Testament.* New York: Oxford, 1993.

Ehrman, Bart D., Gordon D. Fee, and Michael W. Holmes. *The Text of the Fourth Gospel in the Writings of Origen, Volume One* (Atlanta: Scholars, 1992).

Ehrman, Bart, and Zlatko Pleše. *The Apocryphal Gospels: Texts and Translations.* Oxford: Oxford University Press, 2011.

Eichrodt, Walther. *Theologie des Alten Testaments Volume 1,* 5th ed. Stuttgart: Ehrenfried Klotz, 1957.

Eidinow, Esther. "Popular Theologies: The Gift of Divine Envy." Pages 205–32 in *Theologies of Ancient Greek Religions,* ed. Esther Eidinow et al. Cambridge: Cambridge University Press, 2016.

Elliott, W. J., D. C. Parker, and Ulrich Schmid, eds. *The New Testament in Greek IV, 2* vols. Leiden: Brill, 1995–1997.

Ellis, Anthony. "The Jealous God of Ancient Greece: Interpreting the Classical Greek Notion of Φθόνος Θεῶν Between Renaissance Humanism and Altertumswissenschaft," *Erudition and the Republic of Letters* 2 (2017): 1–55.

Emmenegger, Gregor. "Adamantius et le De recta Fide." Pages 393–98 in *Histoire de la littérature grecque chrétienne des origenes à 451,* ed. Bernard Pouderon. Paris: Belles Lettres, 2017.

Engberg-Pedersen, Troels. *From Stoicism to Platonism: The Development of Philosophy 100 BCE–100 CE.* Cambridge: Cambridge University Press, 2017.

England, Emma, and Lyons, William John, eds. *Reception History and Biblical Studies: Theory and Practice.* London: Bloomsbury, 2015.

Eshel, Hanan. "The Bar Kochba Revolt, 132–135." Pages 105–27 in *Cambridge History of Judaism Vol. 4: Late Roman-Rabbinic Period,* ed. Steven T. Katz. Cambridge: Cambridge University Press, 2008.

Evans, C. A. *To See and Not Perceive: Isa 6.9–10 in Early Jewish and Christian Interpretation.* London: Bloomsbury, 2009.

Evans, Robert. *Reception History, Tradition and Biblical Interpretation: Gadamer and Jauss in Current Practice.* London: Bloomsbury, 2014.

Fauth, Wolfgang. "Seth-Typhon, Onoel und der eselköpfige Sabaoth: Zur Theriomorphie der ophitsichen-barbelognostischen Archonten," *Oriens Christianus* 57 (1973): 79–120.

Feine, P. *Das gesetzesfreie Evangelium des Paulus.* Leipzig: J. C. Hinrichs, 1899.

Feldman, Louis H. *Jew and Gentile in the Ancient World: Attitudes and Interactions from Alexander to Justinian.* Princeton: Princeton University Press, 1993.

Feldman, Louis H. *"Remember Amalek!" Vengeance, Zealotry, and Group Destruction in the Bible According to Philo, Pseudo-Philo, and Josephus.* Cincinnati: Hebrew Union College Press, 2004.

Fish, Stanley. "With the Compliments of the Author: Reflections on Austin and Derrida." Pages 37–67 in *Doing What Comes Naturally.* Durham: Duke University Press, 1989.

Fitzmyer, Joseph A. *Luke the Theologian: Aspects of His Teaching.* New York: Paulist Press, 1989.

Fletcher-Louis, Crispin H. T. "'Leave the Dead to Bury Their Own Dead': Q 9.60 and the Redefinition of the People of God," *JSNT* 26 (2003): 39–68.

Fossum, Jarl. *The Name of God and Angel of the Lord: Samaritan and Jewish Concepts of Intermediation and the Origin of Gnosticism.* Leiden: Brill, 1985.

Fossum, Jarl. "Origin of the Gnostic Concept of the Demiurge," *Ephemerides Theologicae Lovanienses* 61 (1985): 142–52.

Foster, Paul, and Sara Parvis, eds. *Irenaeus: Life, Scripture, and Legacy.* Minneapolis: Fortress, 2012.

Fraser, P. M. *Ptolemaic Alexandria.* 2 vols. Oxford: Clarendon, 1972.

Fredriksen, Paula. *Paul: The Pagans' Apostle.* New Haven: Yale University Press, 2017.

Free, K. B. "Thespis and Moses: The Jews and the Ancient Greek Theater." Pages 149–58 in *Theatre and Holy Script.* Ed. Shimon Levy. Brighton: Sussex Academic Press, 1999.

Frend, W. H. C. "The Gnostic-Manichaean Tradition in Roman North Africa," *Journal of Ecclesiastical History* 4 (1953): 13–26.

Fretheim, Terrence. *What Kind of God? Collected Essays of Terrence E. Fretheim,* ed. Michael J. Chan and Brent A. Strawn. Pennsylvania State University Press, 2015.

Frey, Jörg, and Enno Edzard Popkes. *Dualismus, Dämonologie und diabolische Figuren: Religionshistorische Beobachtungen und theologische Reflexionen.* Tübingen: Mohr Siebeck, 2018.

Frohnhofen, Herbert. *Apatheia tou Theou: Über die Affektlosigkeit Gottes in der griechischen Antike und be den griechischsprachigen Kirchenvätern bis zu Gregorios Thamaturgos.* Frankfurt am Main: Peter Lang, 1987.

Furnish, Victor Paul. *II Corinthians Translated with Introduction, Notes, and Commentary.* New York: Doubleday, 1984.

Gadamer, Hans-Georg. *Truth and Method.* New York: Continuum, 2003.

Gager, John G. "Marcion and Philosophy," *VC* 26:1 (1972): 53–59.

Gager, John G. *Moses in Greco-Roman Paganism.* Nashville: Abingdon, 1972.

Gager, John G. *Curse Tablets and Binding Spells from the Ancient World.* Oxford: Oxford University Press, 1992.

Gamble, Harry Y. *Books and Readers in the Early Church: A History of Early Christian Texts.* New Haven: Yale University Press, 1995.

Gantz, Timothy. *Early Greek Myth: A Guide to Literary and Artistic Sources*, 2 vols. Baltimore: Johns Hopkins University Press, 1993.

Gardner, Iain. "Mani's Life." Pages 225–34 in *The Gnostic World*, ed. Garry W. Trompf. London: Routledge, 2018.

Gasparro, Giulea Sfameni. "Addas-Adimantus unus ex discipulis Manichaei: For the History of Manichaeism in the West." Pages 546–59 in *Studia Manichaica* IV, ed. Ronald E. Emmerick. Berlin: Akademie, 2000.

Gaston, Thomas. "The Egyptian Background of Gnostic Mythology," *Numen* 62:4 (2015): 387–407.

Gero, Stephen. "With Walter Bauer on the Tigris: Encratite Orthodoxy and Libertine Heresy in Syro-Mesopotamian Christianity." Pages 287–307 in *Nag Hammadi Gnosticism and Early Christianity*, ed. C. W. Hedrick and R. Hodgson. Peabody: Hendrickson, 1986.

Gilhus, Ingvild Saelid. *Animals, Gods and Humans: Changing Attitudes to Animals in Greek, Roman, and Early Christian Ideas*. London: Routledge, 2006.

Gibbons, Kathleen. *The Moral Psychology of Clement of Alexandria: Mosaic Philosophy*. London: Taylor & Francis, 2016.

Gmirkin, Russell E. *Berossus and Genesis, Manetho and Exodus: Hellenistic Histories and the Date of the Pentateuch*. London: Bloomsbury, 2006.

Goehring, J. E. "A Classical Influence on the Gnostic Sophia Myth," *VC* 35:1 (1981): 16–23.

Goodman, Martin. "Trajan and the Origin of Roman Hostility to the Jews," *Past & Present* 182 (2004): 3–29.

Gowler, David B. *Host, Guest, Enemy and Friend: Portraits of the Pharisees in Luke and Acts*. New York: Peter Lang, 1991.

Grant, R. M. *Gnosticism and Early Christianity*, 2nd ed. New York: Columbia University Press, 1966.

Gray, John. *I and II Kings: A Commentary*, 3rd ed. London: SCM, 1977.

Green, Graham. *The Honorary Consul*. New York: Simon and Schuster, 1973.

Green, Ruth Hurmence. *The Born-Again Skeptic's Guide to the Bible with the Book of Ruth*. Madison: Freedom from Religion Foundation, 1979.

Gregory, Andrew. *The Reception of Luke and Acts in the Period Before Irenaeus: Looking for Luke in the Second Century*. Tübingen: Mohr Siebeck, 2003.

Greschat, Katharina. *Apelles und Hermogenes: Zwei theologische Lehrer des zweiten Jahrhunderts*. Leiden: Brill, 2000.

Griffiths, Gwynn. *Plutarch's De Iside et Osiride*. Cardiff: University of Wales, 1970.

Grindheim, Sigurd. "Jesus and the Food Laws Revisited," *Journal for the Study of the Historical Jesus* 31 (2020): 61–76.

Gruen, Erich. *Heritage and Hellenism: The Reinvention of Jewish Tradition*. Berkeley: University of California Press, 1998.

Hakola, Raimo. *Identity Matters: John, the Jews and Jewishness*. Leiden: Brill, 2005.

Hakola, R. "The Reception and Development of the Johannine Tradition in 1, 2 and 3 John." Pages 17–47 in *The Legacy of John: Second-Century Reception of the Fourth Gospel*, ed. T. Rasimus. Leiden: Brill, 2010.

Halfwassen, J. "Der Demiurg: Seine Stellung in der Philosophie Platonis und seine Deutung im Antiken Platonismus." Pages 39–62 in *Le Timée de Platon: contributions à l'histoire de sa reception*. Leuven: Peeters, 2000.

Hanegraaff, Wouter, ed. *DGWE (Dictionary of Gnosis and Western Esotericism)*. Leiden: Brill, 2006.

Harley-McGowan, Felicity. "The Alexamenos Graffito." Pages 105–40 in *From Celsus to the Catacombs: Visual, Liturgical, and Non-Christian Receptions of Jesus in the Second and Third Centuries CE*, ed. Chris Keith. London: T&T Clark, 2020).

Harnack, Adolf. *Der kirchengeschichtliche Ertrag der exegetischen Arbeiten des Origenes.* 2 vols. Leipzig: Hinrichs, 1918–1919.

Harnack, Adolf. *Marcion: Das Evangelium vom fremden Gott: Eine Monographie zur Geschichte der Grundlegung der katholischen Kirche.* Leipzig: Hinrichs, 1921.

Harnack, Adolf von. *Marcion: The Gospel of the Alien God*, trans. John E. Steely and Lyle D. Bierma. Durham: Labyrinth, 1990.

Harris, Murray J. *Jesus as God: The New Testament Use of Theos in Reference to Jesus.* Grand Rapids: Baker Book House, 1992.

Harris, William V. *Restraining Rage: The Ideology of Anger Control in Classical Antiquity.* Cambridge, MA: Harvard University Press, 2002.

Hayes, Andrew. *Justin Against Marcion: Defining the Christian Philosophy.* Minneapolis: Fortress, 2017.

Hayman, Peter. "Monotheism—a Misused Word in Jewish Studies?" *Journal of Jewish Studies* 42 (1991): 1–15.

Heemstra, Marius. *Fiscus Iudaicus and the Parting of the Ways.* Tübingen: Mohr Siebeck, 2010.

Hegedus, Tim. *Early Christianity and Ancient Astrology.* New York: Peter Lang, 2007.

Heinen, Heinz. "Ägyptische Grundlagen des antiken Antijudaismus: Zum Judenexkurs des Tacitus, Historien V2 2–13," *Trierer Theologische Zeitschrift* 102 (1992): 124–49.

Hengel, Martin. *The Charismatic Leader and His Followers*, trans. James Greig. New York: Crossroad, 1981.

Hengel, Martin. *Crucifixion in the Ancient World and the Folly of the Message of the Cross.* Philadelphia: Fortress, 1989.

Henri, Océane. "A General Approach to *interpretatio Graeca* in the Light of Papyrological Evidence." Pages 43–54 in *Platonismus und spätägyptische Religion: Plutarch und die Ägyptenrezeption in der römischen Kaiserzeit*, ed. Michael Erler and Martin Andreas Stadler. Berlin: de Gruyter, 2017.

Henrichs, Albert. "What Is a Greek God?" Pages 19–39 in *The Gods of Ancient Greece: Identities and Transformations*, ed. Jan N. Bremmer and Andrew Erskine. Edinburgh: Edinburgh University Press, 2010.

Herrmann, F. G. "φθόνος in the World of Plato's *Timaeus*." Pages 53–84 in *Envy, Spite and Jealousy: The Rivalrous Emotions in Ancient Greece*, ed. David Konstan and N. Keith Rutter. Edinburgh: Edinburgh University Press, 2003.

Hill, Charles. *The Johannine Corpus in the Early Church.* Oxford: Oxford University Press, 2004.

Hoffman, R. Joseph. *Marcion: On the Restitution of Christianity: An Essay on the Development of Radical Paulinist Theology in the Second Century.* Missoula: Scholars Press, 1984.

Holladay, Carl. *Fragments from Hellenistic Jewish Authors II: Poets.* Atlanta: Scholars Press, 1989.

Holmén, Tom. *Jesus and Jewish Covenant Thinking.* Leiden: Brill, 2001.

Hooker, Morna. *From Adam to Christ: Essays on Paul.* Cambridge: Cambridge University Press, 1990.

Hopfner, Theodor. *Plutarch Über Isis und Osiris Zweiter Teil: Dei Deutungen der Sage.* Darmstadt: Wissenschaftliche, 1967.

Horbury, William. "Jewish-Christian Relations in Barnabas and Justin Martyr." Pages 315–46 in *Jews and Christians*, ed. Dunn.

Horbury, William. *Jewish War Under Trajan and Hadrian*. Cambridge: Cambridge University Press, 2014.

Horner, G. W. *Sahidic New Testament in the Southern Dialect*. Piscataway: Gorgias, 2010.

Hornung, Erik. *Conceptions of God in Ancient Egypt: The One and the Many*, trans. John Baines. Ithaca: Cornell University Press, 1982.

Hübner, Hans. *Law in Paul's Thought: A Contribution to the Development of Pauline Theology*, trans. James C. G. Greig, ed. John Riches. London: T&T Clark, 1984.

Hultgren, A. J. "Paul's Pre-Christian Persecutions of the Church: Their Purpose, Locale, and Nature," *Journal of Biblical Literature (JBL)* 95 (1976): 97–111.

Irwin, Brian P. "The Curious Incident of the Boys and the Bears: 2 Kings 2 and the Prophetic Authority of Elisha," *Tyndale Bulletin* 67:1 (2016): 23–35.

Jackson, Howard M. *The Lion Becomes Man: The Gnostic Leontomorphic Creator and the Platonic Tradition* Atlanta: Scholars Press, 1985.

Jacobs, Andrew. *Epiphanius of Cyprus: A Cultural Biography of Late Antiquity*. Berkeley: University of California Press, 2016.

Jacobson, Howard. *The Exagoge of Ezekiel*. Cambridge: Cambridge University Press, 1983.

Jacoby, Adolf. "Der angebliche Eselskult der Juden und Christen," *Archiv für Religionswissenschaft* 25 (1927): 265–82.

Jeremias, Gert. *Der Lehrer der Gerechtigkeit*. Göttingen: Vandenhoeck & Ruprecht, 1963.

Jeremias, J. *Der Zorn Gottes im Alten Testament. Das biblische Israel zwischen Verwerfung und Erwählung*. Neukirche-Vluyn: Neukirchener, 2009.

Johnston, Steve. "Le mythe gnostique du blasphème de l'Archonte." Pages 177–201 in *Les textes de Nag Hammadi: Histoire des religions et approaches contemporaines. Actes du colloque international réuni à Paris*, ed. M. Jean-Pierre Mahé, M. Paul-Hubert Poirier, and Madeleine Scopello. Paris: AIBL, 2010.

Jones, F. Stanley. *An Ancient Jewish Christian Source on the History of Christianity: Pseudo-Clementine Recognitions 1.27–71*. Atlanta: Scholars Press, 1995.

Jones, F. Stanley. "Marcionism in the Pseudo-Clementines." Pages 225–44 in *Poussières de christianisme et de judaïsme antiques*, ed. Albert Frey and Rémi Gounelle. Lausanne: Zèbre, 2007.

Joo, S. *Provocation and Punishment. The Anger of God in the Book of Jeremiah and Deuteronomistic Theology*. Berlin: de Gruyter, 2006.

Jorgensen, David W. *Treasure in a Field: Early Christian Reception of the Gospel of Matthew*. Berlin: de Gruyter, 2016.

Karamanolis, George E. *The Philosophy of Early Christianity*. London: Routledge, 2013.

Kazen, Thomas. *Jesus and Purity Halakhah: Was Jesus Indifferent to Impurity?* 2nd ed. Winona Lake: Eisenbrauns, 2010.

Keegan, Peter. *Graffiti in Antiquity*. London: Routledge, 2014.

Keith, Chris, and Loren T. Stuckenbruck, eds. *Evil in Second Temple Judaism and Early Christianity*. Tübingen: Mohr Siebeck, 2016.

Kertelge, Karl, ed. *Das Gesetz im Neuen Testament*. Freiberg: Herder, 1986.

Kim, Seyoon. *The Origin of Paul's Gospel*. Tübingen: Mohr Siebeck, 1981.

Kim, Young Richard. *Epiphanius of Cyprus: Imagining an Orthodox World*. Ann Arbor: University of Michigan, 2015.

King, Karen. "A Distinctive Intertextuality: Genesis and Platonizing Philosophy in the Secret Revelation of John." Pages 3–22 in *Gnosticism, Platonism, and the Late Ancient*

World: Essays in Honor of John Turner. Ed. John Turner, Kevin Corrigan, and Tuomas Rasimus. Leiden: Brill, 2013.

King, Karen. *The Secret Revelation of John*. Cambridge, MA: Harvard University Press, 2006.

Klauck, Hans Josef. *The Apocryphal Acts of the Apostles: An Introduction*, trans. Brian McNeil. Waco: Baylor University Press, 2008.

Klijn, A. F. J. *Jewish-Christian Gospel Traditions*. Leiden: Brill, 1992.

Klimkeit, Hans-Joachim. *Gnosis on the Silk Road: Gnostic Texts from Central Asia*. New York: HarperSanFrancisco, 1993.

Klinghardt, Matthias. *Das ältesten Evangelium und die Entstehung der kanonischen Evangelien*. 2 vols. Tübingen: Francke, 2015.

Klinghardt, Matthias. *Gesetz und Volk Gottes: Das lukanische Verständnis des Gesetzes nach Herkunft, Funktion und seinem Ort in der Geschichte des Urchristentums*. Tübingen: Mohr Siebeck, 1988.

Klinghardt, Matthias. "The Marcionite Gospel and the Synoptic Problem: A New Suggestion," *Novum Testamentum* 50 (2008): 1–27.

Kugel, James. *Traditions of the Bible: A Guide to the Bible As It Was At the Start of the Common Era*. Cambridge, MA: Harvard University Press, 1998.

Koester, Helmut. "Gnostic Sayings and Controversy Traditions in John 8:12–59." Pages 97–110 in *Nag Hammadi, Gnosticism & Early Christianity*, eds. C. W. Hedrick and R. Hodgson. Peabody: Hendrickson, 1986.

Konstan, David. *The Emotions of the Ancient Greeks: Studies in Aristotle and Classical Literature*. Toronto: University of Toronto Press, 2006.

Kuhn, Heinz-Wolfgang. "The Impact of Selected Qumran Texts on the Understanding of Pauline Theology." Pages 153–86 in *The Bible and the Dead Sea Scrolls Volume Three: The Scrolls and Christian Origins*, ed. James H. Charlesworth. Waco: Baylor University Press, 2006.

Kummel, W. G. "Das Gesetz und die Propheten gehen bis Johannes'—Lukas 16,16 im Zusammenhang der heilgeschichtlichen Theologie der Lukasschriften." Pages 89–102 in *Verborum Veritas: Festschrift für Gustav Stählin zum 70. Geburtstag*, ed. Otto Böcher and Klaus Haacker. Wuppertal: Rolf Brockhaus, 1972.

Laato, A., and Johannes C. de Moor, eds. *Theodicy in the World of the Bible*. Leiden: Brill, 2003.

Lahe, Jaan. *Gnosis und Judentum: Alttestamentliche und jüdische Motive in der gnostischen Literatur und das Ursprungsproblem der Gnosis*. Leiden: Brill, 2006.

Lambrecht, Jan. "Gesetzverständnis bei Paulus." Pages 88–127 in *Das Gesetz im Neuen Testament*, ed. Karl Kertelge. Freiberg: Herder, 1986.

Lampe, Peter. *From Paul to Valentinus: Christians at Rome in the First Two Centuries*, trans. Michael Steinhauser, ed. Marshall D. Johnson. Minneapolis: Fortress, 2003.

Lanfranchi, Pierluigi. *L'Exagoge d'Ezéchiel le Tragique: Introduction, texte, traduction et commentaire*. Leiden: Brill, 2006.

Lanfranchi, Pierluigi, and Joseph Verheyden, eds., *Jews and Christians in Antiquity: A Regional Perspective*. Leuven: Peeters, 2018.

Lang, Bernhard. *The Hebrew God: Portrait of an Ancient Deity*. New Haven: Yale University Press, 2002.

Lange, Armin, Hermann Lichtenberger, and Diethard Römheld, eds. *Die Dämonen: Die Dämonologie der israelitisch-jüdischen und frühchristlichen Literatur im Kontext ihrer Umwelt*. Tübingen: Mohr Siebeck, 2003.

Lanzillotta, Lautaro Roig. "The Envy of God in the Paradise Story According to the Greek *Life of Adam and Eve*." Pages 537–50 in *Flores Florentino: Dead Sea Scrolls and Other Early Jewish Studies in Honour of Florentino García Martínez*, eds. Anthony Hilhorst, Émile Puech, and Eibert Tigchelaar. Leiden: Brill, 2007.

Layton, Bentley, ed. *The Rediscovery of Gnosticism*. 2 vols. Leiden: Brill, 1981.

Ledegang, Fred. "The Ophites and the Ophite Diagram in Celsus and Origen." Pages 51–84 in *Heretics and Heresies in the Ancient Church and in Eastern Christianity: Studies in Honour of Adelbert Davids*, eds. Joseph Verheyden and Herman Teule. Leuven: Peeters, 2011.

Leonhardt-Balzer, Jutta. "Yaldabaoth und seine Bande. Die Gegner im Johannesapokryphon." Pages 351–66 in *Dualismus, Dämonologie*, ed. Frey and Edzard.

Levene, Dan. *Jewish-Aramaic Curse Texts from Late Antique Mesopotamia*. Leiden: Brill, 2004.

Levene, David. "Defining the Divine in Rome," *Transactions of the American Philological Association* 142 (2012): 41–81.

Levine, Amy-Jill. "Discharging Responsibility: Matthean Jesus, Biblical Law, and Hemorrhaging Woman." Pages 379–97 in *Treasures New and Old: Contributions to Matthean Studies*, ed. David Bauer and Mark Allan Powell. Atlanta: Scholars Press.

Levieils, Xavier. *Contra Christianos: La critique sociale et religieuse du Christianisme des Concile de Nicée*. Berlin: de Gruyter, 2007.

Lietaert Peerbolte, Bert Jan. "Jewish Monotheism and Christian Origins." Pages 227–46 in *Empsychoi Logoi—Religious Innovations in Antiquity: Studies in Honour of Pieter Willem van der Horst*, ed. Alberdina Houtman et al. Leiden: Brill, 2008.

Lieu, Judith M. *Image and Reality: The Jews in the World of the Christians in the Second Century*. Edinburgh: T&T Clark, 1996.

Lieu, Judith M. *Marcion and the Making of a Heretic: God and Scripture in the Second Century*. Cambridge: Cambridge University Press, 2015.

Lieu, Judith M. "Self-Definition vis-à-vis the Jewish Matrix." Pages 214–29 in *Cambridge History of Christianity*, Vol. 1, ed. Margaret M. Mitchell. Cambridge: Cambridge University Press, 2006.

Lieu, Samuel N. C. *Hegemonius: Acta Archelai (The Acts of Archelaus)*. Turnhout: Brepols, 2001.

Lim, Richard. *Public Disputation, Power, and Social Order in Late Antiquity*. Berkeley: University of California Press, 1995.

Lindars, Barnabas. "All Foods Clean: Thoughts on Jesus and the Law." Pages 61–71 in *Law and Religion: Essays on the Place of the Law in Israel and Early Christianity*, ed. Lindars. Cambridge: James Clarke, 1988.

Lindars, Barnabas. *Jesus, Paul and the Law*. London: SPCK, 1990.

Lindars, Barnabas. *New Testament Apologetic: The Doctrinal Significance of the Old Testament Quotations*. London: SCM Press, 1973.

Lindemann, Andreas. *Paulus im ältesten Christentum: Das Bild des Apostles und die Rezeption der paulinischen Theologie in der frühchristlichen Literatur bis Marcion*. Tübingen: Mohr Siebeck, 1979.

Litwa, M. David. "The Curse of the Creator: *Galatians* 3.13 and Negative Demiurgy." Pages 13–30 in *Telling the Christian Story Differently: Counternarratives from Nag Hammadi and Beyond*, eds. Francis Watson and Sarah Parkhouse. London: Bloomsbury Academic Press, 2020.

Litwa, M. David. *Desiring Divinity: Self-Deification in Ancient Jewish and Christian Mythmaking*. Oxford: Oxford University Press, 2016.

Litwa, M. David. "Did Marcion Call the Creator 'God'?" *Journal of Theological Studies*, forthcoming Autumn 2021.

Litwa, M. David. "The Father of the Devil (John 8:44): A Christian Exegetical Inspiration for the Evil Creator," *VC* 74:5 (2020):540–65.

Litwa, M. David. *Hermetica II: The Excerpts of Stobaeus, Papyrus Fragments, and Ancient Testimonies in a English Translation with Notes and Introductions*. Cambridge: Cambridge University Press, 2018.

Litwa, M. David. *Refutation of All Heresies*. Atlanta: SBL, 2016.

Litwa, M. David. *We Are Being Transformed: Deification in Paul's Soteriology*. Berlin: de Gruyter, 2012.

Llewelyn, Stephen Robert, Alexandra Robinson, and Blake Edward Wassell. "Does John 8:44 Imply that the Devil Has a Father? Contesting the Pro-Gnostic Reading," *Novum Testamentum* 60 (2018): 14–23.

Loader, William R. G. *Jesus' Attitude Towards the Law*. Tübingen: Mohr Siebeck, 1997.

Logan, Alistair H. B. "The Jealousy of God: Exod 20,5 in Gnostic and Rabbinic Theology," *Studia Biblica* 1 (1978): 197–203.

Logan, Alastair H. B. *Gnostic Truth and Christian Heresy: A Study in the History of Gnosticism*. Edinburgh: T&T Clark, 1996.

Löhr, Winrich Alfried. *Basilides und seine Schule: Eine Studie zur Theologie- und Kirchengeschichte des zweiten Jahrhunderts*. Tübingen: Mohr Siebeck, 1996.

Löhr, Winrich. "Christliche 'Gnostiker' in Alexandria im zweiten Jahrhundert." Pages 413–33 in *Alexandria*, ed. Tobias Georges, Felix Albrecht, and Reinhard Feldmeier. Tübingen: Mohr Siebeck, 2013.

Löhr, Winrich. "Did Markion Distinguish Between a Just God and a Good God?" Pages 131–46 in *Markion*, ed. May and Greschat.

Löhr, Winrich. "Die Auslegung des Gesetzes bei Markion, den Gnostikern und den Manichäern." Pages 77–95 in *Stimuli: Exegese und ihre Hermeneutik in Antike und Christentum: Festschrift für Ernst Dassmann*, eds. Georg Schöllgen and Clemens Scholten. Münster: Aschendorff, 1996.

Löhr, Winrich. "Gnostic and Manichean Interpretation." Pages 584–604 in *The New Cambridge History of the Bible Vol. 1*. Ed. James Carleton Paget and Joachim Schaper. Cambridge: Cambridge University Press, 2013.

Lona, Horacio E. *Die "Wahre Lehre" des Kelsos*. Freiburg: Herder, 2005.

Lucarelli, Rita. "The Donkey in the Graeco-Egyptian Papyri." Pages 89–103 in *Languages, Objects, and the Transmission of Rituals: An Interdisciplinary Analysis on Ritual Practices in the Graeco-Egyptian Papyri (PGM)*, ed. Sabina Crippa and Emanuele M. Ciampini. Venice: Cafoscarina, 2017.

Longenecker, Richard N. *Galatians*. Word Biblical Commentary Vol. 41. Columbia: Word, 1990.

Luijendijk, Annemarie. *Greetings in the Lord: Early Christians and the Oxyrhynchus Papyri*. Cambridge, MA: Harvard Theological Studies, 2008.

Lukas, Volker. *Rhetorik und literarischer "Kampf": Tertullians Streitschrift gegen Marcion als Paradigma der Selbstvergewisserung der Orthodoxie gegenüber der Häresie*. Frankfurt am Main: Peter Lang, 2008.

Lundhaug, Hugo, and Lance Jenott. *The Monastic Origins of the Nag Hammadi Codices*. Tübingen: Mohr Siebeck, 2015.

Luttikhuizen, Gerard P. "The Demonic Demiurge in Gnostic Mythology." Pages 148–60 in *The Fall of Angels*, eds. Christoph Auffarth and Loren T. Stuckenbruck. Leiden: Brill, 2003.

Luttikhuizen, Gerard P. *Gnostic Revisions of Genesis Stories and Early Jesus Traditions.* Leiden: Brill, 2006.

Luttikhuizen, Gerard P. "Sethianer?," *ZAC* 13:1 (2009): 76–86.

MacDonald, Nathan. *Deuteronomy and the Meaning of "Monotheism."* Tübingen: Mohr Siebeck, 2012.

MacRae, George. "Anti-Dualist Polemic in 2 Cor 4,6?" Pages 420–31 in *Studia Evangelica IV*, ed. F. L. Cross. Berlin: Akademie, 1968.

MacRae, George W. *Studies in New Testament and Gnosticism*, ed. Daniel J. Harrington and Stanley B. Marrow. Wilmington: Michael Glazier, 1987.

Majercik, Ruth, ed. *The Chaldean Oracles: Text, Translation and Commentary.* Leiden: Brill, 1989.

Mansfeld, Jaap. "Bad World and Demiurge: A 'Gnostic' Motif from Parmenides and Empedocles to Lucretius and Philo." Pages 261–314 in *Studies in Gnosticism and Hellenistic Religions, Festschrift Gilles Quispel*, ed. R. van den Broek and M. J. Vermaseren. Leiden: Brill, 1981.

Marjanen, Antti, and Petri Luomanen. *A Companion to Second-Century Christian "Heretics."* Leiden: Brill, 2005.

Markschies, Christoph. "Die Geburt Mariens." Pages 416–19 in *Antike christlichen Apokryphen in deutscher Übersetzung*, ed. Jens Schröter and Markschies. Tübingen: Mohr Siebeck, 2012. Markschies, Christoph. *Gnosis: An Introduction.* London: T&T Clark, 2003.

Markschies, Christoph. *Gnosis und Christentum.* Berlin: Berlin University Press, 2009.

Markschies, Christoph. "Heis Theos-Ein Gott? Der monotheimus und das antike Christentum." Pages 209–34 in *Polytheismus und Monotheismus in den Religionen des Vorderen Orients*, ed. M. Krebernik and J. van Oorschot. Münster: Ugarit, 2002.

Martin, Ralph P. *2 Corinthians*, 2nd ed. Grand Rapids: Zondervan, 2014.

Martín Hernández, Raquel. "More than a Logos: The ΙΩΕΡΒΗΘ Logos in Context." Pages 187–210 in *Litterae Magicae: Studies in Honour of Roger S. O. Tomlin*, ed. Celia Sánchez Natalías. Zaragoza: Libros Pórtico, 2019.

Martínez, Florentino García. "Galatians 3:10–14 in the Light of Qumran." Pages 51–67 in *The Dead Sea Scrolls and Pauline Literature*, ed. Jean-Sébastien Rey. Leiden: Brill, 2014.

Martyn, J. Louis. *History and Theology of the Fourth Gospel*, 3rd ed. Louisville: Westminster/John Knox, 2003.

Matera, Frank J. *II Corinthians: A Commentary.* Louisville: Westminster/John Knox, 2003.

Matlock, R. Barry. "Helping Paul's Argument Work? The Curse of Galatians 3.10–14." Pages 154–79 in *The Torah in the New Testament: Papers Delivered at the Manchester-Lausanne Seminar of June 2008*, ed. Michael Tait and Peter Oakes. London: T&T Clark, 2009.

Matlock, R. Barry. *Unveiling the Apocalyptic Paul: Paul's Interpreters and the Rhetoric of Criticism.* London: Bloomsbury, 1996.

May, Gerhard. "Marcion in Contemporary Views." Pages 13–34 in *Markion: Gesammelte Aufsätze*, eds. Katharina Greschat and Martin Meiser. Mainz: Philipp von Zabern, 2005.

May, Gerhard. "Marcion und der Gnostiker Kerdon." Pages 233–48 in *Evangelischer Glaube und Geschichte, Grete Mecenseffy zum 85. Geburtstag*, ed. A. Raddatz and K. Lüthi. Vienna: Oberkirchenrat, 1984.

May, Gerhard. "Marcions Genesisauslegung und die 'Antithesen.'" Pages 189–98 in *Die Weltlichkeit des Glaubens in der Alten Kirche. Festschrift für Ulrich Wickert*, ed. Dietmar Wyrwa. Berlin: de Gruyter, 1997.

May, Gerhard, and Katharina Greschat. *Markion und seine kirchengeschichtliche Wirkung*. Berlin: de Gruyter, 2002.

McGowan, Andrew. "Marcion's Love of Creation," *Journal of Early Christian Studies* 9:3 (2001): 295–311.

McKnight, Scot, and Joseph B. Modica, eds. *Do My Opponents Say that I Am? An Investigation of the Accusations Against the Historical Jesus*. London: T&T Clark, 2008.

Meeks, Wayne. "The Divine Agent and His Counterfeit in Philo and the Fourth Gospel." Pages 43–67 in *Aspects of Religious Propaganda in Judaism and Early Christianity*, ed. Elizabeth Schüssler Fiorenza. Notre Dame: University of Notre Dame Press, 1976.

Meier, John P. *A Marginal Jew: Rethinking the Historical Jesus*, Vol. 4. New Haven: Yale University Press, 2009.

Meijering, E. P. *Tertullian contra Marcion: Gotteslehre in der Polemic*. Leiden: Brill, 1977.

Merkelbach, Reinhold. *Abrasax: ausgewählte Papyri religiösen und magischen Inhalts. Band III: Zwei griechisch-ägyptsiche Weihezeremonien (Die Leidener Weltschöpfung-Die Pschai-Aion-Liturgie)*. Opladen: Westdeutscher, 1992.

Messner, Richard G. "Elisha and the Bears," *Grace Journal* 3 (1962): 12–24.

Michailides, G. "Papyrus contenant un dessin du dieu Seth à tête d'âne," *Aegyptus* 32:1 (1952): 45–53.

Miggelbrink, R. *Der zornige Gott. Die Bedeutung einer anstössigen biblischen Tradition*. Darmstadt: Wissenschaftliche, 2002.

Miles, Jack. *God: A Biography*. London: Simon & Schuster.

Miller, Gene. "ΑΡΧΟΝΤΩΝ ΤΟΥ ΑΙΩΝΟΣ ΤΟΥΤΟΥ—A New Look at 1 Corinthians 2:6–8," *JBL* 91:4 (1972): 522–28.

Mills, Michael J. "ΦΘΟΝΟΣ and Its Related ΠΑΘΗ in Plato and Aristotle," *Phronesis* 30:1 (1985): 1–12.

Milobenski, Ernst. *Der Neid in der griechischen Philosophie*. Wiesbaden: Harrassowitz, 1964.

Mitchell, Margaret M. *Paul, the Corinthians and the Birth of Christian Hermeneutics*. Cambridge: Cambridge University Press, 2010.

Modrzejewski, Joseph Mélèze. *The Jews of Egypt from Ramses II to Emperor Trajan*, trans. Robert Cornman. Edinburgh: T&T Clark, 1995.

Moll, Sebastian. *The Arch-Heretic Marcion*. Tübingen: Mohr Siebeck, 2010.

Moll, Sebastian. "Justin and the Pontic Wolf." Pages 145–51 in *Justin Martyr and His Worlds*, ed. Sara Parvis and Paul Foster. Minneapolis: Fortress, 2007.

Moreschini, Claudio. *Apuleius and the Metamorphosis of Platonism*. Turnout: Brepols, 2014.

Moreschini, Claudio. "Tertullian's Adversus Marcionem and Middle Platonism," *ZAC* 21:1 (2017): 140–63.

Moreschini, Claudio, and Enrico Norelli. *Early Christian Greek and Latin Literature: A Literary History*, trans. Matthew J. O'Connell. 2 vols. Peabody: Hendrickson, 2005.

Moses, Robert Ewusie. *Practices of Power: Revisiting Principalities and Powers in the Pauline Letters*. Minneapolis: Fortress, 2014.

Muehlenberg, Ekkehard. "Marcion's Jealous God." Pages 93–114 in *Disciplina Nostra: Essays in Memory of Robert F. Evans*, ed. Donald F. Winslow. Philadelphia: Patristic Foundation, 1979.

Murphy-O'Connor, Jerome. *The Theology of the Second Letter to the Corinthians*. Cambridge: Cambridge University Press, 1991.

Naumann, Victor. "Das Problem des Bösen in Tertullians zweitem Buch gegen Marcion," *Zeitschrift Katholische Theologie 58* (1934): 311–63.

Nicholson, Suzanne. Dynamic Oneness: *The Significance and Flexibility of Paul's One-God Language*. Cambridge: James Clark, 2010.

Noll, Mark A. "The Bible Then and Now." Pages 331–44 in *The Bible in American Life*, ed. Philip Goff, Arthur Farnsley, and Peter Thuesen. Oxford: Oxford University Press, 2017.

Norelli, Enrico. "Marcion: ein christlicher Philosoph oder ein Christ gegen die Philosophie?" in *Markion*, ed. May and Greschat, 113–30.

Norelli, Enrico. *Marie des apocryphes: Enquête de la mère de Jésus dans le christianisme antique*. Geneva: Labor et Fides, 2009.

O'Brien, Carl Séan. *Demiurge in Ancient Thought: Secondary Gods and Divine Mediators*. Cambridge: Cambridge University Press, 2015.

O'Brien, Kelli S. "The Curse of the Law (Galatians 3.13): Crucifixion, Persecution, and Deuteronomy 21.22–23," *JSNT* 29 (2006): 55–76.

Opsomer, Jan. "Demiurges in Early Imperial Platonism." Pages 51–99 in *Gott und die Götter bei Plutarch: Götterbilder-Gottesbilder-Weltbilder*, ed. Rainer Hirsch-Luipold. Berlin: de Gruyter, 2005.

Opsomer, Jan, and Carlos Steel. "Evil Without a Cause: Proclus's Doctrine on the Origin of Evil and Its Antecedents in Hellenistic Philosophy." Pages 229–60 in *Zur Rezeption des hellenistischen Philosophie in der Spätantike: Akten der 1. Tagung der Karl-und-Gertrud-Abel-Stiftung vom 22.– 25. September 1997 in Trier*, ed. Therese Fuhrer, Michael Erler, and Karin Schlapbach. Stuttgart: F. Steiner, 1999.

Orlov, Andrei A. "Adoil Outside the Cosmos." Pages 30–57 in *Histories of the Hidden God: Concealment and Revelation in Western Gnostic, Esoteric, and Mystical Traditions*, ed. April D. DeConick and Grant Adamson. London: Acumen, 2016.

Orlov, Andrei A. *Enoch-Metatron Tradition*. Tübingen: Mohr Siebeck, 2005.

Oropeza, B. J. *Exploring Second Corinthians: Death and Life, Hardship and Rivalry*. Atlanta: SBL Press, 2016.

Pachoumi, Eleni. *The Concepts of the Divine in the Greek Magical Papyri*. Tübingen: Mohr Siebeck, 2017.

Pagels, Elaine. *Adam, Eve and the Serpent*. New York: Random House, 1988.

Pagels, Elaine. "Exegesis of Genesis 1 in the Gospels of Thomas and John," *JBL* 118 (1999): 477–96.

Pagels, Elaine. *Origins of Satan: How Christians Demonized Jews, Pagans, and Heretics*. New York: Vintage, 2011.

Paine, Thomas. *The Age of Reason*. Newburyport: Open Road Media: 2017.

Parris, David Paul. *Reception Theory and Biblical Hermeneutics*. Eugene: Pickwick, 2008.

Parrott, Douglas M. "Gnosticism and Egyptian Religion," *Novum Testamentum (NovT)* 29:1 (1987): 73–93.

Pate, C. Marvin. *Reverse of the Curse: Paul, Wisdom, and the Law*. Tübingen: Mohr Siebeck, 2000.

Pearson, Birger. *Ancient Gnosticism: Traditions and Literature*. Minneapolis: Fortress, 2007.

Pearson, Birger. "Egyptian Seth and Gnostic Seth." Pages 25–43 in *Society of Biblical Literature 1977 Seminar Papers*, ed. Paul J. Achtemeier. Missoula: SBL, 1977.

Pearson, Birger. "Eusebius and Gnosticism." Pages 291–310 in *Eusebius, Christianity, and Judaism*, ed. Harold W. Attridge and Gohei Hata. Leiden: Brill, 1992.

Pearson, Birger A. "Gnosticism as a Religion." Pages 81–101 in *Was There a Gnostic Religion?*, ed. Antti Marjanen. Helsinki: Finnish Exegetical Society, 2005.

Pearson, Birger A. *Gnosticism, Judaism, and Egyptian Christianity*. Minneapolis, Fortress, 1990.

Pearson, Birger A. "Ophites." Pages 895–98 in *DGWE*.

Peels, Rik. "Can God Be Jealous?" *Heythrop Journal* 59:1 (2018): 1–15.

Penchansky, David. *What Rough Beast? Images of God in the Hebrew Bible*. Louisville: Westminster John Knox, 1999.

Penchansky, David, and Paul L. Reddit. *Shall Not the Judge of All the Earth Do Right? Studies on the Nature of God in Tribute to James L. Crenshaw*. University Park: Pennsylvania State University Press, 1999.

Perkins, Pheme. "The Letter to the Ephesians." Page 399 in *The New Interpreter's Bible*. 12 vols. Nashville: Abingdon, 2000, Vol. 11.

Peterson, Erik, and Christoph Markschies. *Heis Theos: Epigraphische, formgeschichtliche und religionsgeschichtliche Untersuchungen: Nachdruck der Ausgabe von Erik Peterson mit Ergänzungen un Kommentaren* Würzburg: Echter, 2012.

Pétrement, Simone. *A Separate God: The Christian Origins of Gnosticism*, trans. Carol Harrison. San Francisco: Harper & Row, 1990.

Pleše, Zlatko. "Evil and Its Sources in Gnostic Traditions." Pages 101–32 in *Die Wurzel allen Übels: Vorstellungen über die Herkunft des Bösen und Schlechten in der Philosophie und Religion des. 1.– 4. Jahrhunderts*, ed. Fabienne Jourdan and Rainer Hirsch-Luipold. Tübingen: Mohr Siebeck, 2015.

Plotz, David. *The Good Book: The Bizarre, Hilarious, Disturbing, Marvelous, and Inspiring Things I Learned When I Read Every Single Word of the Bible*. New York: Harper Perenniel, 2010.

Plummer, Alfred. *Second Epistle of St. Paul to the Corinthians*. Edinburgh: T&T Clark, 1915.

Poirier, Paul-Hubert. "Exégèse manichéenne et antimanichéenne de II Corinthiens 4,4 chez Titus de Bostra (Contre les Manichéens IV, 108)." Pages 273–86 in *Gnose et Manichéisme. Entre les oasis d'Egypte et la Route de la Soie: Hommage à Jean-Daniel Dubois*, ed. A. van den Kerchove and L. G. Soares Santoprete. Turnhout: Brepols, 2017.

Pourkier, Aline. *L'hérésiologie chez Épiphane de Salamine*. Paris: Beauchesne, 1992.

Préaux, Jean-G. "Deus christianorum Onocoetes." Pages 639–54 in *Hommages à Léon Hermann*. Brussels: Latomus, 1960.

Pretty, Robert A. *Adamantius: Dialogue on the True Faith in God*. Leuven: Peeters, 1997.

Procopé-Walter, A. "Iao und Set (Zu den figurae magicae in den Zauberpapyri)," *Archiv für Religionswissenschaft* 30 (1933): 34–69.

Puech, H.-Ch. "Archontiker." Pages 634–43 in *Reallexikon für Antike und Christentum*, Vol. 1, ed. Theodor Klauser et al. Stuttgart: Anton Hiersemann, 1950.

Rainbow, Paul A. "Monotheism and Christology in 1 Corinthians 8:4–6" (D.Phil. thesis, Oxford University, 1987).

Räisänen, Heikki. *The Idea of Divine Hardening: A Comparative Study of the Notion of Divine Hardening, Leading Astray and Inciting to Evil in the Bible and the Quran*. Helsinki: Finnish Exegetical Society, 1976.

Räisänen, Heikki. "Marcion." Pages 301–15 in *The Blackwell Companion to Paul*, ed. Stephen Westerholm. Malden: John Wiley & Sons, 2011.

Räisänen, Heikki. *Marcion, Muhammad and the Mahatma: Exegetical Perspectives on the Encounter of Cultures and Faiths*. London: SCM, 1997.

Räisänen, Heikki. *Paul and the Law*. Tübingen: Mohr Siebeck, 1983.

Rakoczy, Thomas. *Böser Blick, Macht des Auges und Neid der Götter: Eine Untersuchung zur Kraft des Blickes in der griechischen Literatur*. Tübingen: Gunter Narr, 1996.

Rasimus, Tuomas, ed. *The Legacy of John: Second-Century Reception of the Fourth Gospel*. Leiden: Brill, 2010.

Rasimus, Tuomas. "Ptolemaus and the Valentinian Exegesis of John's Prologue." Pages 145–71 in Rasimus, ed., *The Legacy of John*.

Rasimus, Tuomas. *Paradise Reconsidered in Gnostic Mythmaking: Rethinking Sethianism in Light of the Ophite Evidence*. Leiden: Brill, 2009.

Reinhartz, Adele. *Cast Out of the Covenant: Jews and Anti-Judaism in the Gospel of John*. Lanham: Lexington-Fortress Academic, 2018.

Reinhartz, Adele. "How 'the Jews' Became Part of the Plot." Page 99–116 in *Jesus, Judaism, and Christian Anti-Judaism: Reading the New Testament after the Holocaust*, ed. Paula Fredriksen and Adele Reinhartz. Louisville: Westminster/John Knox, 2002.

Reuter, E. "*qn'*." Pages 51–62 in *Theologisches Wörterbuch zum Alten Testament*, Vol. 7, ed. G. Johannes Botterweck and Helmer Ringgren. Stuttgart: Kohlhammer, 1993.

Reydams-Schils, Gretchen. "'Becoming Like God' in Platonism and Stoicism." Pages 142–58 in *From Stoicism*, ed. Engberg-Pedersen.

Reydams-Schils, Gretchen J. *Demiurge and Providence: Stoic and Platonist Readings of Plato's Timaeus*. Turnhout: Brepols, 1999.

Ricoux, Odile. "Des Chrétiens accusés d'onolâtrie à Carthage," *Lalies* 16 (1996): 53–73.

Riess, Werner. *Performing Interpersonal Violence: Court, Curse, and Comedy in Fourth-Century BCE Athens*. Berlin: de Gruyter, 2012.

Robertson, R. G. "Ezekiel the Tragedian." Volume 2, Pages 803-20 in James Charlesworth, ed., *OTP*.

Robinson, Bernard P. "II Kings 2:23–25: Elisha and the She-Bears," *Scripture Bulletin* 14:1 (1983): 2–3.

Roetzel, C. J. "Jewish Christian-Gentile Christian Relations: A Discussion of Ephesians 2.15a," *Zeitschrift für Neutestamentliche Wissenschaft* 74 (1983): 81–89.

Römer, Thomas. "The Origin and the Status of Evil according to the Hebrew Bible." Pages 53–66 in *Die Wurzel allen Übels: Über die Herkunft des Bösen und Schlechten in der Philosophie und Religion des 1.- 4. Jahrhunderts*, ed. Fabienne Jourdan and Rainer Hirsch-Luipold. Tübingen: Mohr Siebeck, 2015.

Roth, Dieter. "Evil in Marcion's Conception of the Old Testament God." Pages 340–55 in *Evil in Second Temple*, ed. Keith and Stuckenbruck.

Roth, Dieter. "The Link Between Luke and Marcion's Gospel: Prolegomena and Initial Considerations." Pages 59–80 in *Luke on Jesus, Paul and Christianity: What Did He Really Know?*, ed. Joseph Verheyden and John S. Kloppenborg. Leuven: Peeters, 2017.

Roth, Dieter. "Matthean Texts and Tertullian's Accusations in *Adversus Marcionem*," *Journal of Theological Studies* 59 (2008): 580–97.

Roth, Dieter. *The Text of Marcion's Gospel*. Leiden: Brill, 2015.

Roubekas, Nickolas P. *An Ancient Theory of Religion: Euhemerism from Antiquity to the Present*. London: Routledge, 2017.

Rowland, Christopher. "The Parting of the Ways: The Evidence of Jewish and Christian Apocalyptic and Mystical Material." Pages 213–38 in *Jews and Christians: The Parting of the Ways A.D. 70 to 135*, ed. James D. G. Dunn. Grand Rapids: Eerdmans, 1993.

Runia, David. *Creation of the Cosmos According to Moses*. Atlanta: SBL Press, 2005.

Runia, David T. *Philo of Alexandria and the Timaeus of Plato*. Leiden: Brill, 1986.

Sagi, Avi. "The Punishment of Amalek in Jewish Tradition: Coping with the Moral Problem," *Harvard Theological Review* 87:3 (1994): 323–46.

Salo, K. *Luke's Treatment of the Law. A Redaction-Critical Investigation*. Helsinki: Suomalainen Tiedeakatemia, 1991.

Sanders, E. P. *Jesus and Judaism*. London: SCM, 1985.

Sanders, E. P. *Paul, the Law, and the Jewish People*. Philadelphia: Fortress, 1983.

Sandnes, Karl Olav. *Paul Perceived: An Interactionist Perspective on Paul and the Law*. Tübingen: Mohr Siebeck, 2018.

Schäfer, Peter, ed. *The Bar Kokhba War Reconsidered: New Perspectives on the Second Jewish Revolt Against Rome*. Tübingen: Mohr Siebeck, 2003.

Schäfer, Peter. *The History of the Jews in the Graeco-Roman World*. London: Routledge, 2003.

Schäfer, Peter. *Jesus in the Talmud*. Princeton: Princeton University Press, 2007.

Schäfer, Peter. *Judeophobia: Attitudes Toward the Jews in the Ancient World*. Cambridge, MA: Harvard University Press, 1997.

Schaller, Berndt. *Jesus und der Sabbat: Franz-Delitzsch-Vorlesung 1992*. Münster: Delitzsch Judaic Institute, 1994.

Schenke, Hans Martin. "The Phenomenon and Significance of Gnostic Sethianism." Pages 588–616 in *Rediscovery of Gnosticism*, Vol. 2, ed. Bentley Layton. Leiden: Brill.

Scherbenske, Eric W. "Marcionite Paratexts, Pretexts, and Edition of the Corpus Paulinum." Pages 71–115 in *Canonizing Paul: Ancient Editorial Practice and the Corpus Paulinum*, ed. Scherbenske. Oxford: Oxford University Press, 2013.

Scherbenske, Eric W. "Marcion's *Antitheses* and the Isagogic Genre," *VC* 64:3 (2010): 255–79.

Schmid, Hebert. *Christen und Sethianer: Ein Beitrag zur Diskussion um den religionsgeschichtlichen und den kirchengeschichtlichen Begriff der Gnosis*. Leiden: Brill, 2018.

Schmid, Ulrich. *Marcion und sein Apostolos: Rekonstruktion und historische Einordnung der Marcionitischen Paulusbriefausgabe*. Berlin: de Gruyter, 1995.

Segal, Alan. "Ruler of This World: Attitudes Toward Mediator Figures and the Importance of Sociology for Self-Definition." Pages 245–68 in *Jewish and Christian Self-Definition Vol. 2*, ed. E. P. Sanders. Philadelphia: Fortress, 1980.

Seifrid, Mark A. *Justification by Faith: The Origin and Development of a Central Pauline Theme*. Leiden: Brill, 1992.

Seifrid, Mark A. *The Second Letter to the Corinthians*. Grand Rapids: Eerdmans, 2014.

Selvidge, Marla. "Mark 5:25–34 and Leviticus 15:19–20: A Reaction to Restrictive Purity Regulations," *JBL* 103 (1984): 619–23.

Sibinga, Joost Smit. *The Old Testament Text of Justin Martyr*. Leiden: Brill, 1963.

Skarsaune, Oskar. "Is Christianity Monotheistic? Patristic Perspectives on a Jewish/Christian Debate," *Studia Patristica* 29 (1997): 340–63.

Skhul, Minna. *Reading Ephesians: Exploring Social Entrepreneurship in the Text*. London: T&T Clark, 2009.

Smelik, K. A. D., and E. A. Hemelrijk. "'Who Knows Not What Monsters Demented Egypt Worships?' Opinions on Egyptian Animal Worship in Antiquity as Part of the Ancient

Conception of Egypt." Pages 1920–81 in *ANRW* Vol. II.17.4, ed. Wolfgang Haase. Berlin: de Gruyter,1984.

Smidt, Corwin E. "The Continuing Distinctive Role of the Bible in American Lives." Pages 331–44 in *The Bible in American Life*, ed. Philip Goff, Arthur Farnsley, and Peter Thuesen.

Smith, Carl B. *No Longer Jews: The Search for Gnostic Origins*. Peabody: Hendrickson, 2004.

Smith, Daniel A. "Marcion's Gospel and the Synoptics." Pages 129–73 in *Gospels and Gospel Traditions in the Second Century: Experiments in Reception*, eds. Jens Schröter, Tobias Nicklas, and Josef Verheyden. Berlin: de Gruyter, 2019.

Smith, Mark S. *God in Translation: Deities in Cross-Cultural Discourse in the Biblical World*. Grand Rapids: Eerdmans, 2008.

Smith, Morton. "The Jewish Elements in the Magical Papyri." Pages 242–56 in *Studies in the Cult of Yahweh*, Vol. 2, ed. Shaye Cohen, 2 vols. Leiden: Brill, 1996.

Spieckermann, Hermann. "The 'Father' of the Old Testament and Its History." Pages 73–84 in *The Divine Father: Religious and Philosophical Concepts of Divine Parenthood in Antiquity*, ed. Felix Albrecht and Reinhard Feldmeier. Leiden: Brill, 2014.

Spittler, Janet E. *Animals in the Apocryphal Acts of the Apostles: The Wild Kingdom of Early Christian Literature*. Tübingen: Mohr Siebeck, 2008.

Stanley, Christopher D. "'Under a Curse': A Fresh Reading of Galatians 3.10–14," *NTS* 36 (1990): 481–511.

Stark, Rodney. *The Rise of Christianity: A Sociologist Reconsiders History*. Princeton: Princeton University Press, 1996.

Stern, Menahem. *Greek and Latin Authors on Jews and Judaism*. 3 vols. Jerusalem: Israel Academy of Science and Humanities, 1974.

Still, Todd. D. "Shadow and Light: Marcion's (Mis)Construal of the Apostle Paul." Pages 91–107 in *Paul and the Second Century*, ed. Michael F. Bird and Joseph R. Dodson. London: T&T Clark, 2011.

Stoyanov, Yuri. *The Other God: Dualist Religions from Antiquity to the Cathar Heresy*. New Haven: Nota Bene, 2000.

Strawbridge, Jennifer R. *The Pauline Effect: The Use of the Pauline Epistles by Early Christian Writers*. Berlin: de Gruyter, 2015.

Stroumsa, Guy. *Another Seed: Studies in Gnostic Mythology*. Leiden: Brill, 1984.

Stylianopoulos, Theodore. *Justin Martyr and the Mosaic Law*. Missoula: Scholars Press, 1975.

Talbert, Charles H. *Ephesians and Colossians*. Grand Rapids: Baker Academic, 2007.

Tardieu, Michel. "Épiphane contre les Gnostiques," *Tel Quel* 88 (1981): 64–91.

Te Velde, H. *Seth, God of Confusion*. Leiden: Brill, 1967.

Thomas, Matthew J. *Paul's 'Works of the Law' in the Perspective of Second Century Reception*. Tübingen: Mohr Siebeck, 2018.

Thomassen, Einar. "Orthodoxy and Heresy at Second-Century Rome," *Harvard Theological Review* 97:3 (2004): 241–56.

Thomassen, Einar. "The Platonic and Gnostic 'Demiurge.'" Pages 227–44 in *Apocryphon Severini Presented to Søren Giversen*, ed. Per Bilde, Helge Kjaer Nielsen, and Jorgen Podemann Sorensen. Aarhus: Aarhus University Press, 1993.

Thompson, Marianne Meye. *The Promise of the Father: Jesus and God in the New Testament*. Louisville: Westminster/John Knox, 2000.

Thrall, Margaret. *The Second Epistle to the Corinthians*, 2 vols. London: T&T Clark, 1994.

Tobias, Nicklas. "'Du bist nur ein Mensch und machst dich selbst zu Gott' (Johannes 10,33): Das Motiv der Gotteslästerung bei Johannes vor dem Hintergrund der Synoptiker." Pages 239–56 in *Studies in the Gospel of John and Its Christology: Festschrift Gilbert van Belle*, ed. Joseph Verheyden et al. Leuven: Peeters, 2014.

Tcherikover, Victor A. *Hellenistic Civilization and the Jews*. Philadelphia: Jewish Publication Society, 1961.

Thiessen, Matthew. *Jesus and the Forces of Death: The Gospels' Portrayal of Ritual Impurity Within First-Century Judaism*. Grand Rapids: Baker Academic, 2020.

Thiselton, Anthony C. *The First Epistle to the Corinthians: A Commentary on the Greek Text*. Grand Rapids: Eerdmans, 2000.

Tripaldi, Daniele. "From Philo to Areimanios: Jewish Traditions and Intellectual Profiles in First–Third Century Alexandria in the Light of the *Apocryphon of John*." Pages 101–20 in *Jews and Christians in Antiquity*, eds. Lanfranchi and Verheyden.

Tsouna, Voula. "Aristo on Blends of Arrogance." Pages 279–92 in *Aristo of Ceos: Text, Translation and Discussion*, ed. William Fortenbaugh. London: Routledge, 2017.

Tsouna, Voula. *The Ethics of Philodemus*. Oxford: Oxford University Press, 2007.

Tsutsui, Kenji. *Die Auseinandersetzung mit den Markioniten im Adamantios-Dialog: Ein Kommentar zu den Büchern I–II*. Berlin: de Gruyter, 2004.

Turner, John D. "The Johannine Legacy: The Gospel and *Apocryphon* of John." Pages 105–44 in *Legacy of John*, ed. Rasimus.

Tyson, Joseph B. "Anti-Judaism in Marcion and His Opponents," *Studies in Christian-Jewish Relations* 1 (2005): 196–208.

Tyson, Joseph B. *Marcion and Luke-Acts: A Defining Struggle*. Columbia: University of South Carolina Press, 2006.

Urbanová, Daniela, and Natalia Gachallová. *Latin Curse Tablets of the Roman Empire*. Innsbruck: Innsbruck University Press, 2018.

van den Berg, Jacob Albert. *Biblical Argument in Manichean Missionary Practice: The Case of Adimantus and Augustine*. Leiden: Brill, 2010.

van den Broek, Roelof, "Archontics." Pages in 89–91 in *DGWE*, ed. Wouter Hanegraaff. Leiden: Brill, 2006.

Van den Broek, Roelof. "Borborites." Page 196 in *DGWE*.

van der Horst, Pieter Willem. *Chaeremon: Egyptian Priest and Stoic Philosopher*. Leiden: Brill, 1983.

van der Horst, Pieter W. "'The God Who Drowned the King of Egypt': A Short Note on an Exorcistic Formula." Pages 135–39 in *The Wisdom of Egypt: Jewish, Early Christian, and Gnostic Essays in Honour of Gerhard P. Luttikhuizen*, ed. Anthony Hilhorst and George H. van Kooten. Leiden: Brill, 2005.

van der Horst, Pieter Willem. "The Great Magical Papyrus of Paris (PGM IV) and the Bible." Pages 269–79 in *Jews and Christians in Their Graeco-Roman Context: Selected Essays on Early Judaism, Samaritanism, Hellenism, and Christianity*, ed. van der Horst, Pieter Willem. Tübingen: Mohr Siebeck, 2006.

van der Horst, Pieter W. "A Short Note on an Exorcistic Formula." Pages 280–84 in *Jews and Christians*, ed. van der Horst, Pieter Willem. Tübingen: Mohr Siebeck, 2006.

van der Toorn, K. "Seth." Pages 748–49 in *Dictionary of Deities and Demons in the Bible (DDD)*, ed. Karel van der Toorn, Bob Becking, and Pieter W. Van der Horst. Leiden: Brill, 1999.

van Henten, Jan Willem "Typhon." Pages 879–81 in *DDD*, ed. van der Toorn et al.

van Henten, Jan Willem, and Ra'anan Abusch. "The Depiction of the Jews as Typhonians and Josephus' Strategy of Refutation in *Contra Apionem*." Pages

271–309 in *Josephus' Contra Apionem: Studies in Its Character and Context with a Latin Concordance to the Portion Missing in Greek*, ed. Louis H. Feldman and John R. Levison. Leiden: Brill, 1996.

Van Kooten, George H. *Paul's Anthropology in Context*. Tübingen: Mohr Siebeck, 2008.

van Oort, Johannes. "The Paraclete Mani as the Apostle of Jesus Christ and the Origins of a New Church." Pages 140–57 in *The Apostolic Age in Patristic Thought*, ed. Anthony Hilhorst. Leiden: Brill, 2004.

Cornelis van Unnik, Willem. "Der Fluch der Gekreuzigten: Deuteronomium 21,23 in der Deutung Justinus des Märtyrers." Pages 483–99 in *Theologia Crucis, Signum Crucis: Festschrift für Erich Dinkler zum 70*, ed. C. Andresen and G. Klein. Tübingen: Mohr Siebeck, 1979.

van Unnik, Willem Cornelis. "Der Neid in der Paradiesgeschichte nach einigen gnostischen Texten." Pages 120–32 in *Essays on the Nag Hammadi Texts in Honour of Alexander Böhlig*, ed. M. Krause. Leiden: Brill, 1972.

van Voorst, Robert E. *The Ascents of James: History and Theology of a Jewish-Christian Community*. Atlanta: Scholars Press, 1989.

Veilleux, Armand. *La seconde apocalypse de Jacques (NH V,4)*. Quebec: University of Laval, 1986.

Viciano, Albert. "The Life and Works of Mani and the Expansion of Manichaeism (216–276)." Pages 647–49 in *Handbook of Patristic Exegesis*, ed. Charles Kannengiesser Leiden: Brill, 2004.

Vinzent, Markus, ed. *Marcion of Sinope as Religious Entrepreneur*. Leuven: Peeters, 2018.

Vinzent, M. "Marcion the Jew," *Judaïsme Ancien - Ancient Judaism* 1 (2013): 159–200.

Vinzent, Markus. *Tertullian's Preface to Marcion's Gospel*. Leuven: Peeters, 2016.

Vischer, Lukas. "Le prétendu 'culte de âne' dans la Église primitive," *Revue de l'histoire des religions* 139:1 (1951): 14–35.

von Lieven, Alexandra. "Translating Gods, Interpreting Gods." Pages 61–83 in *Greco-Egyptian Interactions: Literature, Translation, and Culture 500BC-AD 300*, ed. Ian Rutherford. Oxford: Oxford University Press, 2016.

von Nordheim-Diehl, Miriam. "Der Neid Gottes, des Teufels und der Menschen—eine motivgeschichtliche Skizze." Pages 431–50 in *Emotions from Ben Sira to Paul*, ed. Renate Egger-Wenzel and Jeremey Corley. Berlin: de Gruyter, 2012.

Waldstein, Michael. "The Primal Triad in the *Apocryphon of John*." Pages 154–87 in *The Nag Hammadi Library After Fifty Years*, ed. John D. Turner and Anne McGuire. Leiden: Brill, 1997.

Wassen, Cecilia. "Jesus and the Hemorrhaging Woman in Mark 5:25–34: Insights from Purity Laws from Qumran." Pages 641–60 in *Scripture in Transition: Essays on Septuagint, Hebrew Bible, and Dead Sea Scrolls in Honour of Raija Sollamo*, ed. Anssi Voitila and Jutta Jokiranta. Leiden: Brill, 2008.

Wasserman, Emma. *Apocalypse as Holy War: Divine Politics and Polemics in the Letters of Paul*. New Haven: Yale University Press, 2018.

Watson, Francis. "Jesus Versus the Lawgiver: Narratives of Apostasy and Conversion." Pages 45–62 in *Telling the Christian Story*, ed. Watson and Parkhouse.

Welburn, A. J. "The Identity of the Archons in the 'Apocryphon Johannis,'" *VC* 32 (1978): 241–54.

Welburn, A. J. "Reconstructing the Ophite Diagram," *NovT* 23:3 (1981): 261–87.

Wells, Steve. *Drunk with Blood: God's Killings in the Bible*. Moscow, ID: SAB, 2010.

Wells, Steve. *The Skeptic's Annotated Bible: The King James Version from a Skeptic's Point of View*. Moscow, ID: SAB, 2013.

Werline, Rodney. "The Transformation of Pauline Arguments in Justin Martyr's *Dialogue with Trypho*," *Harvard Theological Review* 92:1 (1999): 79–93.

White, Benjamin L. *Remembering Paul: Ancient and Modern Contests Over the Image of the Apostle*. Oxford: Oxford University Press, 2014.

Whitmarsh, Tim. *Beyond the Second Sophistic: Adventures in Greek Postclassicism*. Berkeley: University of California Press, 2013.

Whitmarsh, Tim. "Politics and Identity in Ezekiel's *Exagoge*." Pages 211–27 in *Beyond the Second Sophistic*.

Wilhite, David E. "Was Marcion a Docetist? The Body of Evidence vs. Tertullian's Argument," *VC* 71 (2017): 1–36.

Williams, Francis E. *Mental Perception: A Commentary on NHC VI,4. The Concept of Our Great Power*. Leiden: Brill, 2001.

Williams, Michael A. "The Demonizing of the Demiurge: The Innovation of Gnostic Myth." Pages 73–107 in *Innovations in Religious Traditions*, ed. Michael A. Williams, C. Cox, and Martin S. Jaffe. Berlin: de Gruyter, 1992.

Williams, Michael A. *Rethinking "Gnosticism": An Argument for Dismantling a Dubious Category*. Princeton: Princeton University Press, 1996.

Williams, Michael A. "Sethianism." Pages 32–63 in *A Companion to Second-Century Christian "Heretics*," ed. Antti Marjanen and Petri Luomanen. Leiden: Brill, 2005.

Willing, Meike. "Die neue Frage des Marcionschülers Apelles—zur Rezeption marcionitischen Gedankenguts." Pages 221–31 in May and Greschat, *Markion*.

Wilson, Stephen G. *Luke and the Law*. Cambridge: Cambridge University Press, 1983.

Wilson, Stephen G. "Marcion and Boundaries." Pages 200–220 in *Crossing Boundaries in Early Judaism and Christianity: Ambiguities, Complexities, and Half-Forgotten Adversaries*, ed. Kimberley Stratton and Andrea Lieber. Leiden: Brill, 2016.

Wilson, Stephen G. *Related Strangers: Jews and Christians 70–170 CE*. Minneapolis: Fortress, 1995.

Winger, Michael. *By What Law: The Meaning of Νόμος in the Letters of Paul*. Atlanta: Scholars Press, 1992.

Winiarczyk, Marek. *The "Sacred History" of Euhemerus of Messene*. Berlin: de Gruyter, 2013.

Witte, Bernd. *Die Ophitendiagramm nach Origenes' Contra Celsum VI,22–38*. Altenberge: Oros, 1993.

Wünsch, Richard. *Sethianische Verfluchungtafeln aus Rom*. Leipzig: Teubner, 1898.

Yang, Yong-Eui. *Jesus and the Sabbath in Matthew's Gospel*. Sheffield: Sheffield Academic, 1997.

Young, Frances M., and David Ford. *Meaning and Truth in 2 Corinthians*. London: SPCK, 1987.

Index of Ancient Sources

Subject Index

Page numbers in *italics* indicate illustrations. Titles of authored works are listed after the name of the author.

Printed in the USA
CPSIA information can be obtained
at www.ICGtesting.com
CBHW071427180324
5454CB00002B/2

9 780197 566428